INTREPID
WARRIORS

INTREPID WARRIORS

PERSPECTIVES ON CANADIAN MILITARY LEADERS

EDITED BY
COLONEL BERND HORN

FOREWORD BY
JOHN SCOTT COWAN

CANADIAN DEFENCE ACADEMY PRESS

THE DUNDURN GROUP
TORONTO

Published by The Dundurn Group and Canadian Defence Academy Press in cooperation with the Department of National Defence, and Public Works and Government Services Canada.

Editor: Michael Carroll
Copy-editor: Nigel Heseltine
Design: Jennifer Scott
Index: Yves Raic
Printer: Marquis Book Printing

Library and Archives Canada Cataloguing in Publication

Intrepid warriors : perspectives on Canadian military leaders / edited by Bernd Horn.

Co-published by: Canadian Defence Academy Press.
Issued also in French under title: Les guerriers intrépides.
Includes bibliographical references and index.
ISBN 978-1-55002-711-2

1. Military art and science—Canada—History. 2. Command of troops—History. 3. Canada—Armed Forces—Biography. 4. Leadership— Canada—History. I. Horn, Bernd, 1959-

U54.C2I68 2007   355.3'30410971   C2007-902053-4

1   2   3   4   5   11   10   09   08   07

 Conseil des Arts du Canada   Canada Council for the Arts   ONTARIO ARTS COUNCIL
CONSEIL DES ARTS DE L'ONTARIO

We acknowledge the support of the **Canada Council for the Arts** and the **Ontario Arts Council** for our publishing program. We also acknowledge the financial support of the **Government of Canada** through the **Book Publishing Industry Development Program** and **The Association for the Export of Canadian Books**, and the **Government of Ontario** through the **Ontario Book Publishers Tax Credit** program and the **Ontario Media Development Corporation**.

Printed and bound in Canada
www.dundurn.com

Canadian Defence Academy Press
PO Box 17000 Station Forces
Kingston, Ontario, Canada
K7K 7B4

Dundurn Press
3 Church Street, Suite 500
Toronto, Ontario, Canada
M5E 1M2

Gazelle Book Services Limited
White Cross Mills
High Town, Lancaster, England
LA1 4XS

Dundurn Press
2250 Military Road
Tonawanda, NY
U.S.A. 14150

TABLE OF CONTENTS

Foreword by John Scott Cowan   7

Acknowledgements by Bernd Horn   11

Introduction by Bernd Horn   13

1   The Power of Patronage and the Value of Knowledge: 21
    The Leadership Experiences of Lieutenant Agar
    Adamson with Strathcona's Horse, 1899–1900
    Craig Leslie Mantle

2   Portrait of a Battalion Commander: Lieutenant-Colonel   59
    George Stuart Tuxford at the Second Battle of Ypres,
    April 1915
    Andrew B. Godefroy

3   The Strain of the Bridge: The Second World War Diaries   75
    of Commander A.F.C. Layard, RN
    Michael Whitby

4   "A Hell of a Warrior": Sergeant Thomas George Prince   95
    P. Whitney Lackenbauer

5   When Leadership Really Mattered: Bert Hoffmeister and   139
    Morale During the Battle of Ortona, December 1943
    Douglas E. Delaney

6   Four Gallant Airmen: Clifford Mackay McEwen,   155
    Raymond Collishaw, Leonard Joseph Birchall, and
    Robert Wendell McNair
    David L. Bashow

7   Leading from the Front: Lieutenant-Colonel Cameron   199
    "Cammie" Ware, DSO
    Tod Strickland

8   Bradbrooke, Nicklin, and Eadie: A Tale of Command   223
    Bernd Horn

Contributors   261

Index   263

FOREWORD

I am grateful to Bernd Horn for asking me to write a foreword for *Intrepid Warriors: Perspectives on Canadian Military Leaders* because it provided me with an opportunity to reflect on the work, both as a particularly accessible approach to military history, and as a source of important contemporary lessons. In 1999, the Royal Military College of Canada substantially altered its undergraduate curriculum in response to the seminal findings of the Withers Report (1998). The research behind those findings and the subsequent report of the Core Curriculum Committee persuaded the Board of Governors that to give officers a reasonable chance at good autonomous judgment in the 21st century, we needed them to reach some basic level of achievement in 17 particular subjects, regardless of other aspects of their specialization. Eight of the 17 were Canadian history, military history, leadership, psychology, ethics, civics, international affairs, and cross-cultural relations. This volume gives insights into all of those eight, and does so in an unpretentious and thoroughly readable fashion.

Indeed, studies of military history and of leadership through biography have become enormously popular in recent years, because the biographical approach confers an eyewitness sort of intimacy to what might otherwise seem a remote and emotionless account. The biographical frame suits the emphases of contemporary society and is especially appropriate when exploring the psychological dimension.

Now I should not want you to think that the only reason for reading this volume is that it's good for you. It is, but so are lots of things, like antioxidants and exercise. The other equally good reason is that it is fascinating. The chapters are all powerful stories, and each seemed to me to carry important lessons without being preachy.

A sampling of chapters demonstrates what I am referring to. In Chapter 3 (Michael Whitby writing on A.F.C. Layard), one sees that doubt and self-criticism are not necessarily weaknesses, but may be exactly the tools needed to have judgment, provided that they do not provoke stasis and indecision. Despite the title of the book, Layard was not a Canadian, but he was most assuredly a military leader of Canadians, in Canadian ships, and sympathetic to Canadians. This gives particular poignancy to the hopes and fears he felt while trying to lead his Canadian men.

In Chapter 4 (Whitney Lackenbauer writing about Tommy Prince), we see a classic early case of post-traumatic stress disorder (PTSD) in an exceptional leader (even though the illness was poorly understood at the time), and realize that leaders and heroes have widely disparate reasons for doing what they do. Indeed, it teaches us to accept the broadest possible range of reasons for desirable behaviours. If we discount everyone who does the right thing for reasons that some might see as other than the right reasons, then there will be no heroes left. And third, this chapter teaches us that the best leaders in combat may not be the best leaders in garrison or in peacetime. Furthermore, in Tommy Prince's era, the easy acceptance and admiration he craved may only have been available to him in those conflict settings where he excelled.

Chapter 5 (Douglas Delaney writing on Bert Hoffmeister) shows us that Hoffmeister's casual and automatic personal courage (being often at the front while commanding his brigade) accomplished two things. It gave him the first-hand information and perspective he needed to have confidence in his own decisions, and it sustained the morale of the men, not just because he was sharing their risk, but because they knew that he understood exactly what they were experiencing.

Chapter 8, by Bernd Horn (this book's editor), deals with Bradbrooke, Nicklin, and Eadie, and reminds us that a variety of styles, strengths, and weaknesses are possible in battalion-level leadership, and reinforces the notion that the qualities needed to lead in garrison and those suited to leadership in the field can be different, and may not all be present in a single individual. Furthermore, it reminds us that the supply of experienced leaders is far from infinite, and that the weaknesses of the best choice available at a given moment can be compensated for by a deputy commanding officer with complementary qualities.

These are timeless lessons. The history of leadership will always be relevant to contemporary leadership issues. One sometimes hears facile arguments that changing conditions and/or technological revolutions have made the older stories of marginal relevance. This is unlikely. Personal qualities will always matter in any setting where the emotional reaction to the leader by those being led is critical, and where decisions must sometimes be taken quickly in conditions of ambiguity and even chaos.

The portraits in this book are not painted with the pastel shades of theory. They are the vivid images of real people trying to tame the unimaginable forces swirling around them and welling up in their souls. And they are etched on the hard metal of the clashes of arms that have shaped our national consciousness. They are worth reading.

John Scott Cowan
Principal
Royal Military College of Canada

ACKNOWLEDGEMENTS

Despite all the labour-saving devices and advanced technology, or perhaps because of it, life in general seems to have greatly increased its tempo. Everyone seems incredibly busy and most lament a pace that is much too quick. In view of this stark reality, I wish to first thank all the contributors who took time out of their busy lives to contribute chapters to this volume. Their dedication to both Canadian history and the profession of arms is greatly appreciated.

I would also like to thank a host of other individuals from the Canadian Forces Leadership Institute who were instrumental in assisting with the compilation of this book. I must thank Joanne Simms and Carol Jackson for the administrative support they provided to the contributors and me, and for their efforts in getting the volume translated into French. I also wish to extend, a special note of gratitude to Craig Mantle for his stellar work at sourcing the graphics needed to support the manuscript.

I also wish to convey my sincere appreciation to the staffs of a number of institutions and organizations that assisted in the completion of our task. As such our thanks go out to Library and Archives Canada, the Directorate of History and Heritage, and the Royal Military College of Canada. Finally, I wish to thank the technical staff at CDA Press/The Dundurn Group, specifically Michael Carroll and Nigel Heseltine, for polishing a raw manuscript into the book you see before you.

In summary, the collective efforts of all these individuals and institutions assisted in the compilation of this volume. However, as always, any errors remain my own.

Colonel Bernd Horn
Deputy Commander
Special Operations Forces Command
Canadian Forces

Introduction

by Bernd Horn

D oes the study of the past, particularly its military commanders and leaders, still hold relevance? After all, today's environment seems so much more chaotic, complex, and different from that of our predecessors. But is it? Ambiguity, chaos, fear, friction on the battlefield, self-doubt in relation to what is the best decision to be made in a moment of crisis are all issues commanders and military leaders have faced in the past and still face today. War and conflict are very human endeavours; as such, participants share experiences that embody all the characteristics and attributes associated with this kind of behaviour.

The timeless nature of the behaviour is the reason that a study of Canadian military leaders is still important for current military professionals and the public at large. The profession of arms, like any profession, demands expertise that can only be attained through continual professional development (i.e., education, training, self-development, and experience). It is the way to maintain a vibrancy and continual evolution of the profession, and to ensure commanders and leaders are as prepared as possible to lead their nation's sons and daughters into harm's way.

In summary, the study of military history provides a better understanding of the military profession. Specifically, the examination of past leaders provides some insight into, and understanding of, warfare, leadership, and command. Current leaders can draw valuable lessons from this rich pool of knowledge for use in their career and/or in operations.

After all, direct combat or battlefield experience is normally in short supply, so professional military personnel often need to gain this vicariously through the experience of others. *Intrepid Warriors* will help them develop the essential knowledge that will provide them with the necessary tools and decision-making ability to anticipate and adapt to the challenges of operations, such as the phenomenon of "friction." For instance, an examination of past commanders and leaders can provide a window — some insight — into how friction affected their command and, equally important, how they dealt with it. This type of study can help current military leaders develop a better grasp of the battlefield. It can also make the public more aware of the challenges and heavy responsibilities their military leaders face in executing the missions their society has entrusted to them. In addition, this book and its focus on military leaders of the past provides a means to understand our own military culture — our nature, ethos, character, and the way we as a nation have gone about doing the "business."

This is not to suggest that one can take a cookie-cutter approach to the study of military leaders. Far from it. Command is a very personal experience. How an individual commands speaks more to the character and personality of the person than it does to the concept of command itself. In essence, command is far more an art than a science. That is why some commanders reach legendary status while others fade into ignominy.

Command, however, is not an arbitrary activity. It can only be exercised by those who are formally appointed to positions of command. It is "the authority vested in an individual of the armed forces for the direction, coordination, and control of military forces."[1] This normally comes from years of formal professional development, assessment, and evaluation, as well as proven ability.

That there is a need to prepare individuals for command is not surprising. First, there is the heavy responsibility command entails — namely, the lives of others. Commanders must accomplish their tasks, but they must do so with the minimum cost in lives and within their allocated resource envelope. This is often an enormous challenge. The all-encompassing scope of command is why it comprises three often reinforcing components. They are authority, management (e.g., allocating resources, budgeting, coordinating, controlling, organizing, planning, prioritizing, problem solving, supervising, and ensuring adherence to policy and timelines), and leadership (i.e., "directing, motivating, and enabling others to accomplish the mission professionally and ethically, while developing or improving capabilities that contribute to mission success").[2] Depending on the mission, subordinates, circumstances, and situations, as well as the commander, different emphasis is placed on each component. It must be noted that command can only be exercised by those who are appointed to the role. Conversely, leadership, although a component of command, also exists outside of the concept of command and can be exercised by anyone.[3]

In essence, command and leadership are exercised in a personal manner. But then this varied approach to command and leadership is exactly why past commanders and leaders should be studied. This examination provides a rich tapestry of approaches, behaviours, and styles. It can help readers become better commanders and leaders; understand the dynamics of war and conflict; gain insight into the why or how of decisions; and improve their understanding of the Canadian military culture and experience.

As such, this book begins with Craig Leslie Mantle's examination of Agar Adamson, a promising militia officer at the turn of the last century who used his operational experience in the South African War to develop his leadership skills. The chapter expertly captures Adamson's journey as an inexperienced commander struggling to learn the responsibilities of leading troops in combat, the loneliness of his command, and his decision-making under fire. Adamson proved to be an able commander, one who demonstrated great concern for the welfare of his soldiers. He strove to know his men and never needlessly endangered their lives. In summary, the examination of Adamson provides an excellent account of the growth of a junior officer in combat. Regardless of the time period, the lessons are timeless.

The next chapter, written by Major Andrew Godefroy, follows a similar track and looks at the leadership of Lieutenant-Colonel George Stuart Tuxford as a battalion commander during the First World War. Tuxford's distinguished wartime career is used as a window to view and reflect on a wider group of senior Canadian officers whose intelligence, skills, personal courage, and ability to learn at the tactical and operational level inspired the Canadian Corps to victory on the Western Front. This chapter examines Tuxford's first experience with command and leadership in combat in April 1915 and how it shaped his later performance as an operational-level commander. It is largely based on Tuxford's own "After Action Report," which provided candid and at times brutally frank personal observations of various events during the battle. His assessment gives a personal critique of his own performance during the engagement and provides invaluable reference to where he was at various times and what he could see. More important, it provides a detailed account of what he knew and when, and what decisions he made based on that knowledge and intelligence. From the point of later assessment, his report on his actions and those of his unit at the Second

Battle of Ypres is a critical document that provides unique insight and education in assessing Canadian combat leadership and command during this engagement.

The third chapter changes the pace of the book. First, it deals with military leadership in the Second World War, which is the focus of the remaining chapters. Second, it concerns a British naval commander and the unusual challenges he faced commanding Canadians during the bitter and hard-fought Battle of the Atlantic. Based on Commander A.F.C. Layard's diary, this chapter by Michael Whitby deals with the officer's personal struggles with naval command and his own self-doubt regarding his ability to measure up to the trials and tribulations of commanding a ship in the rapidly expanding, under-trained, and under-equipped Canadian Navy, which was being sorely tested by German U-boats off the east coast of Canada and in the North Atlantic. This wonderful chapter provides marvellous insight into naval command and is a timeless study of the personal responsibilities and challenges of leading in combat.

Intrepid Warriors continues with its change of pace by next looking at military leadership in combat from the vantage point of a senior non-commissioned officer (NCO), namely, the well-known Canadian aboriginal soldier Sergeant Tommy Prince. In this chapter, Whitney Lackenbauer captures the heroic yet tragic story of an individual who is still held up as the "quintessential Indian at War."[4] A courageous and daring NCO who consistently led by example, Prince became one of the most decorated NCOs in the Second World War. In this chapter, Lackenbauer examines Prince's leadership from his audacious exploits in Italy right through to his enlistment and subsequent two tours of action in Korea. It captures his legendary feats, as well as his eventual breakdown in the field in 1952. This case study is seminal. It focuses on a courageous, dynamic leader who was respected by all and who became a spokesman for aboriginal veterans after the Second World War. However, the chapter also delves into the cost of such leadership responsibility, particularly Prince's eventual collapse because of his physical and psychological injuries. In the end, the chapter provides a great leadership profile, as well as a social statement in regard to post-traumatic stress disorder and the treatment of aboriginal veterans.

The fifth chapter discusses the leadership impact of Brigadier-General (later Major-General) Bert Hoffmeister, the commander of 2nd Canadian Infantry Brigade during the desperate fight for Ortona during December 1943. His formation had already been severely bloodied during the crossing of the Sangro and Moro Rivers. Under-strength and exhausted, they now had to claw their way through the rubble, house by house, to seize Ortona from a tenacious enemy. Written by Major Doug Delaney, a serving infantry officer with operational experience and a doctorate, the chapter captures the essence of Hoffmeister's brilliance — attention to detail, careful planning, and a deep passion for his soldiers. This examination clearly demonstrates the effect of leadership on morale and battle effectiveness.

The trend of soldier scholar continues in Chapter 6. Written by Lieutenant-Colonel David Bashow, a retired fighter pilot and renowned author and Air Force historian, this chapter examines the enigmatic concept of air force leadership through the profiles of four intrepid air force leaders. Leadership in a service that focuses on small crews, if not individual pilots, can be difficult to describe let alone exercise. As such, Bashow lays out how "first and foremost, an effective air leader must lead by example, and must not only be prepared to personally go in harm's way, but must do so in a manner that inspires confidence and a willingness in others to engage the enemy." The narratives of the careers of famous pilots Clifford Mackay McEwen, Raymond Collishaw, Leonard Joseph Birchall, and Robert Wendell McNair provide solid examples of air force leadership in action. Through the filter of Bashow's examination of the careers of these intrepid pilots, it is possible to gain an understanding of the dynamic of the concept of air force leadership, as well as how it differs from the other services.

In Chapter 7, once again, a serving infantry officer, Major Tod Strickland, who also possesses operational experience, took "pen in hand" to examine the leadership of Lieutenant-Colonel Cameron "Cammie" Ware, the commanding officer (CO) of the Princess Patricia's Canadian Light Infantry (PPCLI) who "led his soldiers from the front" through three distinct battles in Italy in 1944, namely, the fight for Villa Rogatti, the cauldron of Vino Ridge and the breaking of the Hitler Line. Throughout, he motivated his soldiers in a style that engendered their loyalty and respect while accomplishing his missions. Accordingly, the author examines two specific questions. First, how did Cammie Ware lead, and second, did his leadership style affect his ability to command? In the end, this valuable chapter provides great insight into military leadership in combat.

Chapter 8, my contribution, concludes the book. In this final chapter, the concept of command, specifically the very personal approaches used by different commanders, is examined. The analysis is conducted through an assessment of three of the four commanding officers in the 1st Canadian Parachute Battalion from its creation in 1942 to its disbandment in 1945. This case study provides an excellent example of how different command approaches can affect the morale and effectiveness of a unit. Moreover, it demonstrates how some command approaches can serve a unit well under some circumstances, but if the commander is unable to adapt or change his approach to meet the required situation, or if there are substantial flaws in his character, he will quickly be seen as ineffective, which may have a dramatic impact on the unit.

In its entirety, this volume looks at the command and leadership practiced by a number of Canada's finest military commanders and leaders. The chapters provide valuable insight into different command approaches, behaviours, and styles that can aid others in becoming better commanders and leaders, while gaining a better understanding of dynamics of war and conflict. In the end, the chapters reinforce two key points. First, command and leadership lessons are timeless and the historical study of leaders will always be relevant to contemporary leadership issues. Second, the character and presence of leaders are critical to military outcomes, particularly during times of ambiguity, uncertainty, and chaos.

NOTES

1.   Canada, *Command* (Ottawa: DND, 1997), 4. Command is the expression of human will — an idea that is captured in the concept of a commander's intent as part of the philosophy of mission command. The commander's intent is the commander's personal expression of why an operation is being conducted and what he hopes to achieve. It is a clear and concise statement of the desired end state and acceptable risk. Its strength is the fact that it allows subordinates to exercise initiative in the absence of orders, or when unexpected opportunities arise, or when the original concept of operations no longer applies. Mission Command is a command philosophy that promotes decentralized decision-making, freedom, and speed of action and initiative. It entails three enduring tenets: the importance of understanding a superior commander's intent, a clear responsibility to fulfil that intent, and timely decision-making. In summary, command is the purposeful exercise of authority over structures, resources, people, and activities.

2.   Canada, *Leadership in the Canadian Forces: Conceptual Foundations* (Kingston: DND, 2005). It is within this powerful realm of influence and potential change that leadership best demonstrates the fundamental difference between it and the concept of command. Too often the terms *leadership* and *command* are exchanged or seen as synonymous. But they are not. Leadership can, and should, be a component of command. After all, to be an effective commander the formal authority that comes with rank

and position must be reinforced and supplemented with personal qualities and skills — the human side. Nonetheless, as discussed earlier, command is based on vested authority and assigned position and/or rank. It may only be exercised downward in the chain of command through the structures and processes of control. Conversely, leadership is not constrained by the limits of formal authority. Individuals anywhere in the chain of command may, given the ability and motivation, influence peers and even superiors. This clearly differentiates leadership from command.

3. Command and leadership are often incorrectly intermixed. Each is a distinct concept. A commander should use leadership, but technically does not have to. He or she can rely exclusively on authority and take a managerial approach (but this is not to say that managers do not use leadership — like commanders, they should). The fact that command is a function of appointment and leadership is a result of a voluntary interaction between someone practicing leadership and those who accept to be led is the greatest defining difference between the concepts of command and leadership.

4. See Janice Summerby, *Native Soldiers, Foreign Battlefields* (Ottawa: Minister of Supply and Services, 1993), accessed at *www.vac-acc.gc.ca/general/sub.cfm?source=history/other/native/prince*; Royal Commission on Aboriginal Peoples, *Final Report v.1: Looking Forward, Looking Back* (Ottawa: Canada Communication Group, 1996); Salim Karam, "Aboriginal Day at NDHQ," *The Maple Leaf* 5/25 (26 June 2002), 3; R.S. Sheffield, *A Search for Equity: A Study of the Treatment Accorded to First Nations Veterans and Dependents of the Second World War and Korea* (Ottawa: National Round Table on First Nations Veterans' Issues, 2001); and Bill Twatio, "Bitter Legacy for Brave Native Soldiers: Out of Uniform They Were 'Just Another Poor Goddamn Indian,'" *Toronto Star*, 11 November 1994.

CHAPTER 1

The Power of Patronage and the Value of Knowledge:
The Leadership Experiences of Lieutenant Agar
Adamson with Strathcona's Horse, 1899–1900

by Craig Leslie Mantle

In a letter home immediately before the impending Canadian attack at Vimy in the spring of 1917, Lieutenant-Colonel A.S.A.M. Adamson, the commanding officer (CO) of the Princess Patricia's Canadian Light Infantry (PPCLI), bitterly complained to his wife:

> Every man in England wants a commission. I get about 15 letters a day.... I am afraid my answers to these wretches will not please them. Fathers write me, M.P.s [Members of Parliament] write me and Mothers and Sisters, and in nearly every case the men are not worth considering and I cannot help telling them that the men out here who have stuck it and are sticking it, are the only ones I can consider. The Corps Commander [Sir Julian Byng] has allowed me to send in the names of 20 N.C.O.s [Non-Commissioned Officers] and men for commissions, which looks as if he expected we would need them fairly soon. It has been quite difficult to pick them out as sahibs won't go round and there are more important factors to consider than Mess and table manners in this serious Push. The power of leadership, which I think is born rather than acquired, I consider first. After that, quick decision and, even in training, quick action and the ability to realize the situation he finds himself in.[1]

After serving continuously since 1914 and having witnessed first-hand the slaughter that became so characteristic of the Western Front,

Adamson was convinced that promotion in the field should be based on merit and ability and not, as had earlier been the case, on overt patronage and political connection. Being responsible for the overall effectiveness of his regiment and being ever aware of the value of life, he was loath to place the welfare of his soldiers in the hands of untested and inexperienced leaders, especially when knowledgeable men were already serving in the ranks, many of whom possessed command experience as NCOs. Politics and patronage would not be pandered to under his leadership, much to the chagrin of certain socially ambitious citizens.

Yet, ironically, nearly two decades earlier during the opening days of the South African War, Adamson himself was exactly the type of man he would later come to describe as "wretched." Ambitious, extremely well-connected, eager to serve and possessing little real military experience, he relied heavily on his political, social, and military acquaintances to secure a commission that would take him to South Africa.[2] Born on Christmas day in 1865, in Montreal, Agar Stewart Allan Masterson Adamson came from a distinguished family that possessed a long and notable association with public service. Living a life of privilege, he received a private education at Trinity College in Port Hope, Ontario, and later travelled to England to read for the holy orders at Corpus Christi, Cambridge. A gifted athlete and rider, Agar rowed and played field sports at university and once rode his own horse to victory in the Newmarket stakes. He returned to Ottawa in 1890 after deciding not to enter the ministry and joined the civil service where his duties took him to the senate.[3]

After connecting himself with the government of the land, he embarked upon a military career that would ultimately prove to be an adventurous and defining period in his life. Undeniably, the time that he spent under arms and his experience of war would transform him from an innocent into a veteran who better understood both the minds of soldiers and the finer nuances of leadership. In 1893, he was commissioned as a second-lieutenant in Number 4 Company of the Governor General's Foot Guards (GGFG) and, by 1899, had been promoted to captain. A host of ceremonial duties provided much of his early military experience.[4] Being a product of the late-nineteenth-century Canadian militia, though, he possessed little real command experience. The act of leading soldiers through the predictable movements of a ceremonial parade could not be equated with leading tired, hungry, and frightened soldiers against a stubborn and resistant enemy. For him, as for many of his contemporaries, the militia was more of a social diversion, a gentle-

Library and Archives Canada PA-110040

The Anderson (Ottawa) hockey team, circa 1885. Agar Adamson is at the top right of the picture.

man's club, which could be used to supplement one's income, however modestly, and to add an element of prestige and pedigree to one's social resume. Truly, "In a society acutely conscious of social status, a militia commission became a badge of social respectability."[5]

Even the annual camps that Adamson attended probably offered little in the way of practical experience that could be put to good use as much of the training was "simple and repetitious" and consisted primarily of drills, some range work and a sham battle.[6] In many respects, he was typical of his peers since he exemplified "the Protestant, middle-class character of the … militia's officer ranks," although his extensive connections set him apart.[7]

HALIFAX

After marrying Ann Mabel Cawthra in November 1899,[8] Agar travelled to Halifax where he served with the 3rd (Special Service) Battalion, Royal Canadian Regiment of Infantry, a hastily recruited unit that allowed the Leinster Regiment, the regular British garrison at Wellington Barracks, to be released for service elsewhere in the empire.[9] The time spent in Nova Scotia's capital afforded Agar with the opportunity to refine and further develop his leadership skills that had begun developing during his early years with the militia. Full-time service, as opposed to the one-night-a-week routine that he had been accustomed to, was indeed a welcome change for it brought him closer to realizing his ambition of serving in South Africa. The garrison was, if nothing else, "a start."[10] In one of his first surviving letters home, he described for Mabel some of his less pleasing, but nonetheless interesting, responsibilities:

> Our duty being to parade the low parts of the town from 8 to10 to gather in all drunken men and search all houses of ill fame, which is done by entering them in the Queens [sic] name back and front, and searching for men, the officer remaining outside. The low part of the town like all garrison and seaport towns is very low. The duty is not a pleasant one and comes round every 16 days. We found men both drunk and otherwise and march[ed] them to the guard room & this morning they received their punishments.[11]

Aside from offering a vivid social commentary on turn-of-the-century Halifax, Adamson's remarks to his wife reveal that he was more than prepared to enforce discipline when required and was resolute in ensuring that his subordinates followed the rules and regulations of the service, an attitude that he continued to hold dear during the months and years that followed.

His duties in Halifax were largely confined to those typical of a garrison setting. Having spent a good deal of time with the GGFG, he probably did not find his service in the provisional battalion to be that much different from his experience in Ottawa.[12] Outside of his regular responsibilities, other opportunities to further develop his practical leadership skills soon presented themselves. As he related to his wife, he was soon:

> given charge of 35 men as a fire brigade for one month. It has to be organized and in a few days the General will send up a staff officer to ring the fire alarm and will make his report accordingly. I am on duty till 1 o'clock tonight. I think I shall ring the alarm after that for practice.[13]

Such comments, although brief and passing, reveal that Agar took to his responsibilities with some interest, vigour, and concern. By taking the initiative, challenging his men, and offering them realistic training, he sought to increase their efficiency and to develop them into a cohesive team that could perform competently. Rather than waiting to see how they would react during an actual fire or during an evaluated exercise upon which their (and his) reputations would hang, he attempted to prepare his soldiers-cum-firefighters with additional practices and ensure that they at least knew the rudiments of their responsibilities. A proactive training regime, he believed, might save him from later exercises to correct deficiencies in the brigade's performance.

Adamson's chance to participate in the fighting on the veldt soon came in April 1900, much to his relief and happiness. A few months earlier, Donald Smith, more familiarly known as Lord Strathcona, the Canadian high commissioner in London, offered to raise a regiment of horsemen at his own expense for service in South Africa.[14] Once these newest soldiers of the Queen had been recruited, organized, and dispatched, all of which occurred under the supervision of their CO, Lieutenant-Colonel Sam Steele, formerly of the North-West Mounted Police (NWMP),[15] the British War Office (WO) asked Strathcona to raise a small draft consisting of 50 men and one lieutenant that could be used to replace casualties in the regiment proper.[16] Inspector D'Arcy Strickland of the NWMP was originally chosen to command the draft, but later declined the opportunity; he did, however, recruit the reinforcements in the western reaches of the country and bring them to Ottawa where they would meet their new officer and be held in readiness until their departure overseas.[17] Recognizing this to be the opportunity that he had long desired and for which he had sacrificed the early days of his marriage to realize, Agar relied on a retinue of influential patrons that included, among other notables, his wife, current Governor-General Lord Minto, and Minister of Militia and Defence, Dr. Frederick William Borden, to recommend his name to Lord Strathcona as Strickland's replacement. With such powerful supporters behind him and an acceptable record of military service thus far, his nomination was immediately accepted.[18]

Upon his departure from Halifax in late April to assume his duties with Strathcona's Horse (SH),[19] a local newspaper recorded:

> Captain Adamson was one of the most efficient officers
> in the regiment. He acted as lieutenant of D company,

and was extremely popular with officers and men.... Before the train left Captain Adamson addressed the men, thanking them for their kindly wishes and assuring them of his deep interest in their welfare.... Three hearty cheers were given for Captain Adamson as the train pulled out from the station.[20]

If such a report can be believed, Agar was apparently one of the better officers of the regiment and was held in high regard by his superiors and subordinates alike.[21] He apparently understood his many responsibilities, both those that fell to an infantry lieutenant and those that had been assigned as secondary duties. Whatever success he experienced in Halifax probably owed much to his past militia service. In the end, his time in the city provided further opportunities to gain experience in exercising command and in being responsible for the good conduct, welfare, and competence of those beneath him, all lessons that would serve him well in the months that followed.

TO THE SEAT OF WAR

After meeting the draft in Ottawa, with whom he "soon became very popular" in the estimation of one of its members,[22] Agar began the difficult process of transforming his western volunteers into a smart, effective, and efficient military body. His efforts, however, were largely interrupted by a devastating fire that scorched large sections of the city and caused his would-be soldiers to be pressed into service as temporary firemen.[23] Adamson and the draft left the nation's capital for Montreal on 30 April and departed for England on the following day. Despite looking smart and neat,[24] the men under his command were soldiers in name only, although "all were riders of experience."[25] Of those who left the familiar air of Canada to assist the empire in South Africa, only a handful, six at most, possessed some form of previous military experience.[26] To compound matters even further, their minimal time in Ottawa had not been spent constructively in training, but in drawing stores and aiding the civilian population. Most definitely, these men had left the city exactly as they had entered it, inexperienced, although they were now somewhat better dressed! Although fighting the fires together started to shape the draft into a cohesive whole, much more work had to be done if bonds of familiarity, loyalty, and trust were to be established. With little or no meaningful opportunities for training or making acquaintances, Agar, who was now expected to properly lead his soldiers through whatever situations presented themselves, was forced to play "catch-up" on both accounts while travelling to the front.

The crossing from Montreal to Liverpool and the journey from London to Cape Town were generally calm and without significant incident. On both legs of the voyage, Adamson endeavoured to provide his men with the rudiments of soldiering in an attempt to compensate for their marked lack of instruction. In a letter to Lord Strathcona written from South Africa, he recalled, "The draft was drilled three hours a day, one hour before breakfast at physical drill, the remainder was such movements as where [sic] possible."[27] Being confined to the available deck space, such training was simple in its evolutions. With some satisfaction, he similarly observed in one of his private letters that "They made very good shooting yesterday in spite of the rifle being quite new to them."[28] Agar was truly relieved when he found his men "keen to learn and not frightened of hard work."[29] He could at least take some comfort in the fact that his men were now on their way to becoming soldiers in both name and ability.

According to David Morrison Stewart, one of the soldiers recruited for the draft, Agar also used this time to give "us a very nice lecture on how to carry ourselves and what we would likely have to go through."[30] During this discussion, he surely set forth his expectations and conveyed the message, whether explicitly or implicitly, that they were not to tarnish the good name of the regiment (and thus their benefactor) with which they now had the privilege of being associated. Judging by their later conduct, however, some of his soldiers misinterpreted his plea to act like gentlemen. How much practical military advice Adamson could offer to his subordinates is questionable given that his experience extended only so far as the Canadian militia in Ottawa and the minimal time that he had spent attempting to assemble a competent garrison in Halifax. Lacking wartime service, and thus the credibility that derived from it, his advice probably consisted of relevant anecdotes and a few interesting stories that he thought applicable at the time. Not having fought in any previous conflict, his counsel was surely limited in value, but he at least attempted to inform his soldiers to the best of his knowledge and ability. The usefulness of his guidance, and the true level of their competence, were soon to be tested.

SOUTH AFRICA

In early June 1900, the draft reached South Africa.[31] Adamson and his men immediately moved to Maitland Camp, a mere seven miles from Cape Town, where he found that "Most of the men and officers are half invalids from the front."[32] The main body of Strathconas had just left the area six days before, having been assigned the task of destroying an important bridge.[33] Being eager to see the front, Adamson became somewhat dejected when he was forced to wait since "I have no orders yet and no horses here for me, but hear they are somewhere."[34] Interestingly, on proceeding inland from the coast, David Stewart noted with some satisfaction that they all had been "Treated to beer & cigars on the way to camp by the Captain."[35] Adamson's munificence on this occasion undoubtedly served as a reward for his men who had worked exceedingly hard on both legs of the voyage from Canada and who had not been able to enjoy the local establishments in any of the cities they passed through owing to their tight schedule. When stopped at St. Vincent to coal the ship, all were forced to remain onboard owing to an outbreak of illness. Given the tedium and restraints of shipboard life, these unexpected gifts surely aided morale, especially among the smokers and drinkers of the draft.

Seeing that Agar was responsible for his soldiers' conduct, it is unlikely that he allowed them to drink to excess, but if he did, he surely removed himself before the effects of intoxication became apparent. A gentleman, to be sure, would never be seen participating in such activities with his subordinates. On this occasion, he undoubtedly maintained his professional distance in order that he might remain impartial should he be called upon to enforce discipline, which he often did with considerable vigour. That he was genuinely interested in their competence and welfare is clear, but he never related to them as his equal, for indeed they were not, seeing that he was from an entirely different social and military class than they.

After being warned to be ready to move on short notice as a separate unit, Adamson kept himself and the draft busy by "drawing extra stores." As he recalled:

> We have all plenty of work to do and the men are kept at
> it most of the time, though no drill to speak of, but my
> darling Mabel, it is very lonely work with no other offi-
> cer to help me and having to decide everything myself
> and act entirely on my own responsibility.[36]

His comments suggest that he was beginning to feel the pressure of command and that he might have been questioning his ability to lead. Serving in an active theatre of operations, instead of the more serene environments of Ottawa or Halifax, seems to have presented Agar with a number of challenges and frustrations that he was not entirely prepared for, or equipped to deal with.[37] The change in his mood after arriving in South Africa, where his enthusiasm or lack of decisiveness could mean the difference between life and death, not only for himself but for his troopers as well, weighed heavily. Mistakes onboard ship or in Canada could largely be forgiven, but overseas, as he was now realizing, most certainly could not.

Agar's sentiments also seem to imply that he was seeking reassurance that his actions were appropriate and right. Without officers around him to validate his conduct, and unable, for professional reasons, to speak to his men about his performance, lest they question his competence, Agar became stressed. He had rarely, if ever, been forced to act entirely on his own for extended periods of time; this novel and uncomfortable situation, then, forced him to rely on his inner-strength to maintain control over the circumstances in which he found himself.

Before leaving camp, a number of changes in the composition of the draft further compounded his mounting problems. By leaving some men behind "with beastly diseases they caught from filthy women,"[38] and simultaneously assuming command of others whom the main body of Strathconas had not taken along for various reasons, Adamson became saddled with a number of new soldiers he knew little about and who knew little about him. The time involved in transporting the draft from Ottawa to Cape Town at least provided an opportunity for him to become acquainted with his soldiers and for them to become familiar with his particular style of leadership, personality, and expectations. This transfer of personnel partially upset some of his efforts and might have, in the end, contributed to his anxiety. If he had felt any degree of comfort in his relations with his men owing to the time that they had spent together thus far, he must have likewise been dismayed at the prospect of starting all over again with his newest soldiers, especially since there were so many other pressing demands that were competing for his attention and effort.

After completing their stay at Maitland, Adamson and his now-altered draft took to the sea again, leaving for Durban in Natal where they, like the main body of Strathconas, would fight with General Sir Redvers Buller's Natal Field Force.[39] Before they reached their final destination, however, their vessel called at Port Elizabeth and East London.

Library and Archives Canada C-000171

Personnel of the Strathcona's Horse en route to South Africa aboard the
SS Monterey, *1899.*

As one member of the draft later recalled, "at the former place a party
of us went ashore and excited some curiosity amongst the townspeople
who had never before seen troops from far-away Canada."[40] Speaking of
the same incident, yet another soldier recorded in his diary:

> Cap't Adamson sticks up for his men in good shape.
> Was telling some of the boys that the people here had a
> very exaggerated account of our capabilities as horse-
> men and he didn't try to undeceive them so we were to
> do the best we can. Said they object to our saddles
> because they were too heavy but he said they were good
> enough for us.[41]

By relating to his men the details of his encounter with some of the
local inhabitants, Adamson undoubtedly instilled a sense of pride by
expressing his confidence and trust in them, even though he had had little
opportunity to observe their martial abilities or their horsemanship. He
apparently saw no reason to deflate a rumour that served the purposes of
building morale. By actively encouraging the unfounded impressions held
by the townsfolk, Adamson implied to those under his command that he
expected them to meet the standard of conduct and performance that he

had just set. Since he publicly expressed his faith in them, regardless of his private opinions, they undoubtedly felt obliged to demonstrate to their leader that his comments were indeed true, well founded, and deserved. Most certainly, the "Cap't seems proud of his men."[42]

Although Adamson did what he could to inspire his troopers and provide them with some soldierly skills, he also strove to maintain a high degree of discipline, a practice that he continued from his days in Halifax and probably before. If he at times appeared friendly and lax with his men, as he surely was when plying them with beer and cigars, he never let this occasional informality become the norm. As before, he maintained order through vigilance and his willingness to punish transgressors. In disgust, he related to Mabel:

> On board the Idaho [the ship that the draft travelled on from Cape Town to Durban] I reduced Sergeant Instructor Bertram to a Corporal for going on shore at Port Elizabeth. This morning he reported sick, and the hospital return has just come in and the brute has a filthy disease caught from a dirty woman at Capetown. He has to be left behind. He was married the day before he left Ottawa and I have been very good to him, although he was never of much assistance to me.[43]

Agar was so sickened with the sergeant's conduct that he opined, with considerable moral overtones, "I think men who subject themselves to such chances when they are on a game of this sort ought to be publicly disgraced as they are very short of traitors."[44]

Being willing to fall back upon his rank when required, Adamson also knew when to cede some of his authority to those beneath him. Before assuming their duties in the field, the draft was allowed to choose their own horses from a remount depot. Unlike the regiment proper, the draft did not bring horses with them from Canada, but rather arranged to be so equipped once in South Africa. After selecting a number of horses for his own use, he "picked five of my men to pick the other 40," a significant responsibility from which they surely derived great personal satisfaction. Since most of his troopers were originally from the Canadian West and thus probably knew more than he did about equine matters, he deferred to their better knowledge and ability in this regard. Although familiar with horses and an excellent rider, he probably did not feel comfortable selecting the horses his men would depend on when engaging the enemy. To be fair, however, his devolution of authority *after* he had chosen his own mounts suggests that he may simply have desired to select the best for himself and leave his rejects for his men to squabble over. Rank had its privileges during the Boer War and the selection of horses may have afforded him the opportunity to exercise his prerogative to his ultimate advantage.[45]

The stress that Adamson seems to have been feeling during his early days in South Africa, when first becoming accustomed to the rigours and difficulties of wartime service, did not recede quickly. When he and his men were ordered to "Charleston alone to scout the country," he accepted the responsibility, but was somewhat uncertain as to his abilities to execute the mission. He later wrote to Mabel, "They are asking a good deal of me. They offered me the job, asked me if I could do it, which of course I said I could, my only chance."[46] Aside from portraying himself in a heroic light, such a statement insinuates that Agar felt that he and the draft had to somehow prove their competence and worth to their British brethren. Whatever his private opinions, he appeared outwardly confident and able, an image that must have reassured his followers. Of course, hesitating to scout ahead would have marked Adamson as a less than efficient officer and, given his ambitions, he was not about to assume this moniker. Conversely, demonstrating his ability, especially during one of his first real assignments, ensured that his career in South Africa would start on a solid foundation.

Shortly after his foray to Charleston, the draft was attached to a fighting column and began more intense field operations. Their duties on the march consisted primarily of acting as either rear or advance guards, or as flanking parties or scouts, to the main body.[47] Their lack of training in open warfare soon became apparent as Adamson observed, "The men are all well and fit but some of them of very little use."[48] Although teaching soldiers aboard ship may have sufficed for drill, physical fitness, and marksmanship, it did not do when it came to imparting the knowledge necessary to move quickly and effectively in the field on horseback. Being ahead of the main column, one of his duties was also to commandeer supplies and to search farmsteads for weapons or other items of value. As he once noted, "Went ahead, with authority to sack a certain Rebel's house, which we did most thoroughly."[49] After arriving in Standerton on 2 July 1900,[50] the draft was attached for duty to the South African Light Horse (SALH).

This association, though temporary, was fortuitous. Owing to the dearth of real and meaningful training for the men, Adamson was genuinely pleased to see that "My men are learning many tips from them."[51]

Faced with the imminent prospect of meeting the enemy, Agar put his "two troops on fighting footing, cancelled all acting appointments and made new ones and fewer, doing away with Carey and three other Lance Corporals who had failed to have any authority over their small commands."[52] In this regard, Agar was genuinely concerned, and perhaps worried, about the draft's effectiveness. By replacing those whom he considered unable to lead with presumably better-qualified or at least more promising soldiers, he demonstrated that competence would be the guiding principle, since only the best and brightest would be advanced to positions of responsibility. Even though Agar had prepared the draft for action, he would still have to wait a little longer to meet the enemy since "Lt. Adamson's party are forty miles in rear but cannot come on [to join the regiment proper] at present owing to the danger of capture by the Boers who are to be seen occasionally."[53] The small, scattered parties of Boers would indeed prove to be trouble as events would show.

CANADA'S FIRST VICTORIA CROSS OF THE WAR — WOLVE SPRUIT

When attempting to link with the main body of Strathconas, who always seemed to be one step ahead of the draft, Adamson's men met with their first real engagement of the war at Wolve Spruit, located some distance from the town of Standerton. Since arriving in South Africa and assuming their duties as scouts and guards for various columns, they had not yet confronted the Boers in any sustained manner. This action would ultimately test the training that the draft had received since leaving Ottawa. For Agar, this short confrontation would compel him to lead competently and decisively in the face of the enemy. Like his men, he would find it a trying and difficult experience.

From Adamson's recollection of events, both immediately after the action itself and some months later, he and his draft, along with a large party from the SALH, started from Standerton early in the morning of 5 July and headed northwest towards a party of Boers on their right flank "who were showing in small numbers at top of hill." As the column approached, he writes, the "Enemy vanished with the supposed idea of drawing us into a trap." At this point, a small party of the SALH was detached from the main body and placed in hiding at the base of the hill occupied by the Boers. The elevated heights provided a commanding view of the "open and undulating" terrain and allowed all movements below to be easily observed. The remaining SALH, who carried with them a Maxim gun and a number of wagons, proceeded north-by-northwest, the idea being to lure the Boers off of the hill to pursue the Canadians, thus capturing them with the smaller force that had been concealed from view. A chess game of sorts was rapidly developing on the field, with each side attempting to outwit the other by strategically placing their forces in those areas where they might meet with the most success. The SALH unfortunately moved too far to the north and thus lost contact with the Strathconas, thus negating any support that they might have offered. Seeing these movements, the Boers wisely remained on the hilltop, thus causing the ruse to fail.

With more Boers appearing on his left flank, Adamson altered course to move against this new position in the north, leaving the concealed SALH to counter the enemy that had been sighted first. To make his thrust, Agar deployed 17 of his men in an advance guard at 50 yard intervals from one another, supported 500 yards back by the remainder of his draft. Suddenly, from a range of about 3,000 yards, the Strathconas in the advance guard came under an intense fire from their front. The men in the rear rank (the supports in reserve) were brought up even with those who were leading. In an attempt to carry the hill, the entire body galloped forward to within 1,000 yards of the enemy. After advancing a fair distance, Adamson's horse was shot in the leg, forcing him to dismount and move on foot to within 500 yards of the enemy. To further compound the Strathconas' difficulties, more Boers appeared to the north on their right flank; the enemy was now positioned in a horseshoe-like formation around the advancing Canadians. Despite the increased volume of fire, Adamson and his men continued to approach and engage the enemy to their front, moving to within 300 yards of the hilltop.

Because the SALH had not supported the attack, they in fact were no where to be seen, Adamson could not overrun the Boer position and was eventually forced to retire. He had essentially advanced too far forward, thereby exposing both of his flanks: The men on his left had moved too far north and west to be of any value and those concealed on his right, who were positioned to capture the Boers coming off of the hill, had meanwhile engaged the enemy to their immediate front and were pushing them eastward, thus increasing the distance between themselves and Adamson. In light of the mounting casualties to both horses and men, Agar fell back to a position some distance away from the enemy to his front. Unfortunately, two of his troopers did not see this sudden movement and continued to advance; they were easily captured by the Boers and made prisoners.

During the general retreat, when most of the men had withdrawn to a safe distance, Sergeant A.H.L. Richardson noticed that Alex McArthur had been dismounted, wounded, and left behind. To prevent him from being captured, the sergeant rode headlong into the advancing Boers (who had by now left the safety of the hilltop and were giving chase), placed him on his horse and rode slowly back in the direction of the waiting Strathconas, all the while under continuous fire. Seeing Richardson and McArthur coming towards him, Adamson ordered George Sparkes, his good friend from Ottawa, and a few others who happened to be close by, to provide as much protection as their rifles would allow.

To avoid the crossfire coming from his front and right, Agar swung his remaining men around to a position on his left. Mounting some extra horses, he advanced somewhat in a northerly direction and gained a position that he held until nightfall, the "Enemy fearing to advance, thinking we had strong reserves." Once he had consolidated his position, he sent some men back to Standerton at a full gallop to bring up reinforcements and an ambulance to tend to the injured. All in all, Adamson thought that his men had behaved "wonderfully cool" throughout their first major engagement. As he later scrawled to Mabel, "The bullets simply flew all around your head and body. It is wonderful how any escaped." He reassured her, as he was apt to do, that "I do not think I was afraid."[54]

Adamson's account of the engagement, on which this brief description is largely based, suggests a sense of orderliness and control. As revealed by the complexity of the draft's movements — breaking into two lines, advancing as one and then retiring, followed by shorter advances in spurts — his directions were apparently heard and understood by all, except the two who were captured. Again in his reassuring tone, he related to Mabel, "The men obeyed my whistle signals wonderfully well, and appeared to do good shooting." From his perspective, the draft failed to capture the hilltop because the SALH had not supported his advance. In essence, they played a minor role in the action; but had they brought their superior numbers and Maxim to bear, the situation might have been concluded very differently. Without the required support, Agar and his men were left to fend for themselves, a dangerous situation considering their lack of experience. As if to justify his actions, he wrote: "I obeyed my orders, and the C.O. of the S.A.L.H. complimented me. My orders were to engage the enemy," he recalled, "and await reinforcements … none of whom arrived."[55]

Another description of the engagement, written by a Strathcona who participated in the fighting, offers an entirely different perspective and, it would seem, places much of the blame for the day's failure squarely on Adamson's shoulders. Thomas Easton Howell, who must have been on the extreme right of the line that Adamson established in front of the enemy, suggests that the action was actually chaotic and confusing. His account more or less parallels the general sequence of events that Adamson offers. He recalled that when the SH came under fire from the front for the first time, at a range of 3,000 yards or so, "Instead of proceeding cautiously the advance was continued at a gallop and 10 minutes later we found ourselves scattered along a wide open ridge, without any support, and exposed to the fire of a rapidly increasing number of Boers." Soon thereafter, events continued to deteriorate for:

> our fellows had realized that they were in a tight corner but no one knew were Adamson was, no orders were given, and part of the troop was in a very exposed position on the wrong side of a barbed wire fence. A few minutes more and we would all have been completely surrounded. The only thing to do, of course, was to bolt and the whole troop was soon galloping away in all directions. At the next ridge some of us pulled up and waited for the stragglers two of whom were riding one horse.[56]

The two stragglers, of course, were Richardson and McArthur.

Howell certainly believed that Adamson had not conducted the operation in a competent and cool manner. The fact that he could not be seen by those who were looking for direction may have resulted from the unfortunate fact that "I was dressed as a trooper without a bandolier, but they [the Boers] were on to me all the time."[57] The loss of his horse, which compelled him to advance on foot, may also have played a role in reducing his visibility since his galloping troopers would have quickly outpaced him. If, on the other hand, the Boers knew that Adamson was in a position of responsibility, he must have been directing his soldiers in a visible fashion that was clearly noticeable despite his attempts at an inconspicuous dress. Although Howell likewise recalled that "Something went wrong … and our support soon completely lost touch with us and did not turn up again," his passing reference to this point, and his concentration on the chaos of the action itself, implies that he blamed Adamson for much of what went wrong.[58] Agar may have acted somewhat impulsively and hastily, being in action for the first time, but as he stated, he was ordered to engage the enemy to his front and that was exactly what he did.

Writing some years later, Andrew Miller recorded the action in his history of the SH in South Africa. His account reinforces Howell's statements that all was not as orderly as Adamson contended. He wrote in 1912:

> On July 5th, at Wolverspruit [*sic*], near Standerton, thirty-eight troopers of Strathcona's Horse started in pursuit of an apparently small Boer force. The chase had not proceeded far, when the Canadians discovered themselves in an ambush, with over two hundred of the enemy on either side of them, who opened fire at less than three hundred yards range. The Boer fire plainly indicated that the Canadians were outnumbered, and that their only safety lay in a speedy retreat.

He added that once Richardson had grabbed McArthur, his horse, being tired and exhausted, would not leap over a single strand of barbed wire about two feet off of the ground, which had formed part of a three-wire fence. Richardson spurred his horse but to no avail. Only when his mount received a wound in its shoulder did the shock of the impact impel it to jump the remaining wire and make for the Canadian lines. After conveying the two soldiers to safety, the horse died of its wounds and the exhaustion of the chase. While waiting for the horse to jump, "The Boers … were reducing the distance, and the Canadians could again hear their calls to surrender."[59]

After the engagement, Adamson returned to camp and pondered the recent events. Impressed by Richardson's bravery, he immediately forwarded a report to headquarters recommending the man for a Victoria Cross (VC), the British Empire's highest award for bravery, believing "it would be a great thing if we could get him a V.C. for Canada, the S.H. and the Mounted Police to which he belongs."[60] In due course, Richardson received his award, the citation reading:

> On July 5, at Wolve Spruit, about 15 miles north of Standerton, a party of Lord Strathcona's Corps, only 38 in number, came into contact, and was engaged at close quarters, with a force of 80 of the enemy. When the order to retire had been given, Sgt. Richardson rode back under a very heavy cross-fire and picked up a trooper whose horse had been shot and who was wounded in two places, and rode with him out of fire. At the time when this act

of gallantry was performed, Sgt. Richardson was within 300 yards of the enemy, and was himself riding a wounded horse.[61]

This action was later described as "one of the most daring feats of the entire war."[62] Incidentally, Richardson was an original member of the Strathconas who had served previously with the NWMP. Owing to a back injury sustained while unloading horses from a transport ship, he had been left behind in hospital and later joined the draft to reconnect with the main body. He was one of the new men that Adamson had received at Maitland Camp before moving inland.

During this brief engagement, from the time that the enemy was initially observed until the concluding act of gallantry, two men were wounded and three were taken prisoner.[63] Despite the casualties, Adamson thought the day beneficial, for the draft "are all working well, and the scrap has had a very good effect, making them look upon the game as not a joke … but a very serious matter."[64] The encounter seemed to bring everyone, Adamson included, to the full reality of the nature of conflict. They had matured quickly in the span of a few hours and now better understood the complexities of war. Having no experience with the Boers in particular, or with fighting in general, the engagement came as a profound shock to all and gave them much to reflect upon. The remainder of Agar's time in South Africa could now be approached with the knowledge that command was not easy, especially in battle, and that orders, if poorly given, could have devastating consequences for those who were obliged to follow.

With limited evidence on which to base an assessment, it is difficult to state with absolute certainty how much Adamson's conduct contributed to the defeat on 5 July. On the one hand, judging by the effectiveness of the Boer ambush and the number of casualties they inflicted, he appears to have acted hastily in ordering his men to the attack. Rushing forward, realizing that he was outnumbered and then retreating in haste is not suggestive of a well-conceived plan. Although "dash and daring" were desirable qualities in officers, as well as attributes Agar later demonstrated he possessed in abundance, he might have realized on this occasion that his lack of battle experience warranted some initial caution. Yet, conversely, he seems to have been in the vanguard of the attack, leading from the front. Owing to the complexity of the draft's movements, his troopers must have heard his whistles; the Boers certainly knew that he was in charge. From the above description, it seems logical to assume that Adamson's conduct on this occasion was the best that could be expected of an untested officer. He made some mistakes, but his men generally performed well under his direction. Now with their first engagement concluded, they could approach the remainder of their time in South Africa with the confidence borne of experience. No longer would they have to ponder how they would perform in battle or what battle itself would be like. A weight had finally been lifted.

THE FOLLOWING MONTHS

After this defining engagement, Adamson continued his journey to join the regiment proper. When not actively engaging the enemy or writing home to tell Mabel about his novel experiences, he thought about the recent action and analyzed his own performance, and that of his men. Agar had reason to be proud of their collective accomplishments considering that it was their first real test of their soldierly abilities, but the costs weighed heavily on his mind. In terms of casualties, this single engagement would ultimately prove to be one of the Strathconas' worst of the entire war.[65]

Adamson attempted to ensure in the days that followed that he and his soldiers would not be lured into an ambush for a second time. In this regard at least, he had learned a great deal about Boer tactics and about the difficulty of leading soldiers in battle and of leading well. Given

Courtesy RCD Archives and Collection

Mounted infantry and Dragoons crossing a South African river.

these circumstances, he now tackled his work with a little more caution than before, being acutely aware that his decisions could exact a heavy toll. Nearly a week later, on 10 July and again on 14 July, the draft recognized a number of Boers in the distance while scouting but did "no firing," nor did they give chase.[66]

The difficulties and hazards of campaigning, which the engagement at Wolve Spruit vividly illustrated, resulted in Agar becoming more forthright and assertive towards his superiors. Being now aware of how quickly situations could deteriorate in the field, he was much more reluctant to accept direction without first anticipating the possible outcomes. Rather than trying to impress his superiors with his willingness to engage the enemy, as had been the case when the draft was given the responsibility of scouting near Charleston shortly after their arrival in South Africa, he now conducted himself with the knowledge of a veteran, who could to some extent predict possible problems. His innocence had been replaced by a soberness that had an eye to the future.

On 10 July, for instance, he immediately objected to orders to escort a convoy of baggage. Although he dutifully "Reported that I was ready to go ahead," he was understandably concerned about the possible dangers owing to "my small knowledge of the direction we were to go in [and] that we were a bit small, as the men of the Devons [Devonshire Regiment] had gone on ahead by train."[67] When later ordered to scout ahead to locate the enemy, he again refused until he had obtained wire cutters, a tool that would enable his force to cut through fences to pursue (or flee from) the enemy.[68] The action at Wolve Spruit may have been playing on his mind at this moment since the wire fences in the area had proved a significant obstacle for some of his men. With only Agar's perspective on the issue, it is exceedingly difficult to gauge the reasons behind his increased hesitancy. Nevertheless, these two successive "objections" raise the possibility that he was somewhat shaken by his first engagement and therefore a little reluctant to meet the enemy again, especially when he was disadvantaged owing to the lack of proper equipment, available reinforcements, and information about the terrain. On the other hand, his initial unwillingness to follow his orders could also be indicative of a well-developed moral courage that enabled him to risk his own reputation (and possibly his career) for a point of principle that he felt deserved strong voice. He certainly had the best interests of his soldiers in mind when informing his superiors of the potential dangers of their orders, for as he admitted candidly, "I do not want to have my good men shot down for the sake of a few waggons of bulley beef and biscuits."[69]

Whatever his reasons for objecting, Adamson took decisive measures to ensure that his next engagement would not be accompanied by significant casualties or defeat. In this regard, he continued to train his men to the best of his ability. On 12 July, he noted, "Took my men out at 8 a.m. … for two hours and a half teaching them to keep proper intervals and dressing when extending which they do not do very well."[70] Such a comment suggests that the men's spacing during the earlier engagement at Wolve Spruit may not have been proper and may have, in the end, contributed to some of their difficulties during their brush with the Boers. After this exercise, he conducted dismounted drill, a kit inspection, and then marched them to water. Once the men had completed a general fatigue, he ordered a saddling harness parade, an inspection of arms, and then he dismissed them for dinner, but not before "reminding them that in future they had better be more careful about keeping their distance and dressing when patrolling."[71] His exhausting and varied regimen on this day seems more consistent with punishment than with meaningful and thoughtful training! In his estimation, mistakes that were made in the past could not, and would not, be made again.

Aside from these incidents, the draft experienced little excitement on their way to join the main body of SH, which they finally did at Watervaal on 17 July. Once Adamson joined the balance of the regiment, he more or less disappears from the historical record, save for letters to his wife, which unfortunately end in mid-August. Several months pass before he is heard from again, meaning that there is a near total lack of references to his later performance.

At first glance, this lack of information implies he was neither so outstanding as to deserve public compliment, nor so incompetent as to warrant public censure. Rather than operating as a separate entity, his fate and fortunes were now tied to that of the Strathconas themselves, and this fact, combined with his valuable experiences to date, may have removed some of the pressures that he had been feeling. In contrast to his time at Maitland, he now had other officers to assist him in his work who could offer the "validation" that he seems to have been seeking. For at least the next month, he continued with the various duties that he and his men had performed since arriving in South Africa. Writing to Mabel, he noted, "Our particular work is to either scout, protect [the] column or gallop up, drawing the fire of the enemy, [and] pretending to retire, endeavouring to draw them out in the open."[72] Other duties also included "rebel chasing, farm burning, and collecting civilians for shipment to concentration camps."[73] Despite these general responsibilities, he was nevertheless involved in the capture of three different towns in quick succession.

In August, in one of his first major actions after Wolve Spruit, Adamson and his soldiers played a key role in capturing Amersfoort. Outlining the general situation for his wife, Agar wrote: "I had the advance guard and 2 small galloping guns under me, with orders to enter if possible, if not hold for main column (flying) to come up." With understandable pride, he also recalled for her benefit, "I was the first to reach the actual Town being in the centre of the semi circle the advance guard formed."[74] His comments clearly indicate that he led from the front on this particular occasion, and by so doing, set the example for all others to follow. Being conspicuously exposed, he encouraged his troopers to follow him as he implied through his actions and presence that he was willing to share the same amount of risk as they. The relative ease with which Amersfoort was captured prompted Steele to write after the war, "The behaviour of the regiment on this occasion was excellent. The whole of it screened the front and flanks during the march, and by skilful work on the part of the corps the enemy's positions were turned and he was forced to retire." Perhaps more important, he also saw fit to mention: "The officers of the regiment worked so well that it would be hard to make individual mention."[75] Steele did not confine his praise entirely to his officers alone, for he noted that his soldiers "behaved splendidly displaying great caution."[76]

Adamson again led from the front as the SH approached the town of Emerlo. As he recalled in a letter to Mabel, "I had a troop on the flank the next day, and owing to the advance guard mixing up their orders, got into Ermilo [sic] ahead of them."[77] Once these two towns had been captured, the SH moved against and captured Carolina where they "blew up the powder magazine."[78]

On 1 September, after the SH had begun their advance through a feature known as Crocodile Valley, they noticed a Boer convoy approaching a long and difficult slope at the other end of the ravine, an obstacle that would surely slow their progress and offer the pursuing British column a chance to capture many valuable stores and to seize many prisoners. After observing such a temping prize, some scouts belonging to SH "pushed their horses forward at the gallop until within four hundred yards of it." Lacking support and being mounted on now-tired horses, they were compelled to retire. Nevertheless, half an hour later:

> a troop of Strathcona's Horse under Lieut. Adamson took up the pursuit, but the convoy had then reached the

head of the valley and was disappearing among the hills. As the pursuit proceeded, the regiment followed at a rapid pace close behind. Overtaking the rear guard near a farm house at the foot of the hills, Lieut. Adamson and his men carried on dismounted action, but as the regiment was halted and ordered to go into bivouac he returned, although the scouts remained out until dark. The troop had retired some distance before it was discovered that one of its number, Pte. McGillivray, was missing. An attempt was made to find him, but the search was fruitless. The Boers had been quick to occupy the ground Lieut. Adamson had vacated, and had made the missing man a prisoner.[79]

Six months later, Adamson learned for himself the true fate of his trooper whom he had thought dead up until this point. His letter to Mabel, in which he relates much of the same story as above, offers an extraordinary glimpse into his character and leadership abilities and thus is worth quoting at length:

My man McGillvery [*sic*] lost and supposed to be killed at Badfontein Valley has turned up in South Africa a returned prisoner. There has hardly been a day that I did not think I should have gone further into the enemy's lines to find him, although at the time had I done so and this I thoroughly understood we must have lost half our men and a whole squadron of the S.A.L.H. under a seasoned officer refused to even support us and declined to even remain with me which we did do for three hours after they left us. As things turned out my judgment was fortunately a proper one as they had a trap for us and not one of us could have pulled out alive had we fought for it, as I fancy we should. It now appears that McGillvray [*sic*] after passing the third donga (after which I thought all my men safe) and well out of fire, went off after some chickens he heard cackling and was collared by the enemy, who thought we would return for him. Had I done so we would all have fallen into a trap and for the sake of a man who says the Boers treated him very well, and he was much more comfortable with them than with us, and was sorry when they were forced to give him up. It is just as well we did not. You have no idea darling how happy this piece of news has made me, and taken a great weight off my mind, for while it was by no means cowardice (much as you may doubt it, knowing how you fancy I value my skin) that prevented my rushing what I felt sure to be a trap. I had 50 men under me and only myself to decide and did not wish to lead them into trouble. The next day I picked 12 men to go over the ground. The rest of this story you know. Anyway it has helped to make my reminiscences of S.A. [South Africa] less unpleasant than they were.[80]

Agar's private confessions to his wife, in which he could scarcely contain his joy, confirm that he was generally interested in and deeply concerned about the welfare of his soldiers. His admission that he felt responsible for the trooper's demise, as well as for the well-being of everyone else under his command, is very much in keeping with his character and personality. His comments further reveal that he did not wish to expose his soldiers to unnecessary danger, however noble and honourable the cause. He again implies that the pressure and solitude of command weighed heavily on his shoulders, but that some of this burden was alleviated by the news that all was indeed well. Agar's concern for his men was not simply a literary ploy to gain credit with and sympathy from his wife. When T.E. Howell recalled the action later, he wrote: "Finally Adamson unwilling to imperil the safety of all for the sake of one gave the order to retire and the troop rode reluctantly away. Once out of range, however, we halted and examined the surrounding country for signs of the missing man."[81]

Unfortunately, little is known about Adamson's activities during the months of September and October.[82] Because his correspondence from this period has not survived, not much can be said about his involvement in the Strathconas' subsequent engagements. The fact that his subordinates neither recorded his activities nor their impressions of him only complicates the matter further.[83] Agar's conduct, along with that of the remainder of the regiment, was sufficient enough to encourage Lord Strathcona to write after the war:

It is hardly necessary for me to say that I am very proud of Strathcona's Horse. The men were evidently all that could be desired and I have every reason to be grateful for the way in which they were led by the Officers who were appointed to command them.[84]

All in all, given his past record, he probably continued to lead from the front while keeping the welfare of his soldiers foremost in mind. If his past behaviour is any indication, he surely maintained discipline within his troop and punished those who transgressed the bounds of acceptable conduct. Additional experience would have given Agar a better understanding of the difficulties of leading men against a determined enemy. That he had much to learn still is suggested by his admission to Mabel, "There are many tricks about campaigning, which had I know [*sic*], I would have bought several things."[85] Almost certainly, he continued to develop into a competent and trusted officer on whom his subordinates could depend; his successes, whether in battle or in overcoming challenges of whatever nature, surely fostered his gradually evolving confidence.

A Premature End

In many of the "glorious little wars" that Great Britain fought during the nineteenth century, disease posed a much greater threat to life than did the enemy. The conflict in South Africa was no different. On the veldt, enteric fever proved to be a significant problem as scores of soldiers either died from this malady or were sent to hospital to recover from it. Within SH, the incidence of disease increased during the months of September, October, and November. As Lieutenant-Colonel Steele observed, "We have a great many suffering from slight attacks of fever, and dysentery, but none serious."[86] Being a constant threat to the regiment's strength and effectiveness, it was only a matter of time before illness of one sort or another claimed more victims. Having thus far escaped the enemy's guns, Adamson soon fell ill in early November and was eventually sent to hospital to recuperate, a transfer that effectively ended his association with SH in the field. At the end of the month, after spending some time in hospital, he was invalided back to England.[87] Leaving Cape Town, he thought about being reunited with his wife, with whom he had corresponded so frequently, and about the regiment in which he had served for roughly four months through an arduous and often frustrating campaign.

After visiting the south of France to further recuperate from his illness, he returned to London where he sat a number of medical boards and attempted to wrestle his pay from a reluctant War Office. Being found unsuitable for further service, he was invalided back to Canada in March 1901. Agar's ambition and quest for adventure, however, would not let him settle back into the stately and privileged lifestyle that he had enjoyed before his first appointment. Perhaps a dinner given by the governor-general to commemorate the battle of Paardeberg rekindled or reinforced his desire for a commission that would again take him overseas to South Africa.[88] Unlike before, when he could only rely on the goodwill and patronage of an impressive retinue of supporters and on the few practical skills that he had gleaned from the militia, he could now cite meaningful military experience as an additional qualification. The time spent with SH, both with the draft and regiment proper, gave him a good appreciation of the confusion of war and, perhaps more significantly, of the difficulties of leading soldiers in battle. The knowledge that he now possessed was based on real and relevant experience drawn from a modern war, rather than from interesting anecdotes and stories. The limited experience that he gained through the militia could only go so far in developing his ability as a competent and effective officer, yet his service in South Africa, where casualties were incurred and the real demands of active campaigning were more fully appreciated, provided him with a complete, if quick, education. His experience, and consequent rise in credibility, was a point that he would not allow to go unnoticed.

Armed with recommendations from many of his former commanding officers, both from the GGFG and SH, Adamson petitioned the minister of militia in late March 1902 for a place "in the contingent now being formed for South Africa."[89] In due course, Adamson received a junior captaincy in the 6th Canadian Mounted Rifles (CMR).[90] As it turned out, Agar was a valuable asset for his new regiment "contained a core of professional officers, [but] few had combat experience."[91] Although the CO and second-in-command, Lieutenant-Colonel J.D. Irving and Major W.D. Gordon, respectively, were both professional soldiers, neither had served in South Africa. Like many of the units raised in Canada, "The officers chosen to command ... were a mix of the tired, the trusted, and the ambitious. For many, advancement in rank provided an inducement to join; all stood a good chance of exchanging their war experience for a promotion upon their return." In a similar manner, most of the men recruited to fill the ranks lacked any previous military experience, while the

Victoria Cross winner Sergeant A.H.L. Richardson.

remainder "claimed only temporary and frequently nominal membership in the Canadian militia."[92]

Agar was intimately familiar with such a situation, having inherited a motley collection volunteers for SH, all of whom lacked military knowledge. The opportunity thus presented itself to impart advice to those above and below him concerning the enemy, their style of warfare and what one could expect while on active service since he had "learned the wiliness of the Boers and knew when and how to strike."[93] In contrast to before, he could now offer more meaningful and realistic advice based on his own personal successes and shortcomings. His credibility as a veteran could be put to good use in heightening the quality and usefulness of his counsel. As he observed in one of his letters, "We have done very little drilling, which is possible [*sic*] a mistake."[94]

Despite the potential of his new assignment, peace was finally attained in May, thus ending the war and the regiment's *raison d'etre.* Adamson reacted poorly to the news. Writing to Mabel, he made it known from Durban that "I am severely disappointed not to have had a chance at doing something, and in this Regiment there would have been more of it than with the Strathconas."[95] A few weeks later, he similarly lamented, "You probably know the bad luck. We have all been ordered home at once."[96] His frustration must have weighed heavily, for his efforts in gaining a second commission so that he might meet the enemy again had amounted to naught. Agar's time in the service of monarch and empire had finally drawn to a less-than dramatic end.

After his two trips to South Africa, Adamson could fairly claim that he was an experienced and seasoned soldier. While his campaign medal would provide a "badge of social respectability" and a certain amount of credibility among his military superiors and subordinates, the lessons he had learned about leadership, about soldiers in general, and about himself in particular were of much greater value. His service during the war gave him much to reflect upon. Despite his early difficulties, he had reason to be proud of his accomplishments. All in all, he had taken a draft of westerners with no military experience to South Africa without major incident; led them through some difficult engagements; provided the best training that space and time would allow; made a determined effort to correct deficiencies in their performance; kept them in good, if not strict, discipline; and become an efficient field officer. As a leader, he employed a variety of techniques to motivate his soldiers such as providing rewards (i.e., alcohol) when his soldiers earned the privilege, perpetuating popular myths about the effectiveness of the Canadian horsemen, and ensuring a degree of responsibility was given to his subordinates. Like other veterans, he now understood that leading in active operations was a demanding, if not a stressful, responsibility that required the greatest care and concern. During his months with Strathcona's Horse, Agar strove to become a better officer by learning from his own experiences. His time on the veldt broadened his horizons and confidence, for the experience and abilities that he took away from South Africa in 1902 did not accurately reflect the knowledge and skills that he had initially brought with him in 1900. War had matured him for the better.

In the autumn of 1914, Agar returned to military service as a captain with the Princess Patricia's Canadian Light Infantry (PPCLI). Over the next four years, he would rise to command his regiment, earn the Distinguished Service Order as a major and ruin his health. Although the pressure of command weighed on him during his time in South Africa, where he met the Boers only occasionally and was responsible for a relatively small number of men, it finally became unbearable during the First World War when he was accountable for an entire battalion that made constant and costly contact with the Germans. While his career with the PPCLI is beyond the scope of this chapter, it seems reasonable to suggest, that the leadership lessons that he learned in South Africa provided a strong foundation for much of his subsequent military behaviour. Having already learned many of the differences between leading citizen-soldiers in a militia setting and leading citizen-soldiers in the field against a determined enemy, he could now strive to replicate his successes and avoid paths that had earlier led to failure.

In France and Belgium, Agar relied on many of the same leadership techniques that he had refined or developed in South Africa, probably because he found them to work so well. During both conflicts, for instance, he always spent time learning about those under his command since, in his opinion, "it is inclined to help the men if they know you take more than a general interest in them."[97] In addition, when serving in the trenches, he, as before, tried to reduce the risks his soldiers faced.[98] During the First World War, Agar could usually be found in forward positions with his soldiers, a characteristic that he continued from his time in the vanguard of attacks in South Africa. One cannot say that simply locating examples of duplicate behaviour between the two wars, of which there are more, conclusively proves that Agar used his earlier experiences to influence his subsequent conduct, but it is an intriguing possibility that deserves attention.

In addition, some of his attitudes changed as a result of his 20 years of service. Reflecting common thought at the turn-of-the-century, for instance, he initially believed that officers should be men of station who possessed the right upbringing, background, and schooling. Patronage was a means for advancement that should be exploited. In contrast, he realized during the Great War that some men from the ranks, regardless of their pre-war social standing or occupation, made very good officers or NCOs owing to the practical knowledge that they had accrued at the front. By this time, in his estimation, ill-used and ill-advised patronage had become a scourge to Canada's professional army and he often attempted to limit its pervasive and destructive influence.[99] This change in perception probably resulted from the many opportunities that he had had to watch his soldiers perform in the face of the enemy. Seeing the successful manner in which they handled men in difficult and trying circumstances probably destroyed his preconceived notions that only the well-bred should be commissioned or advanced. The frequent need to replace casualties, something that he had not been forced to do in South Africa to any great extent, seems to have contributed to this realization as well by compelling him to select those individuals who were best suited to command, regardless of their social pedigree. During the First World War, when he was responsible for the success of an entire battalion, he became more willing to sacrifice social graces and table manners for battlefield efficiency, although competency always remained a guiding principle.[100] Again, examining this and any other attitudinal shifts to further understand his character would be profitable.

All in all, Agar Adamson was a dynamic individual who developed significantly as a leader over time. He was neither static nor inert in his thinking, for he learned from past lessons and allowed them to guide his future conduct, at least in South Africa. His early experiences transformed him into a better soldier and provided him with valuable knowledge about leadership in general and the men he led. Whereas in 1900, his extensive connections with the upper-echelons of society set him apart from his contemporaries, in 1914, it was his status as a veteran of Canada's most recent war that distinguished him from many, but of his fellow soldiers. Now that some of the groundwork has been laid, investigating his accomplishments, character, and personality during the First World War will undoubtedly reveal just how influential his time in South Africa truly was.

NOTES

1. Agar Adamson, Norm Christie, ed., *Letters of Agar Adamson, 1914 to 1919* (Nepean, ON: CEF Books, 1997), Agar Adamson to Mabel Adamson, 4 March 1917, 268.

2. Adamson once served on the staff of Major-General E.T.H. Hutton, the general officer commanding the Canadian militia, at the "autumn manoeuvres." Interestingly, Hutton was a close personal friend of Lord Minto. Agar's acquaintances included other governors-general as well, for he was a friend of Lord Dufferin's son, Lord Ava. See Library and Archives Canada [LAC], Lord Strathcona's Horse [LdSH] Fonds, Manuscript Group [MG] 30 — E166, Vol. 2, File 1, Clouston to Strathcona, 18 April 1900; *Ibid.*, Minto to Strathcona, 18 April 1900; Desmond Morton, *A Military History of Canada*, 4th ed. (Toronto: McClelland & Stewart, 1999), 113; and Sandra Gwyn, *The Private Capital: Ambition and Love in the Age of Macdonald and Laurier* (Toronto: McClelland & Stewart, 1984), 345.

3. Sir Charles G.D. Roberts and Arthur L. Tunnell, *Canadian Who Was Who — Volume II — 1875–1937 — A Standard Dictionary of Canadian Biography* (Toronto: Trans-Canada Press, 1938), 1–2, and, Henry James Morgan, ed., *The Canadian Men and Women of the Time: A Hand-Book of Canadian Biography of Living Characters* (Toronto: William Briggs, 1912), 7. For a brief biography of Agar's father, see W.L. Morton, "Adamson, William Agar," in Francess G. Halpenny, ed., *Dictionary of Canadian Biography*, Vol. 9 (Toronto: University of Toronto Press, 1976), 4–5.

4. LAC, Record Group [RG] 9, II-F-6, Vol. 11 and Vol. 12, Governor General's Foot Guards, Nominal Rolls, 1886–1896 and 1896–1908, respectively.

5. Morton, *Military History*, 96.

6. *Ibid.*, 95. See also, Andrew Greenhill, Cameron Pulsifer, ed., "Narrative of the Volunteer Camp at Niagara, June 1871," *Canadian Military History* 12, 4 (2003), 37–54.

7. Patrick H. Brennan, "Good Men for a Hard Job: Infantry Battalion Commanders in the Canadian Expeditionary Force," *The Canadian Army Journal*, 9.1 (Spring 2006), 13.

8. "Stately Fall Wedding," 1, 15 November 1899, *The Evening Star*. The Cawthras were colloquially known as "'The Astors of Canada.'" See Gwyn, *Private Capital*, 347.

9. Carman Miller, *Painting the Map Red: Canada and the South African War, 1899–1902* (Montreal and Kingston: McGill-Queen's University Press, 1993), 145 and 439.

10. Gwyn, *Private Capital*, 350.

11. LAC, Agar Stewart Allan Masterton Adamson Fonds, MG 30 — E149, Vol. 2, File 1, Agar to Mabel, 3 March 1900. For a highly interesting account of the vices and virtues of Halifax in the 19th century, see Judith Fingard, *The Dark Side of Life in Victorian Halifax* (Nova Scotia: Pottersfield Press, 1989).

12. Being authorized and raised in the span of a few short weeks, the battalion experienced a number of early difficulties, such as recruiting shortages, insufficient rations, and a spate of illnesses, which tested the resolve and ability of officers and men alike. See "Offer of Militia for Garrison Duty Accepted," *Halifax Herald*, 3 March 1900, 1; "Making up Militia Garrison for Halifax," *Ibid.*, 3 March 1900, 1; "New Garrison Coming at Once," *Ibid.*, 6 March 1900, 1; "It Will Not be a Picnic For Them," *Ibid.*, 22 March 1900, 5; "Men Are Not Turning Up," *Ibid.*, 22 March 1900, 7; "Youthful Soldiers to Care for Halifax," *Ibid.*, 23 March 1900, 5; "The Officers Quarters at Wellington Barracks," *Ibid.*, 23 March 1900, 6; "Provisional Regiment," *Ibid.*, 26 March 1900, 5; "Another Hitch," *Ibid.*, 27 March 1900, 7; "Provisional Battalion," *Ibid.*, 30 March 1900, 2; "Canadians 780 Strong," *Ibid.*, 30 March 1900, 8; "Refused to Drill," *Ibid.*, 31 March 1900, 6; "Provisional Regiment," *Ibid.*, 2 April 1900, 8; "The Men Don't Like the Orders," *Ibid.*, 5 April 1900, 5; and, "First Death in Regiment," *Ibid.*, 9 April 1900, 1. Unfortunately, Adamson's role in all of this, whether in minimizing or exacerbating such problems, is unknown and highly unfortunate as his conduct during this period would have shed considerable light on his character and leadership abilities.

13. LAC, Adamson Fonds, Agar to Mabel, 10 April 1900.

14. LAC, LdSH Fonds, Vol. 1, File 3, Strathcona to Laurier, 19 January 1900. See also, Department of Militia and Defence for the Dominion of Canada, Sessional Paper 35a, *Organization, Equipment, Despatch and Service of the Canadian Contingents During the War in South Africa, 1899–1900* (Ottawa: S.E. Dawson, 1901).

15. Details pertaining to the raising of the SH proper can be found in LAC, LdSH Fonds, Vol. 1, File 3, Militia Orders, No. 26, 1 February 1900.

16. *Ibid.*, Vol. 1, File 5, Strathcona to Department of Militia and Defence, 20 February 1900. Details pertaining to the raising of the SH draft can be found in *Ibid.*, Vol. 4, File 3, Militia Orders, No. 92, 23 April 1900.

17. *Ibid.*, Vol. 2, File 1, Borden to Strathcona (Telegram), 16 April 1900; and *Ibid.*, Borden to Strathcona (Letter), 16 April 1900. For an indication of the type of men recruited and the towns and cities from whence they came, see "Hundreds of Recruits Offered," 8, 26 April 1900, *Ottawa Evening Journal;*

"Recruiting in the West," 5, 24 April 1900, *Ottawa Free Press;* LAC, LdSH Fonds, Vol. 2, File 3, Adamson to Strathcona, 8 June 1900; and "Off to the War," *Ottawa Evening Journal,* 1 May 1900, 8.

18. For the various petitions received by Strathcona in support of Agar, see LAC, LdSH Fonds, Vol. 2, File 1, Mabel to Strathcona, 17 April 1900; *Ibid.,* Borden to Strathcona, 18 April 1900; and *Ibid.,* Minto to Strathcona, 18 April 1900. That Agar was an ambitious young socialite is clear, but how much his wife encouraged him to seek advancement is unknown. He certainly relied on her connections and networks, but she may have unilaterally cultivated them on his behalf as well. See, for instance, LAC, Adamson Fonds, Agar to Mabel, 3 March 1900 and 27 December 1901. This line of thought is not altogether unsubstantiated for Sandra Gwyn notes that Mabel once flirted with the minister of militia and defence to obtain a commission for her husband. See Gwyn, *Private Capital,* 328, 422 and 473.

19. Strathcona's Horse did not receive the appellation "Lord" until 1911. Adamson's commission as a temporary lieutenant in SH dated from 12 May 1900. See Sessional Paper 35a, 158. Another document, however, has his commission being gazetted on 11 May 1900. See LAC, LdSH Fonds, Vol. 3, File 5, Under Secretary of State for War to Strathcona, 31 May 1900. Though the prominence of Adamson's patrons and the machinations of his wife surely influenced the awarding of his commission, the possibility also exists that he benefited from mere circumstance. In March 1900, Borden decided that soldiers from the Halifax garrison would be considered first, if and when additional men were required to fill vacancies in the contingents already overseas, namely, the Royal Canadian Regiment of Infantry and the Canadian Mounted Rifles. In fact, "Those joining the Halifax regiment ... have the first chance of seeing service should any vacancies occur." See "Will Get First Chance," *Halifax Herald,* 26 March 1900, 5; and "Impressions of Halifax," *Ibid.,* 18 April 1900, 6. If this decision had indeed set the precedent, then volunteers from Halifax would logically have been considered first when it was eventually decided to raise a draft for SH. With this being said, however, the weight added to his petition by his supporters can neither be dismissed nor overlooked, especially in this era of patronage-driven politics.

20. "A Hearty Send-Off," *Morning Chronicle,* 21 April 1900, 5.

21. The garrison's officers were heavily criticized by some of their subordinates and the *Canadian Military Gazette* for allegedly mistreating those beneath them and for supposedly being inexperienced. See "Provisional Regiment," *Halifax Herald,* 7 April 1900, 11; and "A Grumble from Halifax," *Ibid.,* 9 April 1900, 6.

22. LAC, Thomas Easton Howell Fonds, MG 29 — E20, Narrative, 2.

23. For Lord Minto's accounts of the fire, see Paul Stevens and John T. Saywell, eds., *Lord Minto's Canadian Papers: A Selection of the Public and Private Papers of the Fourth Earl of Minto, 1898–1904,* Vol. 1 (Toronto: The Champlain Society, 1981), 346–47 and 349–51.

24. See "Strathcona Recruits," *Montreal Daily Star*, 1 May 1900, 7; and "Off to the War," *Ottawa Evening Journal*, 1 May 1900, 8.

25. "George Sparks is Going," *Ottawa Free Press*, 28 April 1900, 1.

26. LAC, RG 9, II-A-3, Vol. 30. See also "George Sparks Is Going," *Ottawa Free Press*, 28 April 1900, 1; and "City News in Brief," *Halifax Herald*, 28 April 1900, 2.

27. LAC, LdSH Fonds, Vol. 2, File 3, Adamson to Strathcona.

28. LAC, Adamson Fonds, Agar to Mabel, 27 May 1900.

29. LAC, LdSH Fonds, Vol. 2, File 3, Adamson to Strathcona, 8 June 1900.

30. Diary entry for 8 May 1900, David Morrison Stewart Collection, *Canadian Letters and Images Project* [*CLIP*]. Online collection available at *http://web.mala.bc.ca/ davies/Letters.Images/homepage.htm*.

31. For confirmation, see LAC, Robert Burns Heron Fonds, MG 29 — E50, diary entry for 10 June 1900. Before describing Adamson's brief, if interesting, career in South Africa, it must be made clear that not every action in which he was engaged will be examined. In many instances, he is not at all mentioned in the historical record concerning these events, and thus his participation remains circumstantial. Because he is not mentioned by name, an assessment of his leadership abilities during specific engagements would be based solely on speculation and could only be inferred by the relative success or failure of the SH as a whole. For these reasons, the engagements treated here are all supported by evidence concerning Adamson's involvement

32. LAC, Adamson Fonds, Agar to Mabel, 3 June 1900.

33. For a brief description of the proposed attack, see Miller, *Painting the Map Red*, 309–11.

34. LAC, Adamson Fonds, Agar to Mabel, 3 June 1900.

35. *Canadian Letters and Images Project*, Department of History, Malaspina University College, British Columbia, Canada [*CLIP*], Stewart Collection, diary entry for 2 June 1900.

36. LAC, Adamson Fonds, Agar to Mabel, 9 June 1900.

37. Other officers experienced similar feelings. While serving with the 1st Battalion, Royal Welch Fusiliers, Lieutenant G.E.S. Salt explained, "I am in charge of the maxim gun, rather an anxious job, as it is not an easy thing to work well, and one feels responsible if anything goes wrong." See Salt, *Letters and Diary*, 21 November 1899, 18. In much the same manner, one of his contemporaries once wrote: "There is no question that leadership in war is the most difficult and responsible position in which a man can be placed." See Sir Reginald Rankin, *A Subaltern's Letters to his Wife* (London: Longmans, Green and Co., 1901), 77.

38. LAC, Adamson Fonds, Agar to Mabel, 9 June 1900.

39. The experiences of the SH with the Natal Field Force are beyond the scope of this chapter. Interested readers are encouraged to see Miller, *Painting the Map Red*, 309–39.

40. LAC, Howell Fonds, Narrative, 3.

41. [*CLIP*], Stewart Collection, diary entry for 21 June 1900.

42. *Ibid.*, Diary entry for 16 June 1900.

43. LAC, Adamson Fonds, Agar to Mabel, 23 June 1900. William Bartram held two certificates from the Toronto military school and was apparently well connected, being the son of the Surveyor of Customs. See "Strathcona's Horse," *Ottawa Free Press*, 30 April 1900, 5.

44. LAC, Adamson Fonds, Agar to Mabel, 23 June 1900.

45. *Ibid.*

46. *Ibid.*

47. For instance, Stewart recalled, "18 of us with the Cap't went out scouting." See [*CLIP*], Stewart Collection, diary entry for 30 June 1900.

48. In the same letter, however, Adamson also noted, "With the exception of about six my men are splendid fellows and developing every day." See LAC, Adamson Fonds, Agar to Mabel, 3 July 1900.

49. *Ibid.* For additional information concerning these acts, see Chris Madsen, "Canadian Troops and Farm Burning in the South African War," *Canadian Military Journal* 6, 2 (Summer 2005), 49–58. Contemporary accounts kept by unit members of the activities performed by SH frequently make reference to such endeavours. George Alexander Bowers recorded in his diary, for instance, "I think we will have to move camp soon as we have commandeered almost everything eatable about here as well as all the wood, which is a very scarce article"; "Looting orders read this a.m. as it has been getting too common"; "robbed an orchard"; "burned a mill"; and "We had to do a lot of theiv [*sic*] — commandeering on this trip in order to live." See *Glenbow Museum*, Robson family Fonds, M 7908, George Alexander Bowers's diary entries for 19 December 1900, 22 December 1900, 25 December 1900, 28 December 1900 and 9 January 1901, respectively. See also, for example, *Ibid.*, Ivor Edward Cecil Rice-Jones Fonds, M 1037, diary entries for 26 June 1900, 3 July 1900, 20 September 1900, and 27 December 1900.

50. For confirmation, see LAC, Heron Fonds, diary entry for 2 July 1900.

51. LAC, Adamson Fonds, Agar to Mabel, 5 July 1900. T.E. Howell admitted shortly after the war, "Many of our fellows had been cowboys and had spent the greater part of their lives riding over the prairie looking for lost cattle or shooting dear and antelope. They had therefore all the qualifications required in scouting on active service and quickly settled down to the work the regiment had to perform." See LAC, Howell Fonds, Narrative, 8. While this may have been true for riding, it apparently did not apply to purely military matters. The men, despite their western background, still required some time to learn how to fight.

52. LAC, Adamson Fonds, Agar to Mabel, 5 July 1900.

53. LAC, LdSH Fonds, Vol. 6, File 2, Steele to Strathcona, Greylingstad, 3 July 1900.

54. In the map that Adamson included in his letter to Mabel so that she could follow the battle, he indicated that a third body of SALH was withdrawn a little and eventually circled back towards Standerton from

whence they had just come. He later mentions that they, along with the other SALH left beneath the hill, engaged the Boers in this general area. The objective of this small detachment remains unknown. See LAC, Adamson Fonds, Agar to Mabel, 5 July 1900. The quotations appearing in the text above are taken from this letter.

55. *Ibid.*
56. LAC, Howell Fonds, Narrative, 4–5.
57. LAC, Adamson Fonds, Agar to Mabel, 5 July 1900. It is possible that Adamson may have been ordered to abandon his distinguishing dress in favour of a more inconspicuous garb. Lieutenant G.E.S. Salt was once ordered to dress "as much as possible like the men" because so many officers had been killed since the beginning of the war. See Salt, *Letters and Diary*, 21 November 1899, 16.
58. LAC, Howell Fonds, Narrative, 4.
59. *Glenbow Museum*, LdSH Fonds, M 3608, Andrew Miller's unpublished 1912 manuscript, 89–92. Unfortunately, a portion of page 90 has been excised from the archival copy of this manuscript, thus forcing the present author to rely upon a partially incomplete account of the action.
60. LAC, Adamson Fonds, Agar to Mabel, 5 July 1900.
61. *London Gazette*, 14 September 1900.
62. Arthur Bishop, *Our Bravest and Our Best: The Stories of Canada's Victoria Cross Winners* (Toronto: McGraw-Hill Ryerson Ltd., 1995), 18.
63. Private Alex McArthur and Private G.A.S. Sparkes were both wounded, while Private C.J. Isbester, Private J.C. McDougall, and Sergeant A. Stringer were listed as missing after the action. See LAC, LdSH Fonds, Vol. 6, File 2, Casualty Return, n.d. All these individuals belonged to the draft that Adamson took to South Africa. A brief account of this engagement is provided in "Modest, Brave Chap," *Montreal Daily Star*, 27 November 1900, 12, and repeated in, "Brave Arthur Richardson," *Family Herald and Weekly Star*, 28 November 1900, 22. Robert Rooke also offers an account of this clash in his memoirs. See LAC, Robert Rooke Fonds, MG 30 — E357, 45/321 to 46/320. The accuracy of this account may be suspect because he was not engaged with Adamson's troop, so the version of events that he relates was obviously told to him later; he was also writing (apparently) after the First World War.
64. LAC, Adamson Fonds, Agar to Mabel, 5 July 1900.
65. A return indicating the names of the individuals who died while on active service with SH, along with the squadron to which they belonged, can be found in LAC, LdSH Fonds, Vol. 5, File 13. Similarly, for a casualty summary that lists such categories as the strength of the SH upon arrival in South Africa, the total number killed, whether by action or by disease, the number invalided home, the number appointed to commissions in the British Army, et cetera, see *Ibid.*, Vol. 2, File 19. See also document dated *Ibid.*, Vol. 3, File 2, S.S. Lake Erie, 14 February 1901.
66. LAC, Heron Fonds, Diary entry for 14 July 1900.

67. LAC, Adamson Fonds, Agar to Mabel, 10 July 1900.
68. *Ibid.*
69. *Ibid.*
70. *Ibid.*, Agar to Mabel, 12 July 1900.
71. *Ibid.*
72. *Ibid.*, Agar to Mabel, 2 August 1900. See also, [*CLIP*], Stewart Collection, diary entries for 23 July 1900, 27 July 1900, 29 July 1900, 30 July 1900 and 31 July 1900, in which it is recorded that the draft did a lot of "scouting" and acting as the "advance guard" to the main body of Strathconas or the column in which they were serving.
73. Kyle McIntyre, "'Sons of Good Western Stock': The South African War Artifacts of Private Alexander W. Stewart, Strathcona's Horse," *Canadian Military History* 6, 1 (1997), 89.
74. LAC, Adamson Fonds, Agar to Mabel, 15 August 1900.
75. Sessional Paper 35a, 165.
76. LAC, LdSH Fonds, Vol. 6, File 2, Steele to Strathcona, Tweyfreaar Court, 16 August 1900. Recalling the action, T.E. Howell wrote: "Some resistance was offered and a ridge of hills in front of the town had to be shelled by the big guns.... At dusk when the order came to enter the town the hitherto orderly advance of Strathcona's Horse changed into a wild race to see who would get in first." See LAC, Howell Fonds, Narrative, 9.
77. LAC, Adamson Fonds, Agar to Mabel, 15 August 1900. As Steele recalled, "One squadron under orders from Lord Dundonald was sent forward to seize Ermelo, if possible. This was done. The telegraph and other public offices were taken possession of and posts established in the town." See LAC, LdSH Fonds, Vol. 6, File 2, Steele to Strathcona, Tweyfreaar Court, 16 August 1900. T.E. Howell mentions that Ermelo was occupied "without opposition" after SH had endured "a long and painful march through a blinding dust storm." See LAC, Howell Fonds, Narrative, 10.
78. LAC, Adamson Fonds, Agar to Mabel, 15 August 1900. For comments pertaining to Carolina, see LAC, LdSH Fonds, Vol. 6, File 2, Steele to Strathcona, Tweyfreaar Court, 16 August 1900.
79. *Glenbow Museum*, LdSH Fonds, Miller manuscript, 125–26. The action at Crocodile River was not a total loss, for Steele observed after the war, "Before going into camp the country to the front was scouted and valuable information gained." See Sessional Paper 35a, 167. Immediately after the action, he recalled, "We came in contact with the enemy at Crocodile river. The Pom Pom was brought up and the Boers pressed back. We halted here for the night to enable the rest of the army to catch up. During the day the flankers of the corps captured several prisoners and gained valuable information regarding the enemy's movements which has since proven correct." See LAC, LdSH Fonds, Vol. 6, File 2, Steele to Strathcona, Badfontein, 3 September 1900.

80. LAC, Adamson Fonds, Agar to Mabel, 22 March 1901. A detailed account of the engagement at Crocodile Valley can be found in LAC, Howell Fonds, Narrative, 7–14.

81. *Ibid.*, 16.

82. In late October 1900, after the Natal Field Force had been disbanded, SH, along with a number of other units, began chasing the Boer leader, General Christiaan de Wet. For an account of these activities, see Miller, *Painting the Map Red*, 340–57.

83. No attempt will therefore be made to assess Agar's leadership during this period for any critique would be purely speculative. Commenting without concrete evidence on his involvement in an accidental shooting that occurred in his troop (see Sessional Paper 35a, 171), on his participation in an alleged lynching of Boer prisoners after they had surrendered (see Miller, *Painting the Map Red*, 323–24), or on his role in a drunken riot at Machadodorp (see *Ibid.*, 338–39) would not be wise and will not be pursued.

84. LAC, LdSH Fonds, Vol. 4, File 5, Strathcona to Steele, 3 July 1901.

85. LAC, Adamson Fonds, Agar to Mabel, 2 August 1900

86. LAC, LdSH Fonds, Vol. 6, File 3, Steele to Strathcona, Frederikstad, 4 November 1900. See also, Bowers' diary entry for 20 October 1900, Robson Family Fonds, *Glenbow Museum*.

87. LAC, LdSH Fonds, Vol. 6, File 8, Roll of Officers, N.C.O.'s and Men Invalided to England, 1. Adamson was officially invalided from "A" Squadron on 28 November 1900. See also, LAC, John Edwards Leckie Fonds, MG 30 — E83, Scrapbook, Newspaper Clipping, "Officers Coming Home."

88. "Paardeberg Anniversary Dinner," 1, 28 February 1902, *Globe*.

89. For these various petitions, see LAC, RG 9, II-A-3, Vol. 21, Adamson to Borden, 27 March 1902; *Ibid.*, Vol. 21, Adamson to Jarvis, 5 April 1902; *Ibid.*, Vol. 22, Adamson to Jarvis, 5 April 1902; and *Ibid.*, Vol. 23 "Parties Recommended and Those Recommending," 1 April 1902.

90. In early 1902, at the request of the British government, the Department of Militia and Defence assumed the responsibility of raising a number of additional regiments for service in South Africa. The men so recruited were formed into the 3rd, 4th, 5th, and 6th CMR. Since they did not recruit them personally, the COs of each unit met their soldiers as a group for the first time in Halifax. Each unit consisted of approximately 509 soldiers, all ranks, and a conscious effort was made to give a regional character to each regiment and a territorial identity to each squadron therein. See Miller, *Painting the Map Red*, 414–23.

91. *Ibid.*, 418.

92. *Ibid.*, 417. See also LAC, Adamson Fonds, Agar to Mabel, 12 June 1902, for comments pertaining to the strengths and weaknesses of the officers of 6 CMR.

93. Miller manuscript, 200, LdSH Fonds, *Glenbow Museum*.

94. LAC, Adamson Fonds, Agar to Mabel, 12 June 1900.

95. *Ibid.*, Agar to Mabel, 11 June 1900.

96. *Ibid.*, Agar to Mabel, 28 June 1900.

97. Adamson, *Letters*, Agar to Mabel, 24 November 1917, 317. Agar learned on his voyage to South Africa, for example, that his sergeant-major was the son of an Irish landlord, one Colonel Buchanan. See LAC, Adamson Fonds, Agar to Mabel, 27 May 1900. Also, during the First World War, he wrote: "I am beginning to find out more about the men in the Company sitting about and talking during the day." See Adamson, *Letters*, Agar to Mabel, 24 March 1915, 49.

98. See, *Ibid.*, 21 February 1916, 149.

99. For instance, see *Ibid.*, 11 May 1917, 280, where Agar refused to allow his battalion to become "a training school for the convenience of staff officers." In this regard specifically, he prevented Talbot Mercer Papineau from using the PPCLI for his own ends, namely, to increase his chances of success in post-war public life by adding wartime service to his credentials. Adamson only allowed Papineau to join the battalion if he intended to stay the course, rather than join for a short while and then seek safer employment elsewhere; Papineau was eventually killed at Passchendaele.

100. See, *Ibid.*, 9 January 1917, 252, where Agar writes, "I have twenty commissions to suggest today and find it very difficult to choose. The Company Commanders are poor judges and I am worse. It is so hard to hit a line to go on. I have decided to go on guts and not gamble manners so we will probably have some queer fish but the side will be the stronger for it."

CHAPTER 2

Portrait of a Battalion Commander: Lieutenant-Colonel George Stuart Tuxford at the Second Battle of Ypres, April 1915

by Andrew B. Godefroy

Although central to the analysis of any military history, the study of individual and collective biography remains a weak pursuit in Canada. There are a few reasons for such a state of affairs, not the least of which is the existence of a culture of reluctance and modesty among Canadian soldiers who seldom left behind any memoirs of their wartime exploits. Added to this is an academic and military community also reluctant to engage in military biography, choosing instead to largely ignore the significance of the study of the human element beyond the anecdotal. Nowhere else is this absence more visible than in the biographical study of Canadian senior military leadership in the First World War. Of the 126 generals that served in the Canadian Expeditionary Force (CEF), only its most senior commander, Sir Arthur Currie, has merited more than a single academic examination of his life. Of the remainder, less than six have received any serious biographical attention, leaving one to reconsider the completeness of current assessments of Canadian operational and tactical effectiveness on the Western Front given that still so little is known about the men who shaped it.

Slightly down the chain of command of the CEF the situation improves little. The infantry battalion, consisting of approximately 1,000 men and commanded by a lieutenant-colonel, was the primary unit employed in action in France and Flanders.[1] Yet nearly a century after 260 of these battalions were recruited in Canada for possible combat on the Western Front, information on the infantry battalion commanders who led any one of the 48 fighting battalions[2] remains sparse.[3] In fact, it remains clearly evident that far less is known about the machinations of leadership and command of Canada's Great War army than might be otherwise perceived, let alone how such skills were tested and proven on the battlefield.

The persistent general nescience about the CEF officer corps as an institution, or how these men commanded their forces in the field, has let many popular assumptions become ingrained as historical fact over the last several decades, myths that can neither be validated nor challenged until greater attention is paid to this field of biographical study.

GEORGE STUART TUXFORD

This chapter seeks to shed light on one of these many unknowns, namely, Lieutenant-Colonel (later Brigadier-General) George Stuart Tuxford, CB CMG DSO MiD. Attested as the commanding officer (CO) of the 5th (Western Cavalry) Battalion in 1914, he later rose to become general officer commanding (GOC) 3rd Canadian Infantry Brigade, 1st Canadian Division. An experienced militia officer who understood leadership by example, General Tuxford's distinguished wartime career is reflective of a wider group of senior Canadian officers whose intelligence, skills, personal courage, and ability to learn at the tactical and operational level inspired the Canadian Corps to victory on the Western Front.[4] Yet, like several of his

Library and Archives Canada PA-007936

Brigadier-General G.S. Tuxford, CB, CMG, DSO and Bar and Legion of Honour.

colleagues, as a battalion commanding officer Lieutenant-Colonel Tuxford was tested at the very outset, swallowing tough lessons in hard fought actions at the Battles of Second Ypres, Festubert, and Givenchy in the spring and summer of 1915.

The military career of George Stuart Tuxford provides students of Canadian military history with perhaps one of the best Canadian Army leadership case studies of the First World War. Beginning his service in the CEF as one of only 12 infantry battalion commanding officers assigned to the front line, he survived the slaughter of the Second Battle of Ypres in April 1915 to receive command of the 3rd Canadian Infantry Brigade in March 1916. It was a position that Brigadier-General Tuxford held for over three years, earning him the title of the longest serving brigade commander in the Canadian Corps.[5] While an analysis of his entire wartime career falls beyond the scope of this chapter, it will address his first experience with leadership and command in combat in April 1915 that undoubtedly shaped his later performance as an operational-level commander on the Western Front.

Born in Wales in February 1870, George Tuxford grew to be a man of above average height, standing 5-foot 10-inches, with brown hair, a light complexion, and striking blue eyes.[6] In the 1890s, he and his young wife immigrated to Canada, where they settled as farmers on the Canadian prairies. The Tuxfords ran a healthy mixed farm in Moose Jaw, Saskatchewan, and maintained a sizable herd of livestock. In the summer of 1898, George organized and led a herd from his farm in Moose Jaw to Dawson City, Yukon, transporting "fresh meat on the hoof to this booming town" at the height of the Klondike gold rush.[7] His epic journey across the Canadian Rockies was then the longest cattle drive in Canadian history.

George Tuxford began his association with Canadian military service in the years before the outbreak of war. He served as an officer with the 16th Mounted Rifles (a misnomer as the regiment was intended to be a cavalry unit), the first militia regiment in Saskatchewan, from July 1905 through April 1910. When the militia district headquarters authorized the creation of an independent squadron in Moose Jaw later that summer, Major Tuxford was selected to command it by Minister of Militia and Defence Sam Hughes. The new formation, originally designated "D" Squadron of the 16th Mounted Rifles, was soon after expanded to become its own regiment and renamed the 27th Light Horse. Major Tuxford noted in his memoirs, "I was given authority to organize a new Regiment of mounted troops, to consist of 3 Squadrons for a start. The 3 Squadrons were to be located at Moose Jaw, Swift Current, and Maple Creek."[8] Tuxford also had troops stationed at Moose Jaw, Keeler, Pense, and Morse. A rapidly growing unit, he was promoted to lieutenant-colonel as a result of his new command.

Though Lieutenant-Colonel Tuxford had retired from ranching in 1914, the 44-year-old officer remained active with his militia unit. He naturally offered it for service with the CEF at the outbreak of war in August, but his offer was graciously declined. Colonel Sam Steele, then responsible for forming the cavalry arm of the first Canadian contingent, informed Tuxford that another regiment had already been chosen for the task. Still, Tuxford's desire to serve Canada was not to be denied. He later wrote on the matter, "I, therefore, got Colonel Steele to wire into Ottawa and ask for permission for the mounted units from the West to come down to Valcartier as dismounted troops, if they so desired … Upon application I was authorized to organize two battalions."[9]

After receiving the unorthodox call to arms from Sam Hughes, the Minister of Militia and Defence, Tuxford moved his ad-hoc unit at once to Camp Valcartier, Quebec, where it was amalgamated with other smaller and independent militia units into the 5th (Western Cavalry) Battalion, 2nd Canadian Infantry Brigade, 1st Canadian Division. Secure in his relationship with Hughes, Lieutenant-Colonel Tuxford was selected as its first commanding officer and took the 5th Battalion first to England and later, into action in Flanders and France.

On the morning of 22 April 1915, the 5th Canadian Infantry Battalion was located in the Canadian front line positions east of the town of Ypres. Lieutenant-Colonel Tuxford's battalion started the battle with approximately 30 officers and 996 men.[10] Over the next several days, his unit fought desperately to defend the town against incessant German attacks, bombardments, and the war's latest weapon, gas. His battalion suffered 11 officers and 278

Canadian soldiers in the trenches in France enjoying a quiet moment.

Photographer Horrace Brown, Library and Archives Canada PA-107276

men killed and wounded through 10 May, and although his unit's casualties were relatively light compared to other Canadian infantry battalions engaged at the Second Battle of Ypres, Lieutenant-Colonel Tuxford's own battalion later suffered the brunt of casualties during difficult fighting around Festubert and K.5. at the end of May. By the beginning of July, the 5th Canadian Infantry Battalion received only enough reinforcements to total 698 men, nearly 300 men less than its normal authorized strength.

TUXFORD'S AFTER ACTION REPORT OF YPRES, APRIL 1915[11]

Less than a year after Second Ypres Tuxford, by then promoted to brigadier-general and appointed to command the 3rd Canadian Infantry Brigade, completed an "After Action Report" that provided candid and at times brutally frank personal observations of various events during the battle. His assessment also gave a personal critique of his own performance during the engagement, providing invaluable reference to where he was at various times and what he could see. More important perhaps, it provided a detailed account of what he knew and when, and what decisions he made based on that knowledge and intelligence. For historians, his report on his actions and the actions of his unit at the Second Battle of Ypres is a critical document in assessing Canadian combat leadership and command during this engagement, an

Library and Archives Canada PA-863

The indomitable Canadian infantryman.

assessment that is constantly lacking in contemporary literature on the CEF on the Western Front.[12]

For purposes of clarity and interest Lieutenant-Colonel Tuxford's "After Action Report on Second Ypres" is reproduced below in its entirety. Readers may wish to consult either of the two Canadian official histories of the First World War, the first published in 1938 by Colonel A.F. Duguid, and the second published in 1962 by Colonel G.W.L. Nicholson for a general overview and further details on the events surrounding this battle. Tuxford's report is dated 10 March 1916:

> The Fifth Battalion left Steenhorde on the morning of the 14th of April, being taken by buses the first half of the distance, and remaining under cover with the Welsh Regiment till 5 p.m., then continuing the march through Ypres to the trenches which were at the extreme apex of the salient, the 7th, 8th, and 10th. In the front line trenches, the 5th in brigade reserve.
>
> The front line trenches taken over from the French were in poor shape, being nothing more than isolated non-bullet-proof barricades, with no connections from trench to trench.
>
> The succeeding few days were energetically spent in improving these trenches. The 5th Battalion moved up to the front line trenches, relieving the 10th on the night of the 19th. The 8th Battalion moved over on the left, the 7th in brigade reserve, the 10th in divisional reserve. The 5th held the extreme right of the Canadian Division with the Royal Fusiliers on their right.
>
> Several German attacks were made on different parts of the line during the next two or three days, but were in all cases repulsed. On the 22nd, however, the Germans first threw over gas at the Algerians and Turcos, then holding on the left of the Canadian Division, breaking through and advancing towards St. Julien. During all this time our transports had to run the gauntlet, bringing up rations, and first brought news to the front trenches of the retirement of the Algerians and Turcos.
>
> After the 22nd it was impossible to get any rations up. On the 23rd [the] Germans gassed and apparently broke through the 3rd Brigade. On the 24th Major

Hilliam, my adjutant, called me out about 4 o'clock in the morning to witness a huge wall of greeny, yellow smoke that was rolling up the hillside. We had no idea what it was, but thought it might have something to do with the reported gas attacks of the preceding day. We were not long left in doubt. I immediately rang up Colonel Lipsett on our left for information and he replied personally, choking and gasping in such a manner that I thought he was done for.

This gas rolled over the 8th Battalion front, part of the 5th Battalion front, and both headquarters, being followed up by heavy German attacks in mass, more particularly on the 8th Battalion front.

On the 23rd my reserve company at the bombarded crossroads had been absorbed by Brigade for tactical purposes.

During the morning of the 24th Colonel Lipsett sent me an S.O.S. call, and upon his declaring it as serious, I sent him three platoons of my spare company, retaining one platoon to hold the hill. Again, later in the morning, under a further S.O.S. call I sent him the remaining platoon, thus leaving me nothing but two companies in the front line holding 1100 yards of trench. During this day some 100 to 200 Germans with machine guns broke through on the left of the 8th [Battalion] and took up a position in some cottages about 400 yards away, mid distant from the 5th and 8th headquarters, and started to dig themselves in.

During the night of the 24th Colonel Lipsett and I traveled three times back and forth to the Headquarters of the Royal Fusiliers on our right, asking them to get their brigade headquarters to send up sufficient troops, if possible, to relieve both the 8th and the 5th, who were exhausted, as they had now been fighting [for three days] without rations and water, and had endured the gas.

Major Johnson, commanding the fusiliers was quite in line with this, but it was impossible to supply the troops. We succeeded however, in gathering up details — Cheshires, 8th Durham Light Infantry, Northumberland

Fusiliers, and men from one or two other units, amounting to about 1000 men, which we threw onto the left in the darkness, as well as possible, also relieving two or three companies of the 8th.

Upon returning to Lipsett's headquarters the last time, word was brought up, that there were two British Divisions along the Zonnebeck road, waiting only to be got up. It was midnight, pitch dark, with the exception of flares going up, and nobody knew the way. The position was extremely critical — dead and wounded men lying everywhere. As I have a good general bump of the direction, born of the prairies, I went down by myself to within a quarter of a mile of Zonnebeck but there was not a soul there. Upon returning, we thrashed out the matter of holding on for another twenty-four hours in the hope that relief would be sent, and decided that if we had to retire it would be impossible to do so in daylight and must be carried out at night.

Having done all we could, I then got Lipsett to give me a few men to hold my own line. [H]e offered 150; I took 50. We took these men from the hedges under which they were resting, in a heavy rain, and put them in front trenches on the right of my line. The young officer commanding them was killed before night.

On the road over I met Major Dyer, my second in command, who brought news up that a heavy British attack was going to go through at daybreak, on our left. Naturally, having decided to hold on, we were intensely pleased. However, in the course of events, no British attack eventuated.

Just before daylight Brigadier General Currie, commanding the Brigade, arrived; and at that time, feeling rather pleased, we made preparations for a good breakfast. General Currie could not believe that we really had Germans immediately in our rear, but a practical demonstration of their machine gun fire soon convinced him. About 1 p.m. a number of the Durhams, who were freshly out — unable to stand the intense artillery fire — which had been continuous all these days, came running past my headquarters with their rifles thrown away. They were ordered into trenches on top of the ridge, and Captain Ash, my signaling officer, was given instructions to shoot the first man who broke off afresh.

About 2 p.m. General Currie wrote me the order, transmitted from high authority, to retire and dig in half way to the bombarded cross-roads, which were half a mile in our rear, on the reverse slope. I asked, "When?" — he replied, "Now." I suggested it was impossible in daylight, but the order had to be carried out. Major Hilliam, my adjutant, wrote the order to the two companies holding the front line, and I signed them.

Our telephone lines, which had been continually shot away and repaired, were now taken out completely by a shell, and it was necessary to take these orders down by messenger. Hilliam started with them and Dyer grabbed them, claiming his seniority as entitling him to carry them.

To solve the question I gave the orders to the right company to Dyer and the left to Hilliam. They immediately started out, got clear of the artillery zone, which was extremely heavy, but further down the slope both were shot down, Hilliam through the lung, Dyer within an inch of the heart. Dyer, however, managed to struggle within 10 yards of the trenches, where he was hauled in by the men and the message was delivered.

About this time I persuaded General Currie, who had been in consultation with Colonel Lipsett, to retire, which he did, running the gauntlet of the machine guns of the Germans in the cottages in our rear. Colonel Lipsett and I had arranged, in the event of retirement, that we should do so in succession of companies from the left. However, what was left of the men in the front trenches came out almost as a whole, leaving my A. and B. companies still holding their line. I now started to send my staff away with orders to stop at a position on the Zonnebeck road, keeping clear of the enemy machine gun in the rear. They went one at a time, running the gauntlet of the intense artillery fire, which now sweeping the reverse slopes of the Gravenstafel ridge.

I was now left by myself for some twenty minutes, with the buildings toppling around like a pack of cards. I noticed that the men of the 8th, 7th, and 10th, to the number of some 300, streaming down the river slope, instead of stopping half way to the crossroads to dig in, were carrying on down to the crossroads themselves. This left absolutely no help to my two companies, who had not yet commenced to retire. "A" Company under Major Tenaille, "B" Company under Major Edgar.

I ran down myself to the crossroads and actually found 40 men across the road and heading for Ypres, now in comparative safety. These men I got back across the road and told them all we were going up the hill again to help the two companies of the 5th Battalion in their retirement.

These two companies were absolutely the last of the Canadian Division to leave their trenches. I found Lt. McLeod of the 8th [Battalion], who helped most energetically at this time. The German machine guns, which now opened a heavy enfilading fire from the cottages at 400 yards, seemed to take about a minute to change belts, so that the men laid down whilst the machine guns were firing, and continued immediately [when] they ceased.

About half way up the hill, the enemy machine gun fire ceased, and looking around I saw the cottage in which the gun was placed, blown to pieces. This was one of those lucky circumstances which sometimes occur in war. After I had sent my Regimental S[ergeant] M[ajor] with the rest of the staff from Headquarters, he an old artillery man, made directly for a couple of British batteries on our right rear, and although he could not see the actual cottages, directed their fire by map.

A German shell made a direct hit on one gun of this battery, putting it out of action and killing the crew. Their O.C. whilst wounded and lying on the ground, with his telephone carried away, yelled directions to the other gun, with the result as stated above.

Half way up the hill I found Colonel Lipsett and Major Monroe, his second in command, and we proceeded to the top under a most intense artillery fire. I, however, distinctly remember, during the last hundred yards or so, when the noise was so intense that you had to shout to be heard, and the artillery fire was most incessant, looking over to my right and seeing my cook — Private Purvis — marching jauntily along with his cap stuck aslant over one eye, and grinning at me in a most cheerful manner. My interpreter, who followed me like a dog, escaped with a bullet through the center of his hat.

I saw Colonel Lipsett lying on the ground and shouted to him to go further up the ridge as I knew they had the absolute range of that particular point.

I now want to lay stress on the magnificent morale of these men, some 5th, some 7th, some 8th, and some 10th. They had retired into relative safety, and, upon being ordered, immediately advanced up this half mile slope under heavy machine gun fire at 400 yards, and then under most intense artillery fire, shrapnel, and H.E., and as soon as I had put them in the trenches on the top of the hill and had personally told all N.C.O.s that we were going to hold the ridge till our two companies had retired and until they had arrived when we would then retire altogether, these men immediately snapped their bayonets in and said, "Just tell us what to do sir, and we will do it.," as cheerful as can be.

I now began to look for Colonel Lipsett and went three times over the ground where I had last seen him under this artillery fire, being convinced that he must have been wounded. I could find no trace of him. His batman who was following him was hit where I had last seen him lying alongside him, and he had helped him down to the dressing station just in our rear.

A and B Companies now began to appear. A on our right, B on our left, as had been ordered; and I want to say here that during this retirement, with the Germans yelling behind them, beating drums, and calling out — "We have got you Canadians now" — I never saw a man quicken his step. I ran out on the right and gathered Tenaille's company, forming up a line in continuation of our right, one man per yard, B Company simultaneously doing the same on our left. I posted

Sergeant Bowie and six men on our left flank to guard a rise of ground over which I thought the Germans might possibly appear. This rise was some 80 yards distant. About 150 Germans suddenly appeared over this rise and Bowie could not tell whether they were Germans, British, or French, but immediately challenged. They replied at once, "Do not shoot, ve vas French." Bowie's reply was — "Fire" — and he took off 14 himself and stopped the rush.

The Germans were now advancing and yelling, and I expected a charge, and ordered rapid fire, completely stopping the rush. Dark was almost on hand and I felt that we had control of the situation. However, it would have been madness to have remained there as we should only have been outflanked cut off.

I want to say here that the wonderful retirement of A and B companies, pursued by the German hordes, was greatly assisted by the Royal Fusiliers on our right who still held their trenches, they claiming they had no orders to retire and refusing to do so.

I now arranged with Major Munroe, of the 8th [Battalion] to commence our own retirement, falling back in parties covered by the remaining [men] till about 2 o'clock on the ridge. Upon the comment of the retirement I started down to find General Currie and explain the situation, but not finding him kept on going till I found the two British batteries on our left rear and warned them of what was happening, of which they were entirely ignorant. Continuing, I found the Brigade headquarters to which the Royal Fusiliers belonged, and advised them of the situation.

They were entirely in the dark as to what was happening. Picking up my Sergeant Major we finally made our Brigade headquarters at St. Jean. What was left of the Brigade arrived, about 400, in the morning, dead beat, gassed, starved, and short of water.

At 7 a.m., four hours later, the remnants of the Brigade were marched up towards Fontuin to restore the line. Here we laid in support of the British line that day and night, and the succeeding day under a most intense shell fire and losing heavily, and on the night of the 27th retired through Potijze and Ypres to about two miles to the rear of the canal, moving into huts. We woke next morning with shrapnel bullets breaking through the roofs of the huts.

I immediately got the men out into the fields, where we all laid till the night of the 29th. On the night of the 29th the Brigade again then marched to the canal, the 5th and 10th occupying sectors of the canal, the 7th and 8th in reserve. Here I had to guard some 500 yards of canal adjoining Ypres on the North, with two bridges, No.s. 1 and 2, the blowing up of which I was responsible for.

There was practically no protection in the rear of the canal, and we lay for six days and six nights under most incessant artillery bombardment, losing heavily each day, and were relieved on the night of the 5th by the Essex.

We now marched 17 miles to billets at Outersteen, the other side of Bailleul, arriving about 11 a.m. on the 6th in all stages of exhaustion. Here we were visited by General Smith-Dorrien.

Library and Archives Canada PA-00314

The remnants of the Cloth Hall Tower and surrounding area in Ypres.

CONCLUSION

Lieutenant-Colonel Tuxford was one of only 12 infantry commanding officers that served at the Second Battle of Ypres, but only one of dozens of officers who commanded forces in that battle. Tuxford's report serves as but a single piece of evidence for that analysis, the full assessment still awaiting the attention of serious scholarship from Canada's military historians.[13] Hopefully this chapter, as well as other articles in its wake will encourage a greater study of military biographies of Canada's tactical commanders.

NOTES

1. CEF battalions were recruited at home to a strength of approximately 1,000 men. Units engaged in fighting on the Western Front were almost never at full strength because of constant casualties both in and out of action.
2. Most CEF battalions were broken up in England to provide reinforcements for units already assigned to the Canadian divisions fighting in France and Flanders. Forty-eight infantry and mounted rifle battalions made up the core of the Canadian Corps fighting power.
3. The most notable work recently published has been Patrick Brennan "Good Men for A Hard Job: Infantry Battalion Commanders in the Canadian Expeditionary Force," *The Canadian Army Journal*, 9.1 (Spring 2006), 9–28.
4. The study of leadership and command in the Canadian Expeditionary Force is a largely untouched field with most existing studies dating back several decades. The best detailed institutional studies of the CEF officer corps remain Eyre, K.C. "Staff and Command in the Canadian Corps: The Canadian Militia 1896–1914 as a Source of Senior Officers," (unpublished M.A. thesis, Duke University, 1967), and A.M.J. Hyatt, "Canadian Generals of the First World War and the Popular View of Military Leadership," *Histoire Sociale — Social History*, 24 (November 1979), 418–430.
5. Brigadier General Victor W. Odlum CB CMG DSO was the second longest serving Brigade Commander, leading 11th Canadian Infantry Brigade (4th Canadian Division) from July 1916 to June 1919. Like Tuxford, Victor Odlum had commanded the 7th (British Columbia) Battalion during the latter half of the Second Battles of Ypres after the original CO had been killed, and held the battalion command until his promotion to GOC of 11th CIB in July 1916.
6. Library and Archives Canada [LAC], Record Group [RG] 24, CEF Personnel Record for Brigadier General George Stuart Tuxford, 5th Battalion and 3rd Brigade, 1st Canadian Division. Henceforth referred to as Tuxford — CEF Personnel File.

7. Daniel G. Dancocks, *Welcome to Flanders Fields: The First Canadian Battle of the Great War — Ypres, 1915* (Toronto: McClelland & Stewart, 1988), 23.
8. Cited from the History of the Saskatchewan Dragoons website, accessed at *www.saskd.ca/27Light.htm*.
9. *Ibid*. The first battalion consisted of the 12th, 16th, 27th, 29th, 30th, 31st, 35th Light Horse, and the Corps of Guides. He expected to form a second all-mounted battalion sometime later, however the situation changed and the opportunity never arrived.
10. Colonel A.F. Duguid, *Official History of the Canadian Forces in the Great War 1914–1919* (Ottawa: King's Printer, 1938), Appendix 226. Battalion strength as of 10 February 1915.
11. LAC. RG24, Vol. 1825, File GAQ 5–61, Narrative of Brigadier General Tuxford, CMG, written 10 March 1916.
12. Critics may argue that Tuxford may have wished to cast himself in as positive a light as possible for posterity, but as his report shows he was not afraid to criticize himself or his organization during the action. For example, Tuxford admits that mistakes were made and that the enemy was able to penetrate behind his position, something that may have been considered embarrassing to leaders less sure of their abilities.
13. Tuxford is also one of the few senior Canadian commanders to have produced a memoir after the war, but to date it remains unpublished. The author is currently seeking to rectify this.

Chapter 3

The Strain of the Bridge: The Second World War Diaries of Commander A.F.C. Layard, RN

by Michael Whitby

Picture the North Atlantic on Saturday, 22 April 1944. Four frigates of the Canadian support group EG-9 are on an offensive anti-submarine sweep west of Ireland with the escort carrier Her Majesty's Ship (HMS) *Biter* and the British group EG-7. They have been out for 11 days and have already destroyed one submarine, and made promising attacks on others.

On the bridge of Her Majesty's Canadian Ship (HMCS) *Matane*, the senior officer of EG-9, Acting Commander Frank Layard, Royal Navy (RN) was restless and uneasy. To put it simply he was not sure if he was measuring up. After HMCS *Swansea* and HMS *Pelican* destroyed U-448 following a skilful four-hour hunt the week before, he wrote in his diary "*Swansea* is certainly doing its stuff. Everybody on board here is desperately jealous — except me. My only reaction is one of fear and doubt whether in similar circumstances I would make a balls of it."[1]

That was what he thought he did on 22 April. His diary reveals:

> Not a very nice day with SW'ly wind force 6. We got an H/F D/F bearing at 5.15 and we weren't certain of distance [so] I turned the group to the bearing and steamed along it till 11.00 but saw and heard nothing. I planned my movements for the night so as to be in the eastern edge by about 0600 when I was going to shape course for Loch Foyle but a signal arrived ordering us to operate with a Leigh Light Wellington aircraft during the night in another small area which quite upset my previous plans. We were just about in the middle of the area spread out in line abreast when at 2000 we got an

A/S contact to port. It was a cracking echo and soon it became obvious that this really was a U boat. I went slow, meaning to take my time, but the range closed very rapidly and I found myself in to about 300 yds with the bearing going rapidly right and the ship's head swinging as fast as possible to Std [starboard] to keep pointed. Suddenly, ahead appeared the swirl of the thing, that must have been very shallow. I was still worried that I was going to get so close as to lose contact before ready to attack when the periscope was reported just off the Std bow. I then got thoroughly rattled and in case he should fire a torpedo or gnat [acoustic torpedo] I reckoned I must go for him. Went full ahead and forgetting we were still in A/S contact dropped a pattern by eye, that as it turned out was a good deal too early. However, we picked him up astern and the other ships were now on the scene. Swansea then attacked and although we held him and so did Stormont for a time the A/S conditions, that were never good, suddenly became awful and we simply couldn't get our reverbs out at all and that was the last we heard of him. I started [an] Observant patrol and then a parallel sweep but it was dark soon after losing contact and if he got away he could make off on the surface.

I went through agonies of suspense and worry. What I've always dreaded has happened. We find a U-boat and I make a balls and lose it. It must be admitted the lack of daylight, the bad A/S conditions and the periscope all made it difficult but I feel I've let the ship and the group down and feel suicidal with shame.[2]

This disclosure reveals the personal struggle that Commander Frank Layard faced in command. His impressions of daily life, runs ashore, of people, places and things, and of naval warfare are all laid out in remarkable detail in his diary. It is truly a fascinating document that opens a unusual window on the demands associated with naval command in war.

Layard got the idea of keeping a diary from his mother and he firmly believed it should contain everything of note. "A diary is like a confessional," he wrote in later life, "in that all one's sins and omissions are exposed and recorded. Unlike the confessional, however," he continued,

Courtesy Raymond Layard

Commander Frank Layard, RN.

"the good is there as well as the bad and although in life there is much that I regret and am ashamed of, there are also some redeeming features and it is for the reader to form an opinion and to decide whether there is a reasonable balance between the debits and the credits."[3]

Layard wrote virtually a page a day from when he entered HMS *Osborne* as a cadet in 1913 to when he first retired in 1947 — he later returned to service during the Korean War. There is just one gap in 1919–1920, when along with hundreds of other young officers he was sent to Cambridge University to make good the education lost although serving at sea in the Great War. In a poem about this program Rudyard Kipling pleaded, "Far have they come, much have they braved. Give them their hour of play."[4] Layard obviously played for he did not write.

This chapter covers Layard's sea-time during the Second World War — and he can be said to have had a good war — focusing primarily on his command of EG-9 during the challenging inshore campaign against the U-boats in the waters off Britain. A look at how he confronted a totally new type of anti-submarine warfare; at how he handles people he has great difficulty understanding, namely, Canadians; and, finally, how he dealt with the strain of seemingly endless operations provides a fascinating insight into the war at sea at the sharpest end — on the bridge. Layard's brutal honesty provides a near spotless window into the strain that accompanies command. It reveals the burden of wartime operations on a person who was by all accounts a fairly typical naval professional. There are no great lessons here, beyond how the average officer copes with the strain associated with years of command in wartime. But perhaps that, in itself, is worth understanding.

Concealing one's innermost fears is a necessary attribute of a leader. Layard's diary presents a picture of an officer lacking confidence, and wracked by indecision and doubt. However, those who served with him paint a totally different picture. They describe a professional with a cool, decisive demeanour. One officer referred to him as our "beloved Captain"[5], and Allan Easton, an experienced Royal Canadian Naval Reserve (RCNR) officer who sailed with him as commanding officer (CO) of HMCS *Matane* recalled, "I respected his ability and admired his knowledge, yet I admired more his reticence in displaying it…. I could have served no finer officer."[6] Even the great U-boat killer, Captain F.J. "Johnny" Walker, RN, evaluated him in 1942, "as a capable destroyer captain, who has shown marked coolness and good judgment under fire."[7]

Layard was obviously like the infamous duck that appears to be moving gracefully and calmly on the surface but is paddling like heck underneath. The contrast between what can be termed the "inward" and "outward" Layard is obvious, but both must be taken into account when considering the entirety of an individual. However, when dealing with the pressure of command, it is the internal persona that is most revealing and that is the one that this chapter will focus upon.

It is important to first, establish Frank Layard's pre-war record.[8] He joined the navy in 1913 because his parents selected that career for him. Nonetheless, he was happy with the choice and never had any regrets. For most of the First World War, he served in the battle cruiser HMS *Indomitable* and witnessed the Battle of Jutland from its foretop. He transferred to destroyers later in the war, and became a confirmed destroyer man, loving the freedom and responsibility that service in those ships brought.

Throughout the 1920s, besides some big ship time, he served as first lieutenant in destroyers in the Atlantic, Mediterranean and Far Eastern fleets. He appears to have been highly thought of for when his CO went down with pleurisy at Hong Kong he was appointed acting captain and brought the ship home to England even though there were relief commanding officers on station.

From September 1930 to December 1933, Layard, by then a lieutenant-commander, commanded three destroyers in the Mediterranean and Atlantic Fleets. He appears to have been an average CO; a fairly good ship-handler, but one that lacked panache; a level-headed leader, but one who could never be considered dynamic. He was steady and competent, but lacked the aggressive confidence that characterized most successful destroyer officers of the day. Promotion lists were short and when Layard was passed over for promotion to commander for the final time in December 1933, it devastated him. He thought himself, pure and simply, a failure.

After much reflection he decided to stay in the navy but was dismayed at how quickly he was pushed out of the mainstream. Instead of getting another destroyer or a staff job in Gibraltar as he requested, he was made physical fitness officer for the reserve fleet. That was followed up by command of a minesweeper; considered to be the scrapings of the barrel for the sea-going executive branch.[9] In 1936, he was appointed to the Experimental Department at Whale Island There, he did extremely well, exhibiting an understanding of technical matters and becoming extremely comfortable in the gunnery world, which is ironic given earlier complaints in his diary about promotion lists being "gunnery benefits." After war broke out Layard continually requested sea duty, but was consistently rebuffed because the work he was doing at HMS *Excellent* was considered too valuable. Finally, in July 1941, he got his way and was appointed commanding officer of the destroyer HMS *Chelsea*. Except for an eight-month break in 1943, he was to be at sea for the duration of the European war.

Although this chapter concentrates more on the latter part of the war, incidents from 1941 and 1942 provide insights into the face of naval battle as seen through Layard. The first concerns his preparation

HMCS Matane *in the North Atlantic on convoy duty. By the end of the war, frigates such as this were effective U-boat hunters.*

for the job at hand. HMS *Chelsea* was attached to the West Approaches local escort force operating out of Liverpool, escorting North Atlantic and Gibraltar convoys on the first or final stages of their passage. Within a week of taking over *Chelsea*, he met his first convoy — "It quite reminded me of the Grand Fleet at sea in the last war," he wrote[10] — and on just his second trip he was horrified to learn that he was to be senior officer of the escort (SOE), responsible for coordinating the defence of the convoy. He had not been to sea for five years and his preparation for the job as senior officer, and indeed for convoy escort generally, was practically nil. He was given no formal training and did not even have the luxury of a "shake-down" cruise in his new ship. All he was able to do was hurriedly glance over convoy instructions and tactical manuals, and consult experienced escort commanders who were part of his large network of friends. But he even had difficulty absorbing that information as he also had to re-learn the job of being captain of a warship, which, to make matters worse, was an old American four-stacker that he thought a pig to handle. Consequently, it is fair to say that Layard was relatively lost during his first few weeks at sea, and never really appears to have been comfortable over the next year.

An example from August 1942 reveals the challenges of convoy warfare. By then Layard had taken over the destroyer *Broke*. Although already at sea with another convoy, he was ordered to reinforce SC 94, which was being attacked by U-boats in the North Atlantic air gap. Again Layard was horrified to learn that he was to take over as senior officer. When he joined the convoy, he found it in complete disarray. Under attack for four days, six merchant ships had been sunk and two escorts damaged in encounters with U-boats. Faced with a tactical situation that was as murky as the thick fog shrouding the convoy, unfamiliar with the escorts now under his command, with no opportunity to be briefed by the previous SOE or convoy commodore, Layard was confronted by what can only be described as a desperate situation that he attempted to sort out as best he could.[11] After being with the convoy for only about 12 hours, and handling myriad decisions, Layard took over the bridge watch:

> It was very dark & when I took over I couldn't really make up my mind where we were. Then suddenly torpedoes were reported passing the ship & I saw one cross the bows from Starboard to Port & then on our Std. bow appeared the swirl of a U-boat, loud H.E. effect also reported on the A/S. At that moment some ship to the

Std. blew 6 blasts [the collision alarm]. I didn't know where anybody was & I turned towards the U-boat & went on to 20 knots sweating with fear lest I was going to get across the bows of the convoy for whom I was heading directly or ram one of the escorts. I was quite unable to concentrate on the U-boat owing to this worry but found myself somehow pointing there. At close range we picked up good echoes & dropped a 14 charge shallow pattern. When it had gone I could only think of how I could turn before getting in among the convoy & had to give up all thought of the U-boat.[12]

That is the face, the strain, of naval battle.

The attacks on SC 94 continued over the next three days, and U-boats claimed four more merchant ships. At the end of it all an exhausted Layard despaired at how he handled the episode: "Looking back on the whole thing I felt I'd made a thorough balls of both the night & the day episodes with that we'd been concerned & I felt depressed & fed up. There is no doubt about it, I'm not a man of action & when faced with an emergency I just can't compete." Layard was being unfair with himself. But the point is that the mental strain associated with such responsibility was immense, and SC 94 was just one episode of many. Each time Layard put to sea with a convoy he suffered over the many command decisions that had to be made: Will I miss the rendezvous? Who should I send out on an anti-shadow sweep and how far should they go? What's our position? How long should I stay over the contact? Should I join the hunt? Should I stop and rescue survivors? Could I have done something differently? Was the loss of that ship my fault? Layard was surely not the only captain to suffer this angst but his attitude certainly contrasts with the confidence that permeates accounts of escort leaders such as Donald Macintyre, Johnny Walker, and Peter Gretton.

In his self-recrimination over SC 94, Layard complained that he was not a man of action, but the momentous events of 8 November 1942 demonstrate otherwise. As part of the opening moves of Operation Torch, the invasion of North Africa, the destroyers HMS *Broke* and HMS *Malcolm* were dispatched to force the boom guarding Algiers harbour and land troops to control the port facilities before they could be destroyed by the French. When HMS *Malcolm* and Layard's *Broke*, with Captain H.L. Fancourt, senior officer of the operation on board (another source of

Commander Layard eases HMS Broke *alongside the cruiser* Sheffield *to embark American soldiers for the attack on Algiers.*

strain to be sure) made their first run in, they lost their bearings in the glare of French searchlights and had to circle around again, all the while under shellfire.

> Twice more we tried to find the entrance & failed both times. Malcolm 2nd time came under heavy fire & retired with 3 boilers out of action. We then stood well away & decided in spite of only now having 1/2 our force to have another shot. I had got the position of 2 buoys now taped, both burning dimmed lights. As we rounded the breakwater I felt quite confident & in spite of Fancourt's advice to pull out again I went on to full speed & sure enough we were right & went slap through the boom like cutting butter.[13]

Layard put *Broke* alongside in harbour and landed his troops but was forced to shift berths when the ship came under shellfire. When the French guns again zeroed in Fancourt correctly decided their position was untenable and ordered Layard to withdraw. *Broke* was hit several times while escaping and the next day it lost steam and foundered in heavy seas; Layard and most of the crew were rescued by the destroyer HMS *Zetland*. Waking after his first sleep in more than 48 hours the loss of *Broke* hit home; "The more I thought about yesterday the more I felt I hadn't done all that I might have in shoring up & jettisoning more top weight & I got so depressed that I burst into tears … Reaction I suppose." Today, that would be recognized as post-traumatic stress.[14]

Two aspects of the Algiers operation and its aftermath reveal something of Layard's character. HMS *Broke* was under heavy fire and suffered nine killed and 20 wounded. Everyone is curious about how they would react under fire, and Layard was no different. In his diary he noted of his crew, "I thought there was a rather unpleasant tendency to fall flat every time a rifle went off & I was delighted to find I didn't want to do it myself. I was simply overjoyed at finding I was able under fire to at least conceal any feelings of fright…" This was not just self-serving, other officers remarked upon Layard's coolness. Perhaps an even more courageous act occurred when he gave a personal report of his experiences to Admiral Sir Andrew Cunningham, the naval commander for TORCH, whose short-fuse and irascibility were legendary: "I gave him an account of our little affair & told him the loss of the ship was because of a bad error of judgment on my part." Cunningham's final report on the attack on Algiers reflected that honesty; Layard had performed gallantly under fire but had erred in not keeping his damaged ship close by Algiers.[15] Despite this assessment, Layard's performance earned him a Distinguished Service Order (DSO) "for outstanding zeal and enterprise." "Fancy me getting a DSO. It's terrific," a surprised Layard wrote in his diary.[16]

War can bring together some strange bedfellows, and there is no question that Frank Layard and Canadian sailors fit into that category. Layard began to work closely with the Royal Canadian Navy (RCN) in November 1943, but in February 1944, when he took command of the RCN support group EG-9 he became totally immersed in the Canadian naval milieu, commanding Canadian sailors in Canadian ships. Although EG-9 was one of the more effective support groups in the inshore campaign, the buttoned-up Brit professional and the loosey-goosey Canadian volunteers were not always a good fit. The relationship is worth exploring since working with allies is a constant of naval warfare, and the cultural differences that exist between navies, and the different ways they do things can affect operations. It also adds to the strain of command.

After Algiers, Layard served nine months in the Miscellaneous Weapons Division at the Admiralty working on projects such as "Highball," the naval version of Barnes Wallis's dam busting weapon. Interestingly, he had a fair amount of time on his hands and spent it devouring every biography of Nelson he could get his hands on. In the late summer of 1943 he was informed that he was appointed to lead a new British support group operating out of Halifax. Although disappointed because he would be far from his family he was happy to get back to sea and finally get the brass hat of an acting commander. From the start, however, there were bad omens about service with the Canadians. When he stopped by Derby House in Liverpool to pay his respects to the commander-in-chief (CinC) Western Approaches, the chief of staff greeted him with "What have you done to be sent out there?," that Layard grumbled, "seems to imply it is a God awful job."[17]

When he arrived at Halifax, he immediately suffered what we would now call culture shock — he was flabbergasted when a Canadian officer picked up a bone off his plate and started gnawing on it; "A very nice chap but strange table manners." The comparative dinginess of Halifax, its conservative liquor laws and the lack of culture in the sense that Layard understood it greatly dismayed him. But the institutional shock was even greater. Since 1939, the RCN had expanded fifty-fold and with that expansion had come some severe teething troubles, both at sea and ashore. The greatest problem was with officer training. There were not enough regular officers to fill all the important positions and, unlike the RN, the RCN had no reserve of experienced officers like Layard to call upon. Junior officers were thrown into the Battle of the Atlantic with little experience and only the most basic training. On shore the RCN was simply overwhelmed; in 1939 it barely had the infrastructure to support a small force of about 3,500 but by mid-war had to deal with some 60,000.[18] Chaos and disorganization reigned. Soon after arriving in Halifax, Layard went to see the film "Corvette K-225," a Hollywood propaganda piece about the wartime RCN. "Very good" he wrote: "but to my mind it depicted something so entirely different from the RN as to be almost completely unrecognizable. But of course the RCN *is* very different."[19]

Layard took over the destroyer HMS *Salisbury* from Commander B.J. de St Croix, RN whom he later referred to as the "great Canadian hater,"[20] and who called the RCN the Royal Chaotic Navy.[21] On assuming command Layard observed, "The attitude in this ship initiated by the Captain is intensely hostile to the RCN. I think it is deplorable and I shall do my best to alter it."[22] That he did, but he was never completely comfortable with Canadians. Witness this passage written on 21 March 1945, when the EG-9 slipped from Scapa Flow: "At about 1500 we shoved off. I've never been so ashamed of a ship's company. There were men in khaki trousers, in filthy duffel coats, sea boots, jerseys, mostly smoking, and not one man in No 3s. The RCN [destroyer] *Iroquois* was on the other side of the oiler with every man in rig of the day. Thank God we were only seen by another RCN ship. I felt furious and despairing because obviously apart from me there wasn't another officer who saw anything wrong with it."[23]

Although Layard consistently complained about his Canadians, he realized he had a professional duty to adapt to them and he adjusted his leadership style to do so. Normally a distant, hands-off captain, with the Canadians he became more involved in the day-to-day running of his ships. Due to the inexperience of certain officers, and depending on each ship's effectiveness — he ultimately rode in five different RCN frigates — he sometimes informally filled the role of first lieutenant, as well as captain. He also seized every opportunity for individual ship and group training. Finally, he assumed the role of teacher and role model, educating his officers about the most basic skills associated with leadership and service at sea.

To ease the underlying tension that often existed between RN and RCN personnel, Layard also worked hard to build bridges between senior British officers and the Canadians serving under them. In Plymouth, after the group had killed a U-boat in a particularly good attack, Layard persuaded the Admiral's chief of staff to come on board HMCS *Saint John* to say "Well done." "I told him I thought the R.N. treated the R.C.N. unfairly — all criticism and no help and we'd never seen a senior R.N. officer on board." There were also problems in EG-9's usual homeport, Londonderry, home to commodore D (destroyers) Western Approaches, the legendary Commodore G.W.G."Shrimp" Simpson. As the senior officer responsible for RCN operational effectiveness on the eastern side of the Atlantic, Simpson faced a significant challenge in transforming under-trained, poorly-equipped RCN ships into effective escorts. Unhappily, he was occasionally quite scornful of Canadians, and although he reviewed matters with Canadian COs after each operation, he rarely visited RCN ships. On one occasion Layard tactfully suggested to Simpson's chief of staff "what a pity it was [the Commodore] didn't try to get to know the Canadian COs better." For his part, Simpson recognized the challenge faced by Layard. In his final flimsy he wrote: Layard had performed "entirely to my satisfaction. He has led with distinction a difficult team of individualistic Canadian officers."[24]

Layard was completely professional in his approach to the Canadians under his command — something they recognized and appreciated.[25] After the frigate HMCS *Saint John* left the group, the frigate's ASDIC control officer, Lieutenant J.R. Bradley, RCNVR, sent Layard a letter recounting his conversations with some of the crew: "Since leaving Scapa Flow large numbers of the ship's company have come to me expressing their admiration for you as captain of the ship, and senior officer of the group. They said that you always made them feel that their job was very important no matter how small it was; that you never forgot about leave and mail whenever opportunity to obtain them presented itself; that you were always concerned about the welfare and safety of the ship. They have expressed their wish to serve with you again." This was high praise, but having to work at the relationship took a toll on Layard at a time he was already under heavy strain because of the challenges of inshore anti-submarine warfare.

The Battle of the Atlantic has been described as a game of chess, although it can be argued that some convoy battles also had a large element of checkers in them. The inshore campaign in U.K. waters was completely different, and the board game it best resembles is *Battleship*, where players search a grid for the other's ships. Various tactics are used to find a contact among the maze of squares and once a ship is found it has to be localized before final "destruction" can be achieved. Then the search/hunt/localize sequence begins anew until all ships in the opposing "fleet" are destroyed. Luck, logic and patience are all keystones to victory.

A situation like this existed in U.K. waters from June 1944 until the end of the war in Europe. When the *U-bootwaffe* moved inshore in an attempt to thwart the build-up of materiel to Normandy, they let the convoys come to them, lying along the obvious coastal shipping routes amid the thousands of wrecks that littered the ocean floor. *Rudeltaktik* — wolf-pack tactics — were not used nor was there much occasion for communication between boats at sea and U-boat command in Berlin. *Schnorkel* largely negated the need for surfacing, making U-boats more like true submarines. For the Allies, the effectiveness of many of the weapons and tactics they had used to win the mid-Atlantic convoy war — radar, air power, HF/DF [high frequency/direction finding], code-breaking, evasive routing — diminished in varying degrees as decisive factors in the anti-submarine war. Consequently, finding U-boats in the new environment was similar to searching for ships in the *Battleship* game. Surface ships had to pick their way among the myriad wrecks and rock formations that lay on the ocean floor, classifying each and every one, which were all the time subject to powerful tidal currents. It was painstaking work and revised search and localizing tactics, equipment such as echo-sounders and the radio navigation aid called QH, and accurate, up-to-date wreck charters became the new war winners.[26] And like *Battleship*, luck, logic and patience, above all patience, were the keys to success.

Frank Layard's diary well describes the face of that battle. EG-9 was at the forefront of the inshore campaign for its duration — its only real break coming when the group supported a Russian convoy in November 1944; Layard's reaction to that was a succinct "Ugh!"[27] The burdens associated with inshore operations fell heavy on Layard and came from many sources. In July 1944, Layard's frigate HMCS *Matane* was badly damaged when it was hit by a glider bomb off Brest. In a wonderful feat of seamanship — and no doubt learning from his experience in *Broke* after Algiers — he got the ship back to Plymouth where he was cheered ashore by his crew. Six days later he was back at sea in another ship. In fact, over the course of the inshore campaign Layard rode in five ships and was sometimes double-hatted as CO and SOE. On each ship he had to adjust to a new crew. "I feel depressed and disheartened" he complained on one occasion, "and haven't the energy to start all over again in another ship."[28] These sources of strain aside, two others were particularly challenging; the tactical decision-making associated with the inshore campaign and fatigue.

Decision-making for senior officers in the inshore campaign essentially involved classifying a contact and deciding what to do with it. Consider one all too typical day for Layard and EG-9:

> In the course of the forenoon a signal arrived ordering us to carry out a gamma search of 20 miles in our old position up and down from C. de la Hague to about the centre of the Channel. At about 1330 we turned to the E[ast]. in order to get into our new position and almost at once picked up a contact. Ran over with the echo sounder and found it was definitely some thing on the bottom so went to action stations and attacked with H[edge]/H[og], that immediately produced oil. Meon and St. J. joined up although the attack was in progress and altogether we gave it 2 H/H salvos and 2 10 charge Deep D[epth]/C[harge] patterns, but still nothing but fish and

oil and the echo sounder trace looked nothing like a S[ub]/M[arine]. Reported I was attacking but thought it probably wreck. After 3 hours I finally decided it must be a wreck as those attacks were accurate and must have killed it had it been a S/M and at about 1730 we all went on and took up our new gamma search at about 1900. I reported classifying it as wreck and was very worried when at about 2200 a signal arrived asking on what I'd based my classification and implying they thought I'd left it too soon. I was still further fussed when Cooke reported to me that the paper speed on the echo sounder had been too slow and so the trace that had influenced my decision quite a bit was completely meaningless. Infuriating to have to signal that. To think I've done the wrong thing naturally puts me into an absolute lather.[29]

As Canadian historian Doug McLean has described, "EG-9 was one of many groups who learned the lesson of shallow water ASW [anti-submarine warfare] the hard way in the difficult school of experience."[30] New tactics had to be developed, and, as opposed to his earlier experiences in convoy warfare, Layard was as well off as any other officer commanding a support group. When contacts were found, the first step was to consult the wreck chart to see if it had already been classified as a known wreck. This took precise navigation and Layard quickly realized the value of QH, the naval version of a radio navigation aid called GEE, that gave accurate positions at virtually the push of a button. "This Q.H. is a joy and delight," he noted on one occasion, "Had a sniff round a wreck giving off oil on two occasions, on the N'ly leg and S'Sly leg. Q.H. tells me once it is the same contact and there is no movement."[31] But it was seldom that straightforward. Few contacts could be readily classified, even with the help of QH and wreck charts, or by continual runs from a variety of angles using the echo sounder. Those about which there was any uncertainty were plastered with depth charges and hedge hog. "One just has to attack every echo and there is no way of telling whether he is a S/M on the bottom or not." Ships took a real beating but patience and persistence, which Layard had in quantity, were keys to success.

It was tedious work, and the stress was considerable. Each contact required many command decisions, especially in the sense of when to move on. "We seemed to get a contact very nearly every 1/2 hour," he wrote in the midst of one patrol, "Some were known wrecks and others needed investigation but I had to turn out for every one and fix the ship and decide whether or not to go on. This sort of thing is really exhausting but on the route between Hartland Pt. and Trevose Head where the bottom is littered with wrecks it happens unceasingly. Contact, investigate, check position, probably attack, examine result, classify.... I shall be thankful to leave this patrol tomorrow and have a spell. It has been a particularly wearing 10 days."[32]

Courtesy Raymond Layard

Commander Layard on the bridge of HMCS Swansea. *This photograph captures some of the tedium of the inshore campaign.*

Layard was an old salt in a young sailor's game. After sitting down for a glass of gin with two fellow destroyer captains in September 1942 he complained, "When I hear these young 2 1/2 stripers talk I realize what an awful old cup of tea I am by comparison."[33] Old, and increasingly worn out, in 1944 Layard spent 211 days at sea, almost two out of three, and the weight of command exacted a heavy toll. On each of those days, Layard had to make dozens of command decisions involving the running of his ship or the direction of his group, some potentially involving life and death. Whether he was hunting U-boats or steaming routinely, Layard spent many hours on the bridge — 16 to 18 on some days. During that time he had to remain alert, ready for any eventuality. Meals, often taken on the bridge, were hurried affairs. For rest, he retired either to the small chart house at the back of the bridge or to his cramped sea cabin one deck below. Sleep would be fitful at best, his ear tuned to activity on the bridge, his body feeling any fluctuation in engine revolutions or movement of the rudder, and his troubled conscience reminding him that inexperienced officers had control of the ship. It was not an existence conducive to vitality or stability.

To some, the strain became overwhelming. One escort officer, Commander D.A. Rayner, RNVR, who had been at sea almost continuously since the outbreak of war, described the effects well. When his corvette nearly went aground because of a steering failure in late 1944, Rayner wound up shaking uncontrollably on the bridge. "'Well,'" he said to himself after getting his ship safely alongside in Londonderry, "'this is it — you are round the bend.' It was true. I could no longer trust my own body to obey orders. Catching sight of myself in the mirror made me pause. There had been a time when people ashore had said, 'You look very young to be a Commander,' but they hadn't been saying that recently. There wasn't any reason they should. The candle was burned out."[34] Rayner immediately requested a shore appointment. Layard's colleague, the Canadian escort leader Commander J.D. "Chummy" Prentice, did the same in November 1944 when he asked to be relieved of command of EG-11 because he thought fatigue was beginning to affect his judgment. In yet other examples, the Canadian officer Alan Easton went ashore because of ulcers and Captain Johnny Walker died in the saddle in July 1944. There were many others.

Strain and fatigue also pushed Layard to the limit. The winter of 1944–45 took a severe toll; not only did he beat himself up more than usual but he expressed more than his usual angst about going to sea. In February 1945 he agonized in his diary, "Deep depression of course setting in … not to mention worry and nerves. Oh Dear, oh dear I sometimes feel I can't go on competing anymore."[35] The war, moreover, seemed like it might last forever. On 19 April 1945 — three weeks before the European war actually ended — he lamented "it is obvious there is going to be no order to stop fighting and the Germans will continue to resist until every square mile is ours and that includes Norway and so it is still a long time before we can celebrate V.[E.] day." But even that would not be the end: "then 2 or 3 years more fighting in the Far East. I suppose I shall have to do my duty and go out there if required."[36]

Layard recognized the strain he was under, but it was his wife Joan who pushed him to seek relief. At her prodding he asked Canadian authorities about being replaced but, interestingly, he did not harp about the issue in his diary as he did when bothered by other matters. Moreover, he took the matter of his relief up with a Canadian civilian authority instead of an officer in the chain of command. One therefore is left with the impression that he was prepared to stick it out, and his comments about the continuing role he might have to play in the war bear that out. So how did he carry on? What got him through?

He had a vast network of fellow officers, known through past service, and he took every opportunity to tap into it. Whether it was exchanging gin in each other's cabins or meeting on runs ashore, he relied upon his fellow officers to give him the "gen," and to discuss common experiences. Although he was usually in awe of their accomplishments, their common experience probably told him that he was performing to expectations.

He also sought diversions. During lay-overs ashore he consistently went for long walks and always tried to avail himself of the local culture, be it inspecting old cathedrals or going to the theatre. He also loved impromptu parties. And at sea he always had a book going, and would grab a few minutes whenever possible to read modern novels, classics, and even Shakespeare. He also took great interest in the progress of the war, and piped the news over the ship's broadcast each day so that his crew knew what was going on.

He had a strong family network as well. He and his wife Joan were extremely close and he cherished her letters. In the most trying days of the inshore campaign when he was close to the brink, he was fortunate to operate out of Portsmouth or Plymouth and was thus fairly close to his home in Hampshire, of that he took good advantage. And even on lay-overs in Londonderry or Liverpool he would bring Joan up and involve her in wardroom activities as a way of extending his naval family.

Certainly, the diary was critical to him getting through. Keeping a diary was against regulations but officers who served with him often observed him scrawling away at something — they didn't know what — at all times of the day and the night. Quite simply, the diary was his release, his way of getting things off his chest. Without it, the mental anguish he suffered could have got the best of him.

In his excellent study on courage and morale among American and British aircrew in the Second World War, historian Mark Wells suggests that the ability to identify with a group was important in overcoming combat stress.[37] That was the case with Frank Layard. Identification with the long-established values and traditions of the Royal Navy was probably the key factor in enabling him to rise above the many challenges or obstacles thrown his way, including the strain of command. Although loyalty to an institution or a profession seems almost trite today, it was a vital part of Layard's character.

More than anything, his long education and experience in the Royal Navy ingrained in him the concept of the infallibility of duty. No matter how much his confidence waned; no matter how tired he became, his devotion to duty drove him to persevere. Abstract concepts like duty are difficult to define in concrete terms, but three diary entries from the first months of the Second World War shed light on Layard's attitude. At that time he was ashore at Whale Island, and the war at sea was just beginning to take its grim toll. On 19 October 1939 he learned that a colleague, Commander R.F. Jolly, RN, captain of the destroyer *Mohawk*, though mortally wounded in an air attack, only succumbed to his wounds after he had taken his ship safely into port. "Stories of that sort make an enormous impression upon me. It makes me wonder if I could ever be heroic like that."[38] A week later he volunteered for hazardous duty: "I hope I am not required as I don't think I'm brave enough but I feel I must make an effort to do something better worth while than just sitting comfortably back here."[39] In late November 1939 came news of the sacrifice of the armed merchant cruiser *Rawalpindi* at the hands of the battle cruisers *Scharnhorst* and *Gneisenau*, as well as word that another friend had been killed when the destroyer *Gypsy* was mined. "With every fresh naval disaster I get a return of this awful complex: 'How would I meet a similar circumstance.' Should I have done my duty bravely or should I have disgraced myself in a blind funk?"[40]

Frank Layard had an unshakeable understanding of what his duty was, not just duty to his country or the Royal Navy, but to his profession. That was the foundation of his success, and that is what motivated him to try one more time to enter Algiers, to work with and not against his Canadians, and to persist in trying to fathom the intricacies of inshore ASW. Yes, he was full of self-doubt but his experience can provide a level of comfort to those who have similar doubts in their ability. And there is a lesson, though a trite one. Navies need traditional thrusting heroes in the mould of the Walkers, the Vians and the Cunninghams but where would they be without a cadre of solid professionals like Frank Layard?

Finally, the U-boat attack in April 1944, mentioned at the beginning of the chapter, that Layard thought he had botched — was in fact a success. In 1986, after a reassessment by the Admiralty Historical Branch, he learned that he had sunk U-311. Once again, Frank Layard did far better than he gave himself credit for.[41]

NOTES

1. Layard Diary, 9 April, 1944. The original of the diary is in the Royal Navy Museum at Portsmouth. The copyright remains with the family.
2. Layard Diary, 22 April 1944.
3. Layard manuscript, 1. After retirement, Layard condensed portions of his diary into a manuscript. It remains in the family's possession.
4. Rudyard Kipling, *"The Scholars"* in *Rudyard Kipling's Verse: The Definitive Edition* (New York: Doubleday, 1940), 795–7.
5. J.R.S. "Broke, 1942," *The Naval Review*, Vol. 56, 1958, 442–444.
6. Alan Easton, *50 North: An Atlantic Battleground*, (Toronto: Ryerson Press, 1963).
7. Captain D Western Approaches, Form S-206, 26 November 1942. Layard Papers.
8. Details of Layard's career are either from the diary or the Royal Navy's *Navy List*. He also wrote a number of articles on his early naval service that appeared in *The Naval Review* in the 1970s. Accounts of some of his First World War experiences also appear in Max Arthur, *The True Glory: The Royal Navy, 1914–1939* (London: Hodder Stoughton, 1996).
9. Commander J. Baker-Creswell (Retired) to Vice-Admiral Peter Gretton (Retired), 5 October 1981. National Maritime Museum, Greenwich, Gretton Papers, Vol. 23, Part 1, MS 93/008.
10. Layard Diary, 28 July 1941.
11. For SC 94 see Anti-Submarine Warfare Division, Public Record Office [PRO], ADM 199/2007, "Analysis of U-Boat Operations in the Vicinity of Convoy S.C. 94, 31st July–13th August, 1942," 15 September 1942; *Ibid.*, Captain D Liverpool, "S.C. 94," 20 August 1942; *Ibid.*, "Report of Proceedings Received from Commanding Officer Her Majesty's Ship (HMS) *Broke*," nd.
12. Layard Diary, 9 August 1942; see also Library and Archives Canada [LAC], Record Group [RG] 24, Vol. 11334, 8280-SC-94, HMS *Broke*, "Report of Attack on U-Boat," nd.
13. Layard Diary, 8 November 1942.
14. See also PRO, ADM 199/224, Commanding Officer Operation TERMINAL to Commander Eastern Naval Task Force, "Operation 'TERMINAL'" — Report, 11 November 1942; *Ibid.*, CO HMS *Broke*, Report of Proceedings, 11 November 1942.
15. PRO, ADM 199/904, Report of Naval C-in-C Allied Expeditionary Force for Operation Torch.
16. DSO citation, Layard Papers. The award was gazetted on 16 March 1943.
17. Layard Diary, 7 September 1943.
18. For the growth of the RCN see, W.A.B. Douglas, Roger Sarty, and Michael Whitby, *No Higher Purpose: The Official Operational History of the RCN, 1939–43* (St Catharines, ON: Vanwell, 2003).

19. Layard Diary, 17 October 1943. Film historian Thomas Doherty describes "Corvette K 225" (Universal Studios 1943) "a good-neighborly nod to the Canadian Navy." Thomas Doherty, *Projections of War: Hollywood, American Culture and the Second World War* (New York: Columbia University Press, 1993), 153.
20. Layard Diary, 22 January 1944.
21. Layard manuscript, 1943, 66.
22. Layard Diary, 11 October 1943.
23. Layard Diary, 21 March, 1945.
24. Commodore D Western Approaches, Form S-206, 25 June 1945, Layard Papers.
25. The devotion to Layard by those who sailed with him is quite remarkable. For a testimonial of his time in one ship in particular see Fraser M. McKee, *HMCS Swansea: The Life and Times of a Frigate* (St. Catharines, ON: Vanwell 1994).
26. For the inshore campaign see W.A.B. Douglas, Roger Sarty, and Michael Whitby, *Blue Water Navy: The Official Operational History of the RCN, 1943–45* (St. Catharines, ON: Vanwell, 2006).
27. Layard Diary, 21 November 1944.
28. Layard Diary, 27 July 1944.
29. Layard Diary, 1 August 1944.
30. Naval History Collection, Directorate of History and Heritage, 2000/5, Lieutenant Commander D.M. McLean manuscript, "A Canadian Escort Group in British Waters: A History of Escort Group 9."
31. Layard Diary, 6 July 1944.
32. Layard Diary, 9 September 1944.
33. Layard Diary, 1 September 1942.
34. D.A. Rayner, *Escort: The Battle of the Atlantic* (London: William Kimber, 1955), 230.
35. Layard Diary, 2 February 1945.
36. Layard Diary, 19 April 1945.
37. Mark K. Wells, *Courage and Air Warfare: The Allied Aircrew Experience in the Second World War* (London: Frank Cass 1995), 61.
38. Layard Diary, 19 October 1939.
39. Layard Diary, 26 October 1939.
40. Layard Diary, 25 November 1939.
41. F.M. McKee, "Some Revisionist History in the Battle of the Atlantic," *The Northern Mariner*, Vol. 1, No. 4 (October 1991), 27–32.

CHAPTER 4

"A Hell of a Warrior": Sergeant Thomas George Prince

by P. Whitney Lackenbauer

> *As soon as I put on my uniform I felt a better man.*
> — Tommy Prince[2]

O ver the last decade, there has been a flurry of scholarly and popular interest in the Aboriginal men and women who served in the world wars and Korea.[3] No one is more famous than Sergeant Thomas George Prince, MM (1915–77), one of the most decorated non-commissioned officers (NCOs) in Canadian military history. Awarded 11 medals in all, including the Military Medal (MM) and United States (U.S.) Silver Star, Prince is held up as the prime example of the important contributions that Native peoples made to the Canadian war efforts of the twentieth century: he is the quintessential "Indian at War."[4] In biographical terms, his story is also tragic: That of a soldier whose commitment to his people and his country was never matched by his country's support for him. Overseas he was a bold, audacious, and courageous warrior. At home, he was a "fallen hero," fated to spend his final years as an alcoholic on the streets of Winnipeg.[5]

Given this duality, journalists and historians mobilize the story of Tommy Prince to represent Canada's treatment of its Native soldiers and veterans. In 2005 Remembrance Day ceremonies, for example, Native veterans received significant attention — including a special "spiritual journey" to Europe and high-profile photo sessions with the governor general. Sergeant Prince was frequently mentioned in the tributes to Aboriginal peoples' wartime contributions that accompanied these events.[6] Although he remains the most famous Native soldier of the modern era, that does not diminish the need to retell his story and recount his accomplishments. Prince's life as a soldier and veteran merits study on its own terms, and

deserves analysis beyond the uncritical hagiographical tributes that dominate the literature in Native-military relations. His qualities of courage and
daring, and his individualism on the battlefield, led to recognition that cat-
apulted Prince to a leadership role as an Native spokesperson after the
Second World War. He enlisted with the Canadian Army Special Force
(CASF) in 1950 and completed two tours in Korea, where physical injuries
and psychological trauma took their toll. His little-known breakdown in
the field in December 1952 revealed that this proud warrior was not superhuman. Acknowledging that Prince ended up a psychological casualty,
however, does not diminish his heroism or his courage. Instead, his story
serves as a reminder that operational stress can prey upon even the most
committed soldiers.

Thomas George Prince was born into a large family on the Brokenhead
Reserve, about 42 miles northwest of Winnipeg, Manitoba, in 1915. The
great-great grandson of Saulteaux Chief Peguis, Prince's relatives had
served the Crown during the Red River resistance in 1870, as Nile River
voyageurs in 1885, and on the battlefields of Europe during the First World
War.[7] One of 11 children, Tommy went to residential school at age five. "I
was a regular Tom Sawyer," he remembered. "I was a real rascal." His teach-
ers recalled that Prince had high hopes for the future, but that he was more
interested in hunting and fishing than in his studies. While he was away at
school, like many Native youth, he received his first taste of military life
with the army cadets. "I liked being in the cadets at Elkhorn," he later told
a reporter. "As soon as I put on my uniform I felt like a better man. I even
tried to wear it to class."[8] He became an excellent marksman. As a teenag-
er, he had great aspirations of becoming a lawyer. Instead, he finished
grade eight and quit school at age fourteen. "I didn't want to leave school,"
Prince later lamented, "but my father had no money." In the midst of the
Great Depression, he worked as a lumberjack and at other odd jobs.[9]

The onset of war offered new opportunities. In June 1940, at the age
of 24, Prince enlisted in the Royal Canadian Engineers (RCE). After six
weeks training with the 1st Field Park Company, Sapper Tommy Prince
was sent to England. Filled with anticipation early on, he soon grew disillusioned with operating a lathe and performing home guard duties. He
found an outlet for his energy in sports, and became one of his regiment's
"star athletes" — one of his fellow soldiers recalled him running down the
football field "like greased lighting."[10] It was simply a way to cope with the
monotony in England. John Haslam, who served in the RCE, explained

that the tedium was "driving Prince mad." To keep busy, Prince ran up to five miles each day and boxed regularly. "I joined the army to fight, not to sit around drinking tea," Haslam remembered Prince telling him before the call for volunteer paratroops went out in mid-1942.[11]

The Canadian Army sought volunteers for its new parachute corps from every possible source, including units already overseas. However, it imposed the highest standards on potential recruits. In fact, individuals were required to revert to the rank of private to join. Prince was the first to step forward from his regiment — parachuting was relatively new and exciting, and offered the possibility for Prince to actually see combat. He was accepted into the 1st Canadian Parachute Battalion (1 Cdn Para Bn), and was one of the nine volunteers (out of a hundred) in his student squad who earned his wings at the British parachute school at Ringway near Manchester. However, before 1 Cdn Para Bn was fully established, its members were recruited for a newly forming commando unit.[12]

The First Special Service Force (FSSF), formed in mid-1942, was a unique Canadian-American combined military force. Drawing officers and men from both countries' armies, it was originally conceived as a brigade-sized, special operations unit intended to raid and sabotage Nazi-occupied regions of Europe. Although this particular role never materialized, historian James Wood recently concluded, "the Force came to symbolize the united purpose of the democratic nations. Today, it is remembered … for its outstanding combat record and its distinctive bi-national composition."[13] At the time, it was referred to as a "super-commando unit," a "combined special force for offensive warfare" using "U.S.-Canadian super-specialists" in parachute attacks, marine landings, mountain fighting, and desert warfare. Troop selection emphasized "youth, hardness, and fitness."[14]

Al Lennox, a platoon sergeant with the FSSF during the war, recounted, "Tom was ideal for this type of a unit. He was brave. He was intelligent. In his early days as a young man, he was out living off the land, getting their own game, learning how to track, and how to walk right, without making a noise. So all those attributes came in very handy in this type of a unit."[15] Indeed, an original proposal suggested that the Force might be named the "Braves," its subunits named after Native American tribes, and its badge bearing crossed tomahawks.[16] Tommy Prince fit the bill in every respect. Along with the others, he qualified as a parachutist and headed to Montana to train in small arms, demolitions, unarmed combat, and vigorous physical exercise. They also practiced skiing, mountain climbing, cold climate survival, and use of snow vehicles. By late 1942, developments in the strategic situation indicated that it would be useful to send the FSSF to the Mediterranean in a combat role. The intensive training program expanded to include new weapons and tactics, including amphibious operations.[17]

Prince earned a solid reputation.[18] His prowess in the field was celebrated by his comrades, wrote McKenzie Porter, a journalist for *Maclean's*, particularly his "natural instinct for 'ground.'" When the Forcemen arrived at the front, Prince would "creep forward on his belly with the speed and agility of a snake and take advantage of small depressions in an otherwise flat field to stay out of view. He was a crack shot with a rifle and crafty as a wolf in the field." Prince claimed that it was "born in him" — he never let his fellow soldiers forget that he was a Native. Whenever mail arrived from home, Prince always exclaimed "I've got a smoke signal from the chief."[19] His biographers later suggested that his propensity to stress his Native-ness at every opportunity puzzled his men. "Once a man was in an army uniform no one cared

Courtesy Canadian Forces Airborne Museum

Members of the FSSF load a mule with heavy weapons in the Italian mountains.

about his origin. Prince, however, felt it necessary to represent Natives as a people and never let the men forget his racial origin."[20]

"All my life," Prince explained, "I had wanted to do something to help my people recover their good name. I wanted to show they were as good as any white man."[21] These considerations provide insight into Prince's motivation for military service and his daring exploits in uniform. Several scholars, particularly in the United States, intimate that Natives enlisted to secure the approval of mainstream white society. Prince's own statements reveal this sentiment, but this should not be used to deny Native American servicemen (including Prince) agency, as it tends to do when they are portrayed as subservient "Tontos, Natives whose greatest aim and sole identity is to be 'faithful and trusted companions' of whites."[22] Prince did not seek a supporting role; he would be front and centre of the action. He sought profile, and married his actions to his general appreciation of the Native situation. "Prince is not very precise in what he wants for Indians but you can tell in his conversation that he is comparing their past with their present and is concerned largely with their prestige," Porter concluded after interviewing Prince. "Consciously or unconsciously he made a personal contribution to the Indians' good by his heroism."[23] He would prove his courage, cleverness, and daring in the field.

The first opportunity for the FSSF to test their mettle came in North America. In the summer of 1942, the Japanese captured the Aleutian Islands of Attu and Kiska. In mid-August 1943, the First Special Service Force landed at Kiska as part of a combined operation to dislodge the Japanese. Although prepared to sustain high casualties, the Force encountered no resistance because the Japanese had already evacuated the island.[24] For his part, Tommy Prince was disappointed. "He was exultant at the prospect of combat," Porter said, "and dejected on arrival to find the enemy had withdrawn. It seemed to him that he was never going to get a chance to test his courage."[25]

Allied High Command decided that the FSSF would fight in Italy. In the fall of 1943, the force sailed for North Africa and then on to Italy to join the U.S. 5th Army. Allied troops had landed at Salerno (south of Naples) in early September and established a bridgehead. The German commander in Italy, Field Marshal Albert Kesselring, ordered his troops to defend every inch of ground and the campaign was soon "transformed into a remorseless, attritional grind."[26] On 20 November, Prince and the other members of the FSSF arrived in theatre to participate in the Naples-Foggia Campaign. They quickly moved to the rugged

mountain range south and east of Casino, where the Germans dominated the battlefront from a series of hilltop strongholds. "Throughout
November," a journalist reported, "the entire U.S. 5th Army had been
stopped by a series of heavily-fortified mountains.... From these tower-
ing vantage points strong German forces had been able to beat back
every Allied effort to advance." Although the FSSF was still without battle experience, its special training and equipment for mountain operations meant that it was tasked to wrest the daunting peaks from battle-
hardened German divisions. Its soldiers did not disappoint.[27]

Early in the New Year, Prince finally got his baptism of fire. His regiment was ordered to oust the enemy from Mount La Difensa, whose
1,259-metre-high peaks dominated the valley northeast of Casino. Under
the command of a Canadian, Lieutenant-Colonel Thomas P. Gilday, 1st
Battalion led the 3rd Regiment assault on the night of 6–7 January. It drove
a battalion of the German 132nd Grenadier Regiment from "its rock-
ribbed positions."[28] During the attack "Prince saw for the first time men
riddled by bullets from the Spandau light machine gun which fired so fast
it sounded like a motorbike engine revving up," Porter recorded. "He
learned to walk at the crouch whenever he heard the Nebelwerfer mortar
softly coughing up nine big bombs that came fluttering through the air
with no more sound than the beat of a bird's wings, then burst around him
with the loud flat report of slamming doors and tore men to pieces." War
is slaughter, Carl von Clausewitz described bluntly in his famous On War,
and Prince learned this first-hand. During his first night in combat, he saw
anti-tank mines toss gun carriers into the air and crush their crews. He saw
bodies dismembered by anti-personnel mines. "Through that demonic
night, lit by flares and gunfire, Prince heard men who had never been to
church calling on their Maker, and saw men who had looked like lions turn
into gibbering loons, and trod on sickly sweet tumescent puff balls that
had once been men." He "pressed on, regardless":

> When he got to the top of the mountain in the dawn,
> vaguely aware of the ragged line of staggering comrades
> on either side, and of green-faced Germans jumping out
> of holes and running away, his bursting lungs sum-
> moned the breath for a great exultant shout, for in this
> moment he had come to know the meaning of that
> ecstasy which unites infantrymen in beer parlors and to
> realize that on a twentieth-century warpath an Indian
> brave can still be worth more than many a paleface.[29]

The FSSF repelled repeated German counterattacks in the weeks ahead.[30] Nevertheless, fierce enemy artillery, sleep deprivation, and continuous night patrolling wore on the front-line soldiers. The weather was bitter, the terrain difficult, and German resistance fierce. The 1st Canadian Special Service Battalion's war diary described the nature of operations on 8 January 1944: "Today's casualty return … lists 100 names, half of them frostbite and exposure, the rest battle casualties. The weather in the hills is very cold, with high wind and snow. German resistance is quite severe, artillery and mortar fire is taking its toll." It was tough slogging until the Force was withdrawn to reorganize for offensive operations. By that time, nearly half the strength of the combat regiments had become casualties.[31] The FSSF was also earning a reputation on the battlefield. "The Germans dubbed these gallant commando-paratroopers 'men with funny pants and dirty faces,'" journalist Ross Munroe informed Canadians back home.[32]

Corporal Tommy Prince was also earning a reputation for his fieldcraft. Lieutenant-Colonel Gilday first met Prince near Casino, when "he went ahead to scout a route that avoided enemy patrols and mines, then quickly returned with the information of an enemy placement." Gilday was impressed: "I immediately adopted him for my battalion headquarters and decided he was my man. He knew that he had the superior ability to find his way around … to know where other people were, and they'd never know where he was."[33] Given Prince's prewar experience in the Manitoba bush, he soon earned renown for silence, swiftness, and daring. One of his comrades recounted how:

> He used to carry a pair of moccasins in his bag with him. He would never tell anyone where he was going, but would just slip away in the night. The Germans thought he was a ghost or a devil. They could never figure out how he passed the lines and the sentries. He was deathly quiet…. Instead of sneaking in and killing them, he would steal something like a pair of shoes right off their feet. Or he would leave articles behind, like a calling card; just to let them know he had been there. Once in a while he would kill one of them, slit his throat so as not to awaken anybody. When those Germans woke up and found one of their own lying dead in the midst of them that's when they got scared. They didn't believe that Prince

could be real so they figured he must be an evil spirit or better yet the devil. We were known as the Devil's Brigade to the Germans.[34]

The reliability of this insight into German thinking may be questioned, but the aura that Prince exuded to his fellow soldiers was clear. He was a warrior, and was promoted to sergeant. His métier was reconnaissance, and stubborn enemy resistance in mountainous terrain offered ample opportunity to hone his craft.[35]

By January 1944, after four months of gruelling combat, the U.S. 5th Army had advanced only 70 miles beyond the Salerno bridgehead. To break the deadlock, the Allies launched a daring amphibious invasion to outflank German defences and take the port of Anzio, 35 miles south of Rome. The assault force achieved tactical surprise on 22 January and established a beachhead, but German commander Kesselring hastily improvised a force to oppose the Allied invaders. Rain, terrain, and defenders conspired against a decisive Allied breakthrough. On 2 February, the FSSF took over an 11,000 yard sector (about one quarter of the entire bridgehead perimeter) along the Mussolini Canal, which formed a natural barrier between the German 316th Division and the Allied forces on the east flank of the beachhead. With the rest of the beachhead ground in stalemate, the Force took the offensive using highly-effective raiding tactics and aggressive patrols. For 90 days the FSSF managed to keep the Germans off balance, prevented any major counterattacks from developing in their sector, and thus "played an important role in the beachhead defense."[36]

At Anzio, Sergeant Prince earned his first decoration for bravery. German tanks and artillery were inflicting serious damage to Allied soldiers and material near Littoria, so Prince volunteered to set out alone for a special reconnaissance mission on 8 February. Under cover of darkness, he ran a telephone wire 1,800 yards into enemy territory and established an observation post in an abandoned farmhouse, 200 yards in front of the enemy lines. It was a precarious position but his daring paid off. Using his field telephone in the house, Prince passed along exact enemy dispositions, otherwise invisible to Allied artillery. Around noon the next day, communications suddenly ceased and Prince correctly surmised that shellfire had cut the wire. Prince quickly appraised the situation. If the Germans suspected his presence, they would continue to shell the house. If he tried to withdraw, he would be mown down. If he did nothing, he could not pass along vital information to his comrades. His solution was bold, audacious, and courageous.

"Using his own ingenuity," his citation later announced, "Sgt. Prince donned available civilian clothes and, under direct enemy observation, went out to repair his line, to re-establish contact for target observation." Prince donned an old black Italian hat, black jacket, and white muffler that the former resident had left in the house, and ran outside imitating an Italian farmer. In plain sight of the Germans, he inspected the chicken coop for damage, grabbed a hoe, pretended to weed his crops (actually tracing the wire until he found the breach), bent down as if to tie his shoe laces, and spliced the line. He maintained his charade, shaking his fists at the Germans and the Allies, then returned to the house and resumed communications with his unit. Obviously, the ruse succeeded in convincing the Germans that he was a peasant farmer, and they stopped shelling the position. After 24 hours of surveillance, he returned to his lines under darkness. "You crazy fool," an officer told him. "If you'd been taken prisoner in those clothes you'd have been shot out of hand." His superiors were suitably impressed: Prince's information allowed their artillery to destroy four German positions. Lieutenant-Colonel Gilday recommended that his superiors award Prince the Military Medal for "exceptional bravery in the field." His citation attested that "Sergeant Prince's courage and utter disregard for personal safety were an inspiration to his fellows and a marked credit to his unit."[37]

Photographer C.J. Woods, Library and Archives Canada PA-142287

Prince was obviously well-suited to the active patrolling at Anzio. Nevertheless, his comrades "had mixed feelings about his patent disregard for safety." Bill Johnson served with the FSSF in Italy, and later recalled hearing one soldier remark, when Prince set out on one of his many patrols, "There goes Prince trying to win another medal to prove he is brave."[38] The risks were high, but so too were the payoffs,

Sergeant Tommy Prince (right), now a member of the 1st Canadian Parachute Battalion, photographed at Buckingham Palace after receiving his Military Medal.

and Prince achieved results. On 9 May 1944, the Force withdrew from the front to prepare for further offensive operations. Two weeks later, the 1st Regiment spearheaded the FSSF breakout from the Anzio Beachhead. They faced stiff resistance and fierce counterattacks, but led General Keyes's 2nd Corps in the final drive into Rome. Prince was among the first Allied units into the Italian capital on 4 June, when the FSSF secured the seven Tiber bridges in the northern part of the city. This ended the Force's operations in Italy, and it was withdrawn in late June to prepare for its next assignment. General Mark Clark, commander of the U.S. 5th Army, paid the men high tribute:

> The part played by your elite American-Canadian Force is so well known that it hardly needs to be rehearsed at this time. The grueling fighting which you went through on the main front in the dead of winter, the important part which you took in the establishment and in the defence of a beachhead during its historic four months' siege, the way in which your relatively small Force maintained an aggressive offensive on a front equal to that held by a full division, and finally your brilliant performance in the final breakout and in the strong fighting which culminated in the capture of Rome have entered history and forged a bright new link in our military tradition.[39]

Prince had been through it all, had tasted victory, and forged a reputation for bravery.

As a member of the FSSF, Prince continued to find himself involved in actions apart from the main body of Canadian Army troops through the war. Exactly one year after his unit invaded the Aleutian Island of Kiska, it participated in another amphibious operation: the invasion of southern France. The Force easily accomplished its objectives on 15 August 1944 by capturing the two easternmost Îles d'Hyères to protect the invasion's left flank during the French Riviera landings. Transferring to the mainland a few days later, the First Special Service Force re-entered operations just west of Cannes as part of 6th Army Group. They made rapid progress pushing eastward along the narrow coastal plain of the Riviera, but faced stiff resistance in the mountainous terrain behind Nice at the end of the month. It was difficult slogging for Tommy Prince and his fellow countrymen in the FSSF, who were the only Canadian soldiers to serve in southern France. Once again, he did his part to ensure they were noticed.[40]

On 1 September, Sergeant Prince led a two-man reconnaissance patrol 15 miles behind enemy lines near L'Escarène, France. Over rugged, mountainous terrain, he and his partner gained "valuable and definite information [about] the enemy's outpost positions, gun locations, and a bivouac area." On the way back to their lines to report their findings, Prince and the accompanying private came upon a skirmish between a German platoon and a squad of Free French partisans who were being encircled. Taking up concealed positions to the rear, Prince and his comrade began to pick off Germans — he killed at least six and was presumed to have injured more. The German platoon commander, shaken by the high casualties and oblivious to the two Canadians, withdrew. When the Free French officer asked Prince "Where is the rest of your company?," Prince pointed to the private and said "Here." "*Mon Dieu,*" said the officer, "I thought there were at least fifty of you!"[41]

Prince's patrol, accompanied by the Free French partisans, returned to the FSSF lines on 3 September and provided details on the German positions. "So accurate was the report rendered by the patrol that Sergeant Prince's regiment moved forward on 5 September 1944, occupied new heights and successfully wiped out the enemy bivouac [encampment] area," declared his ensuing recommendation for the American Silver Star. In the previous five days, Prince had covered fifty miles by foot and had little rest. "The keen sense of responsibility and devotion to duty displayed by Sergeant Prince is in keeping with the highest traditions of the military service and reflects great credit upon himself and the Armed Forces of the Allied Nations."[42]

By 9 September the FSSF had advanced quickly along the Riviera coast, covering 45 miles. It settled into a position on the border with Italy, holding a large front by active patrolling — and sustaining heavy casualties in the process. It was a thankless battle. German artillery and numerical superiority confined the men to their foxholes for large stretches, with no prospect for relief. The number of battle exhaustion cases rose: "the men had been in the line for too long without rest."[43] Sergeant Tommy Prince, however, did not seem to suffer. He continuously sought out danger, and came up with creative ways to harass the enemy. The fate of the FSSF, however, was sealed back in North America. By late 1944, administrative difficulties diminished its appeal, and its specialized training and operational techniques were no longer required. On 5 December, the Force was inactivated near Villeneuve-Loubet. Because Prince had trained as a parachutist, he soon returned to England to reinforce the 1st Canadian Parachute Battalion.[44]

In practical terms, Prince's war was over. He returned to England in early 1945, and was summoned to a ceremony at Buckingham Palace. His brother Morris, who also served in the war, joined him on the momentous occasion. King George VI decorated Tommy Prince with both the Military Medal and, on behalf of the president of the United States, the Silver Star with ribbon. The King actually recognized him from an inspection in Surrey in 1942, and they discussed Prince's service, as well as his life on his Manitoba reserve. "He spoke to me for two minutes," Prince later boasted, "but most of the others only got about thirty seconds." Only 59 Canadians received the Silver Star, only three of whom also wore the Military Medal. Prince was in elite company.[45] Victory in Europe was achieved before Prince could actually join 1 Cdn Para Bn in the field. He did join them, however, for the voyage back to North America.

His story was front page news when he returned to Winnipeg on 24 June. "He is very quiet and extremely humble about the job he has done since he joined the army approximately five years ago," a reporter observed upon his arrival. "If you were to ask what he has done to receive his decorations, his answer would shed as little light on the subject as possible. His friends can tell you better what he did to deserve his medals." Readers of the *Winnipeg Free Press* learned that he was one of the most decorated men in the Canadian Army, with his Military Medal and Silver Star, mentions in dispatches, as well as his rumoured eligibility for more decorations. Prince, however, downplayed his exploits at Anzio. "It wasn't very much to get a medal for," he told journalists. "I set up an artillery post and got rid of a few enemy emplacements." He described his deeds as nothing more than his duty; he had a job to do and he did it. So had others. "That is only one thing — the boys in the infantry and other branches have done as much and more," he explained. "We just haven't heard about it yet. You have to go a long way to beat those boys." Prince was a team player, and seemed prepared to serve in the Pacific War. "I'm still A-1 in the army and it is up to them whether or not they wish me to stay and fight in the Pacific. Certainly I will go if they want me — if not, I'll start establishing myself." In the meantime, he stayed with friends in Winnipeg to await the verdict from army headquarters on his future in the forces. He received his discharge on 21 August 1945.[46]

Warrior Tommy Prince returned to civilian life. As a child, Doris Small met him several times and remembered him as a "joyful, impish, laughing man when around children ... but he was quiet and reserved around adults." She recalled how he shared his overseas experiences with elementary students to put their lives in perspective:

> Tom Prince arrived at our school to render a history lesson; to tell us how lucky we were because we had a roof on our school, with books for reading and scribblers with pencils for writing, when many children in war torn villages, towns and cities in Europe did not. He used to carry chocolate bars and he would break them into pieces and pass them around, should we entertain with a song, a poem, or a story. He was a very kind and gentle man. He came often and then he came no more. The military bases closed at the edge of our town and life went back to some form of normality.[47]

There was no return to "normality" for Prince. Like many other veterans, he found that his life had changed. He divorced his first wife, and his father passed away.[48] When a woman attacked him with a broken bottle at a dance in 1946, he was left with a facial laceration requiring 64 stitches and the determination to leave the Brokenhead Reserve for good. Even a veteran with a heroic record had a difficult time finding a job in peacetime. He made his living cutting pulpwood and soon found that he was "just another Indian" once again. After working as a janitor in Winnipeg, he decided to start his own cleaning business and purchased a panel truck and supplies using re-establishment support from the Department of Veterans Affairs. Soon his small business began to make a profit.[49]

The 30-year-old veteran was called upon to serve as a voice for his people. "Before you could say 'Big Chief Sitting Bull,'" one over-zealous journalist noted, "this young Chippewa brave was back on the warpath. Only his sniper rifle was replaced by words and writing."[50] In early December 1946, the Manitoba Indian Association asked Prince to serve as vice-president and chief spokesman for their organization, believing that his war hero status would provide leverage when he spoke to federal officials.[51] He agreed to represent his people's interests, motivated by the awareness that Native peoples faced dismal prospects after the war. "On his return from overseas he visited some northern Indian reservations and was appalled by the prevailing conditions," one editorial explained. "My job is to unite the Indians of Canada so we can be as strong as possible when we go to the House of Commons," Prince said.

His testimony as a witness before the Special Parliamentary Joint Committee established in 1947 to look into the Indian Act represented his finest hour as Native spokesman.[52] His statements were bold, unequivocal, and visionary. If the Indian Act was abolished and the original treaties honoured, Prince believed, Natives would regain their confidence and self-sufficiency. It was time for renewed Native-White relationships built on trust and partnership.[53]

Prince had a particular interest in the Brokenhead Band, and expressed deep resentment that sacred treaty promises had been broken. He complained about the curtailment of fishing, hunting, and trapping rights, and pushed for a "long-range programme" of financial support, hospitals, improved sanitation, and schools.[54] "I returned to this band after I was discharged from the armed forces," he told the committee, unable to make a living on the reserve "as there is nothing there to make a living." He saw a future in agriculture — after all, the reserve had "ideal land for agriculture, real rich black soil." A fire had swept through the year before, preparing about one-third of the reserve for breaking the land. With the timber gone, Prince wanted young men to take a leadership role and secure a government loan to begin farming. "We have a few veterans who can really handle machinery," he noted. "They showed it by holding their own in the army." But the band chief, who Prince stressed could not read and write, had quashed the plan. The chair of the joint committee noted that Prince's "objective is not only to get himself set up as a farmer, but he also wants to give a lead which others can follow as closely as possible." To bring about change would require the education of "the older men," and the chair saw Prince as a progressive Native who was "trying to help his fellow Indian to help themselves [sic]."[55]

If any group could bring about meaningful change, Prince believed it was Native veterans who had served overseas. Instead, they were constrained inequitable and insufficient veterans' benefits compared to non-Natives. "There are some 3,000 young Indian men who fought on the other side of the water for their King and for their country," Prince highlighted. "Those Indian veterans had responsibilities in the army and they carried out those responsibilities to perfection." The $2,320 in veterans' grants available to them, however, was paid directly to the Minister of Mines and Resources "and the Indian veteran has nothing to say about it and he is treated just as a common labourer. How can we better conditions for the Indian veteran if we do not give them the privilege of practicing their ability and showing their fellow Indians an example?"[56] To Prince, it all came back to leading by example. It was action not rhetoric that mattered.

"I should like to know why a man like Mr. Prince, who has had a fine record and who has spoken here in a very able manner, is not in the Indian department somewhere," MP Raymond MacNichol pondered during the 1947 hearings. The committee chair replied that he could probably "take that up with the Civil Service Commission and get [Prince] on the staff of the Indian Affairs Department. If you could do so, I know you will be performing a great service to this committee and to the Indians of Canada."[57] Prince pursued no such course. Prince was "bewildered and frustrated by the legal verbiage used to counter his arguments." As the hearings dragged on, Prince tried to convince other Indian leaders to appeal directly to King George VI for change. It did not happen. Although amendments eventually removed some of the most offensive provisions of the Indian Act, Prince left Ottawa disillusioned. He was convinced that the myth of the simple-minded, backward Native needed to be shattered. "The changing of this view became an obsession with him," his biographers observed. "Somehow or other, the prestige of the Indians had to be raised as a first step towards future progress." Unfortunately, he could not accomplish this with his cleaning business as Prince returned to find that his "friends" had smashed his truck and the rest of his equipment was missing. He went to work as a lumberjack, in a pulp and paper mill, and at a local cement plant.[58]

In early August 1950, when the Canadian Government appealed for volunteers to fill the Canadian Army Special Force to serve in the Korean War, Tommy Prince re-enlisted immediately. Why did he sign up? "I owed something to my friends who died" in the earlier war, he explained later in life.[59] On 17 August, Private Prince was taken on strength by the 2nd Battalion, Princess Patricia's Canadian Light Infantry (2 PPCLI), a regiment with an established military tradition. On 14 September, he was reinstated as acting sergeant to conduct pre-deployment training for inexperienced recruits at Camps Sarcee and Wainwright in Alberta. Range training focused on small arms, machine guns, anti-tank rockets, grenades and demolitions, and mines. Prince also conducted camouflage and concealment training.[60] His previous achievements, coupled with his forceful personality, made an impression on his subordinates. "You're in the Princess Patricia's now," he was overheard telling a group of enlisted men in basic training. "You are hard! You drink hard! You play hard! You love hard! You hate hard! You can decide what you drink, how you play, who you love. We'll decide who you hate and who you fight."[61] He had high personal expectations, and high expectations for the men under his command.

The 2 PPCLI was the first Canadian infantry unit to arrive in the Korean theatre. It proved to be a gruelling campaign in a cold and mountainous land, bereft of the comforts of life at home. The infantry in Korea "led a life of extreme hardship and deprivation," historian Brent Watson noted in his superb social history of the CASF, living "like tramps without even the most basic comforts."[62] Prince, for his part, was pleased to be back in military action. If the first contingent was seen as "bums from the slums," Prince was the seasoned "hunter" back in his element.

Robert Hepenstall concluded that two major problems plagued the army in Korea: alcohol and sleeping on guard duty.[63] Prince was a hard-drinker, but he had no tolerance for sleeping on guard duty; the latter was a serious military offence that could place an entire platoon in danger. Private Dan Johnson recounted this story:

> Sergeant Tommy Prince, while making his rounds one night, found a soldier, leaning over the lip of his trench, asleep at his post. He came up behind him, grabbed him around the neck and began choking him. Some off-duty soldiers, awakened by the noise, grabbed Prince and with some difficulty managed to pry him off the soldier's back.
>
> "You know what I could have done to him!" exclaimed Prince.
>
> "Yes" came back the answer.
>
> "Well," Prince yelled, "that's what the next guy gets who sleeps on guard duty."[64]

In a war zone where danger abounded, Prince had little tolerance for ineptitude that could jeopardize the lives of his men. In late March, Prince's platoon joined the rest of the company on the crest of a hill. From an adjacent feature, a Chinese sniper began to pick off Canadian soldiers. Private Herman Thorsen recalled how Sergeant Prince scanned the ground with his binoculars and called him over. "See that tree with the rock beside it?" Prince asked. "Well, that's not a rock, it's the shadow of a hole, and in the hole is the sniper." Thorsen looked more closely and saw movement. Prince raised his rifle and fired a shot. "We didn't receive any more fire from that point again," Thorsen confirmed.[65] On another occasion, Prince's platoon was resting on the reverse slope of their own position when they received a radio call announcing that their artillery would be ranging on targets far out in front. Shells began to burst all around them, however, and "a sizeable chunk landed between Prince's thumb and index finger." Lieutenant Brian Munro explained that they quickly "jumped in our slit trenches and notified battalion."[66] Prince remained cool under fire, and his courage set an example to his men.

On the night of 24–25 April 1951, 2 PPCLI fought in the most famous Canadian battle of the Korean War when the Chinese launched their offensive at Kapyong. Although outnumbered and isolated, historian Brent Watson explains, "the Princess Pats repulsed wave after wave of attacking Chinese infantry from their positions atop Hill 677 overlooking the Kap'yong River Valley."[67] For his part, Sergeant Prince "set his men an example of courageous calm when the Chinese prepared for attack with bugle blasts, whistles, and shouting."[68] As the Chinese approached, panic spread through the Canadian ranks in their slit trenches, eroding morale and prompting comments such as "Let's get the hell out of here!" Sergeant Prince and the other NCOs quashed these notions, and passed orders that they would only leave together.[69] The company stayed in place and, with its experienced leadership, specialized training, and high morale, succeeded in defending Hill 677. For its important contribution to the Commonwealth victory at Kapyong, 2 PPCLI was awarded the United States Presidential Unit Citation — the only Canadian unit to ever earn this distinction. Although soldiers did not receive individual insignia of the citation to adorn their uniforms until after the war, it was the men, like Tommy Prince, who had displayed the rewarded "extraordinary heroism and outstanding performance" in combat.[70]

During his first Korean tour, Sergeant Prince had the respect of his subordinates, but he did not enjoy easy relations with his company commanders. Major George Flint, a permanent force soldier from the 1st Battalion, PPCLI, was rigid in his thinking and had difficulty relating to the men of his company. Prince, who was close to his men, recognized that the soldiers lacked confidence in Flint's leadership. He worried that they might harm the major; but passing along this message to Colonel James Stone could not have improved relations between the NCO and the major. "There was a conflict between Prince, Major Flint, his platoon officer, and the men of his platoon," Robert Hepenstall later recorded. "There was some jealousy between Prince and the officers because the men respected his [Prince's] fighting ability." Flint, for his part, distrusted Prince, believing that he was too reckless with himself and his men — as an officer, he was ultimately responsible for all of them.[71] Although his feeling about the sergeant could have reflected personal animus and jealousy, Prince's comrades later echoed similar concerns.

Prince's previous service provided him with important experience, but had also taken its toll physically. He had varicose veins in his legs and patrolling in the rugged Korean terrain caused him great discomfort. His comrades noticed that Prince was exhausted, dragging himself up and down hills "with a wooden staff, plus guts and determination."[72] When he finally agreed to a physical examination, the medical staff found "an arthritic condition of the knee that must have kept him in perpetual agony and seriously impaired his agility." In October 1951, over his strident objections, Prince was posted home from Korea.[73] He was duly posted to a training position at Camp Borden.

Prince hardly welcomed the transition to a less bellicose role. "He was a misfit," Hepenstall later recorded, Prince was "excellent in battle, but unable to function in any other situation. There was a problem finding him employment within the army. He was not a good parade square man, nor with his limited education was he a good lecturer." The sergeant was put in charge of stores, but had the nasty habit of insulting young officer cadets when they picked up equipment. He also made enemies in the sergeants' mess when he heaped scorn on those who had not seen combat overseas.[74] In mid-1952, Porter visited the military camp and encountered an obviously uncomfortable situation:

> Ageing warriors of thirty-five and more, looking for a cushy billet in which to await their pensions, sometimes say that a sergeant instructor's appointment at Camp Borden, with its five-day week, white tablecloths, leather armchairs, swimming pool, movies, organized sports, beer and spirits, bed lamps and white sheets, is "just the job." But Sergeant Prince longs to get back to the fighting, even though he is thirty-six and has an arthritic knee from too much crouching in slit trenches. He lets his wishes be known vociferously in the Sergeants' Mess, respectfully in the Orderly Room, and bitterly, out of the corner of his mouth, when he delivers a case of "thunderflash" fireworks to the young officer cadets so they can play at throwing hand grenades.

In general Sergeant Prince's comrades find his gripe irritating. Most of his fellow instructors have had combat service too and accept with phlegmatic satisfaction the truism that their life in war was "ninety percent tedium and ten percent sheer hell." None is afraid to admit that he'd have traded the hell for still more tedium. Yet here's a man who should know better still demanding hell all the time. "Well," says one sergeant, tongue in cheek, "I guess there just isn't enough hell to go around."

Young recruits seemed intimated by Prince's achievements, NCOs thought that Prince was "medals mad." Although he already had "ten ribbons on his chest," they told Porter, "more than any other NCO in the Canadian Army, he still wants more."[75]

What accounts for Prince's enthusiasm to return to Korea? Was it a psychological need to return to the bloody meritocracy of combat? Although a decorated hero, did he feel compelled to prove that he was still a warrior? Was his desire tied to proving that courage was part of his cultural identity? "Unlike many Indians Sergeant Prince is loquacious," Porter noted in his article. "When he is not talking about fighting he is talking about Indians. There comes a period, after a few beers, when these two subjects get all mixed up. 'He lets you know,' says one sergeant, 'that he has no inferiority complex about his color.'"[76] Prince may not have seen himself as inferior, but he certainly had something to prove. He continued to see himself as a representative of his people, and the only place that he believed he had succeeded in demonstrating his leadership was on the battlefield.

Ever the warrior, Prince felt that his knees had improved enough to apply for a second tour of duty in Korea. In October 1952, the military approved his application and he disembarked with the 3rd Battalion, Princess Patricia's Canadian Light Infantry (3 PPCLI). On the voyage across the ocean, he met Saskatchewan Native soldier Allan Bird and told him "I'm not coming back until I win the Victoria Cross in Korea."[77] Prince immediately encountered problems when he arrived in the Far East. Professional NCOs that Prince had insulted at Camp Borden were no longer untested soldiers: they had served a year in combat, and were "in no mood to brook any slurs from Prince, nor were they willing to listen to his war exploits." In one episode during a party, emotions boiled over and Prince got into a drunken fistfight with Sergeant Dick Buxton, also a well-decorated senior NCO. More generally, Prince's relationship with his new platoon was not as easy as it had been during his first tour:

> In the Second Battalion, his men had been eager and willing to listen to his wartime exploits. They were also willing to overlook, or ignore, or not acknowledge the aggressiveness and eagerness to win further medals.

This was not so in the Third Battalion. By now there had been too much talk about Sergeant Prince from his detractors. He had a reputation as a bull-shitter, his wartime exploits were no longer accepted, and his men did not trust him on patrol.[78]

Indeed, some Korean veterans who served with Prince suggested that he had a reputation for unnecessarily placing his men in harm's way. Ed Higham later reflected at Prince's funeral:

> How do you judge a man like Prince? He was a glory seeker who, although admirable in so many ways, was also a danger to everyone else. Men feared patrol work with Prince, for he took too many chances and unduly endangered their lives. It was obvious that even the battalion leaders were restraining Tom at times, much to his resentment. Yet, most of the men admired that very daring — as long as Tom didn't demand the same disregard of personal safety from them.[79]

Prince's zealous approach to combat seemed out of sync with the new realities of the Korean battlefront. By the fall of 1952 it had become a defensive war. While diplomats tried to negotiate an end to the war, the Canadian Army fought "a war of patrols" on the ground. There were no more company raids; at most the Canadians launched platoon-sized offensives. Fighting patrols of up to 30 men might attack an enemy outpost, take a prisoner, or carry out diversionary actions. Ambush patrols (usually 15 to 30 men) were designed to dominate no man's land, remove the possibility of an enemy surprise

Sergeant Tommy Prince as a member of 3 PPCLI on his way to Korea for a second tour of duty in that conflict, 6 October 1952.

Photographer J.J. Schau, Library and Archives Canada PA-128264 attack, and keep the enemy off balance. Reconnaissance patrols, led by an officer or sergeant with up to four men, gathered information on enemy movement patterns, routes, defences, and obstacles. Standing patrols, a short distance in front of the company positions, provided early warning of Chinese activities. "Patrolling was exacting work where mistakes could be costly," Lieutenant Robert S. Peacock recalled.[80] It was perilous, but hardly conducive to bold acts of heroism.

In late October, 3 PPCLI entered the front lines for the first time at "the Hook" — a three-kilometre fortified crest at the easternmost end of a series of hills ending at Sami-Ch'on. The Hook was the crux of the Jamestown Line in this sector and was subject to continuous bombardment of Chinese artillery and rocket fire, as well as frequent enemy probes. The Patricias' first operational role was to counterattack the Hook and other positions held by the 1st Black Watch if they fell to the Chinese. By this point in the war, historian David Bercuson has explained, this "steep and craggy feature" was a formidable position: "its three main defended localities were honeycombed with deep firing bunkers connected by tunnels and sandbagged, lined crawl trenches. They were ringed with barbed wire. The men slept in four to six-man bunkers built on the reverse slopes." These subterranean accommodations, as deep as four metres below the surface, protected the men from enemy artillery.[81] It was a dismal landscape. Historian William Johnston described the Hook as "littered by what can literally be described as shattered humanity. It is not known how many dead there were in forward areas in dead ground or in enemy forming up places."[82]

On 18 November, the Chinese began intensive shelling before launching a battalion-sized infantry assault on the Hook at 2100 hours. They managed to secure a foothold on the forward positions. That night, "B" and "C" Companies (3 PPCLI) were ordered forward to defend Hill 146, reinforce the British unit clearing the main position, "ferret out Chinese stragglers," and evacuate casualties. By dawn the Allied counterattack had succeeded, but sporadic shelling had caused a number of Canadian casualties: Five Patricias were killed and nine wounded. Prince sustained a leg injury but remained in action.[83] Korean War veteran Claude Petit recalled seeing Prince in a dug-out, using his bayonet to pick shrapnel out of his leg. Someone told the sergeant to go back to have his leg examined, but he retorted: "Hell, I don't have time for that." As Petit put it, "that's just the kind of guy he was."[84]

Prince always held himself to ridiculously high standards. Platoon commander Robert Peacock told a documentary filmmaker that

"Tommy was always pushing, pushing … He had a reputation to maintain and he shouldn't … have been pushed, or allowed to be pushed, into his final [bit] where he literally collapsed … it was too bad, because, it was a great legend there."[85] The daily grind of occupying front-line positions and mounting patrols took its toll on Canadian soldiers, and proved particularly damaging to Tommy Prince.[86]

Christmas Eve was a cold, crisp night, with hard snow encrusting the Canadian positions, but it was no time for relaxing or home sickness. Soldiers in 3 PPCLI went out on seven standing patrols, one reconnaissance patrol, and one ambush party. Battalion headquarters sent Prince out with a small party of men to search the "Warsaw" position, a large hill about a 1,000 yards across the valley in front of the "Hook." They were told to find out if the Chinese were building shelters in preparation for an assault. Lieutenant Robert Peacock recalled that the patrol left through his platoon area and therefore he made a head count as the patrol passed him on its way out. "Quite a while" after they left, Peacock's men heard explosions or mortar bursts in front of their position. Prince's patrol had been attacked on the way back. At 2330, the patrol arrived at "B" Company. The men were quickly identified and Peacock asked Prince, "the sergeant [in command] as to what had happened and where the missing man could be located." Prince responded that the patrol was complete and that he had to get back to battalion headquarters immediately, to report to the battalion adjutant. When Lieutenant Peacock questioned the other patrol members, they explained that Chinese mortar bombs had landed towards their rear during their return and that the last man in the patrol (Private Power) was missing. Quickly, Peacock ordered his own platoon sergeant to organize a search party. Four soldiers were sent out to look for him, found the mortar holes in the snow, and recovered the wounded, unconscious soldier at 2355 hours.[87]

In Peacock's memoirs, it is telling that the officer did not mention Prince by name — obviously out of respect to his comrade. He only referred to him as "a very experienced and highly decorated sergeant." Regardless, Peacock and the others recognized that Tommy Prince had pushed himself too far:

> The sergeant still maintained that the patrol was complete. At this stage it was obvious that the patrol leader had panicked and lost control when the mortar bombs hit the rear of the patrol. I placed him under arrest and

sent him back to battalion HQ, separately from the rest of the patrol, informing battalion HQ of the circumstances. The matter was eventually dropped by those in charge as the sergeant was obviously worn out from desperately trying to achieve too much. His psychological fitness to cope with the pressures of patrolling had deteriorated before his physical strength, and he had almost caused a wounded man to die of exposure or to be captured. The sergeant had had extensive combat experience in World War II and had a previous tour in Korea. He was regarded by all of us as a first-class fighting soldier. In both campaigns he had served with distinction but he had tried to continue when he knew he was pushing himself beyond his limits. I felt that his immediate superiors should have recognized that the man was wearing out emotionally and should have taken some action to place him where he could have rested and regained his stability. Each us felt that 'there but for the grace of God go I' and was relieved that the situation was ended.[88]

"In my view, that was a sad, sad situation," Platoon Sergeant Don Ardelian opined. "Here was a fine outstanding soldier, one of the best this country has ever produced, and [we] let it end that way." Ardelian was careful to clarify that responsibility could not be left with Prince alone. "It didn't have to be that way at all, in my view. If his officers had been on top of the job, they would have had 'indicators' that they were working this one too far, [he]'s not going to make it. And he didn't...."[89] Fortunately, his superiors did not insist on a court martial; in their informal assessment, Prince was clearly suffering from "battle exhaustion." Instead, Prince was relegated to an administrative job and spent several weeks in hospital between January and April 1953.[90] Prince did not see combat again.

In light of his comrades' assessments it is appropriate to deduce that, by the end of 1952, Prince was suffering from post-traumatic stress disorder (PTSD), a psychological injury caused by the reaction of the brain to severe stress. Operational stress injuries have always been a part of war, but the serious study of acute anxiety neuroses brought on by combat began in the twentieth century. Soldiers were first diagnosed with traumatogenic "shell shock" during the Great War, but practical interest in the disorder declined after the conflict ended. American psychoanalyst Abram Kardiner codified its critical features in 1941, and terms like *physical exhaustion, battle exhaustion,* and *combat exhaustion* entered the lexicon during the Second World War. The psychiatric establishment, however, failed to officially recognize PTSD as a classification of psychiatric malady until 1980.[91] Since that time, researchers, clinicians, and military officials have devoted significant attention to exposing its causes and effects. Recent studies observe that the more missions in which an individual soldier participates, the more likely s/he is to develop the disorder or PTSD-related symptoms.[92]

Diagnosing operational stress injuries is always difficult. Terry Copp and Bill McAndrew, in their seminal study on battle exhaustion, said, "[I]ndividual, situational and organizational factors all played a part in determining an individual's breaking point."[93] Furthermore, memory is intrinsically connected to a person's conception of "self," thus linking self-awareness to the past and present.[94] In Prince's case, he held high expectations for himself as both an Native and a soldier, had been on repeated combat tours, faced debilitating physical injuries, and found himself in a frustrating operational situation. When emotional trauma compounded physical trauma, it seems to have produced pathophysiological effects.[95] Prince was never assessed nor diagnosed with PTSD in his lifetime, however, and no "smoking gun" can be produced to prove that his symptoms were definitely a product of this disorder. Nonetheless, the suffering was real, the symptoms were real, and thus Prince's psychological scars were real. While contemporary practice demands intensive counselling and treatment, peer support, and a clinical milieu in which patients can confront their traumatic memories, Prince had to battle his inner demons on the rough streets of Winnipeg.[96]

Does the assertion that Prince suffered from PTSD diminish his heroic stature? Does the assumption that it would harm his reputation explain why his experiences in late December 1952 were (and are) concealed from the public in media and political statements?[97] Must Sergeant Prince be depicted as a superhuman soldier from start to finish to be recognized as a Canadian war hero? The story of Lieutenant-General (now Senator) Roméo Dallaire, who commanded peacekeeping forces during the mass genocide in Rwanda, has recently drawn attention to the effects of PTSD on Canadian soldiers. Dallaire was haunted by his perceived failure to stop atrocities abroad, and he spiralled into a deep depression after returning to Canada. On 20 June 2000, he was found partially clothed, drunk, and unconscious under a park bench; the incident generated national headlines and drew attention to PTSD. Thanks largely to

Dallaire's openness about a disability that he once described as best "kept in a drawer," PTSD is now recognized as "a public rather than a private problem." In Dallaire's estimate, as many as 3,000 Canadian soldiers suffer from the disorder — many of them silently.[98]

The silence on the part of veterans like Prince is partially explained by the perceived stigma of admitting human fallibility in a hyper-masculine military culture that prioritizes selfless service, loyalty, and duty. "Those succumbing to PTSD face a classic military Catch 22," Scott McKeen reported in the *Edmonton Journal* on 14 April 2001. "Seek help, and perhaps the nightmares, the chronic anxiety and the unchecked anger will be treated. But asking for help raises questions from fellow soldiers, suspicion of dereliction of duty." Prince, like many Second World War and Korean War veterans, did not seek medical help for his psychological injuries. Before Vietnam War veterans politicized shell shock in the 1970s, historians explain, neuro-psychiatric casualties were scarcely discernible from cowardice.[99] For a fierce individualist decorated for courage and utter disregard for his personal safety on the battlefield; who held himself up as an example for his people, it would have been devastating to ask for help.

Library and Archives Canada PA-114890

Sergeant Tommy Prince in Korea with a PPCLI sub-unit command group.

PTSD is now recognized as a legitimate medical condition, "no less real or legitimate than physical health problems," and often occurs in combination "with other personal, social, spiritual and mental health difficulties." This can include "depression, anxiety, alcohol and drug abuse, and difficulty dealing with family, friends, and co-workers."[100] Common reactions to trauma include: feelings of panic or anxiety; avoiding anything attached to the event; feeling sad, tearful, hopeless, depressed, angry, or guilty; consuming alcohol or abuse of other substances; feeling a change in personality; difficulty concentrating, disorientation, and/or memory problems; sleep disturbances or excessive alertness; being easily startled; trouble controlling moods, especially anger; difficulty with relationships; reliving the event (while awake or asleep); and intrusive thoughts about the event.[101] Prince's postwar experience reflected many of these reactions. In mind and body, he returned to Canada a broken man.

By the time his Korean War service ended, Prince walked with a limp. He required knee surgery for arthritis and cartilage damage, and could no longer soldier on. In October 1953, he was honourably discharged from the army with a disability pension. Prince returned to civil life with little hope of securing sustainable employment. "Unskilled and unable to fit into the post-war boom," his biographers noted, "Prince retained only menial jobs and was the subject of scorn from white workers ignorant of his wartime gallantry. His skills as a hunter that made him one of the best soldiers had no value in the urban centre of Winnipeg in the early 1950's."[102] Prince earned headlines in June 1955 when he pulled a drowning man from the Red River. After pulling the struggling man to safety on the dock using an army "stranglehold," Prince simply walked away. A bystander recognized Prince, however, and gave his name to police and reporters. "I knew how I'd have felt if I were in the water unable to swim and someone just stood looking at me, not doing a thing," Prince said at the time. In the eyes of a local journalist, the war hero had proven to be a "peacetime hero" as well.[103]

Heroism, however, hardly translated into postwar comfort — after all, "you can't eat medals."[104] Without a uniform, Prince found that society no longer treated him as an equal. Although Native peoples in general faced discrimination, a Senate Committee observed in the mid-1990s, "the wartime experiences and sacrifices made by veterans made it all the more intolerable and frustrating upon their return to civilian life. Continued prejudice and unequal treatment left them feeling disillusioned and betrayed."[105] Prince found a job at an ice cream factory in Winnipeg soon after his return, but he discovered that some men refused to work with him simply because he was an "Indian." Obviously his achievements overseas were not enough to quash racial prejudices. Although the plant manager supported Prince, the former soldier could not stand the humiliation and quit. "It was a bitter lesson to learn," Bruce Sealey and Peter Van de Vyvere explained, "and it changed his personality."[106]

Prince's life lacked stability. He and his new common-law wife, Verna Sinclair, had five children after 1953, and they moved the family back and forth between Winnipeg and the Brokenhead Reserve. Haunted by painful wartime memories, he had trouble sleeping and his arthritic knees got worse. By 1961, he had descended into alcoholism and poverty. Allegations of abuse followed, and he and Verna separated in 1964. Their children were placed in foster homes.[107] Around this time, a social worker's report revealed that Prince was a man of intense contradictions:

> In many respects this veteran continues to leave me puzzled. There is little doubt that he is intelligent and that he was a very brave and competent soldier but unfortunately he does not appear to possess the qualities required to adjust to civilian life. While it is easy to blame his adjustment difficulties on the fact that he is Indian and therefore is subject to a prejudiced society- and he constantly projects this blame in defense of his actions-this does not justify all of the difficulties he experiences. He is a very impulsive individual with poor self control despite his years of army discipline. He can at times display intense warmth and understanding for his family and particularly his common law wife but can also be markedly paranoid and brutal at other times.[108]

Prince found himself isolated and lonely: Depression, alcohol, and chronic pain took their toll. Prince tended to be a loner when sober, but he was gregarious after a few drinks. When his old army buddies grew tired of his drunken reminiscences, he found "new friends" who encouraged his drinking. "The excessive use of alcohol hastened his physical deterioration," his biographers observed, "and people were shocked to discover how rapidly he was aging."[109]

Tommy Prince remained fiercely independent. Although war injuries (and alcoholism) prevented him from working full-time, he eked out a meager existence by working odd jobs in construction and later with Winnipeg Help-All. By 1976, he was living out of a suitcase in the Salvation Army's Social Service Centre, his six-by-eight foot room furnished only with a sagging bed, four-drawer chest, and a wooden chair. Prince's only possessions were newspaper clippings describing the honours he received at Remembrance Day ceremonies.[110] Claude Petit recounted:

> I was hearing that he was drinking quite heavily and down on skid road, "hawked" his medals and "everything else," it's bad stuff, you know … the thing is, somebody should have … especially the [regiment] … he spent his life in there, that's all he knew … You get into [the army system], the routine … and that's probably why he … wouldn't hang on to a job, or he got fired and would start "boozing.…" That's bad stuff, they should have took care of him.[111]

The Winnipeg police, some of whom knew Prince well, always drove him home rather than to the "drunk tank." This was their way of recognizing and taking care of the hero. For Prince, who insisted that he was fine and happy, it remained a lonely existence.[112]

As a decorated soldier, however, Prince was not forgotten. The PPCLI housed at Kapyong Barracks in Winnipeg always invited him to Remembrance Day ceremonies, and in August 1975 honoured Prince with a special ceremony on the Brokenhead Reserve. During Indian Days celebrations, the PPCLI band played a forty-five minute concert and he received a special salute and citation.[113] When it was over, Prince slipped back into obscurity on the rough streets of Winnipeg. The next year he was beaten by some young thugs, and was later stabbed by a young man who mistook Prince for someone else. He became disillusioned. When a reporter asked Prince if he would fight for his country again, he replied "No, absolutely not. I wouldn't go back and fight for these punks." He quickly added that he would fight "for the people of my generation anytime."[114] His children eventually found him at the National Hotel or the Salvation Army Hostel, and their reunions helped to restore his faith. In the end he managed to beat alcoholism, but could not conquer his nightmares. Prince disclosed to a local journalist that "his final years were spent reliving the terror of the two wars and every night his bed was wet from the tears and sweat."[115] Prince never overcame the operational stress injuries he had sustained in wartime.

In 1977, at age 62, Tommy Prince died at the Deer Lodge Hospital for Veterans. Although destitute, he remained a hero to Manitobans and to his regimental comrades. More than 150 people attended his funeral, representing "a mixture of ages," a journalist reported, "native and white, pensioners in threadbare topcoats, ladies in fine furs, privates and high-ranking officers, the lieutenant-governor, two foreign consuls, and an old man with a cane who shuffled to the coffin to view 'Warrior Prince, serial H-25272, Sergeant Thomas.'"[116] Five Native men beat a black drum and chanted a song of grief as his coffin was lowered into the ground:

> Beryl and Beverly Prince, Tommy's daughters, shed tears. When the officer in charge presented Beverly with the Canadian flag which had been draped over the coffin the flow of tears increased. Who were all these strangers, both military and civilian, honouring her father with apparent sadness and great respect? Where had they been these past years when her father, crippled from machine- gun wounds, was forced to do menial jobs to keep alive? Were the honour and respect given only after his death? Did these people really care or was this just a colourful pageant performed by white people for entertainment?[117]

Difficult questions lingered. What was clear, however, was the sentiment shared by Don Genaille, one of his army comrades: "He was a hell of a warrior."[118]

Recently, the Canadian Forces have taken deliberate measures to acknowledge and recognize Aboriginal peoples' contributions to the military, and Prince's name has figured prominently in these initiatives. It adorns the Tommy Prince Barracks at Canadian Forces Base Petawawa and the Tommy Prince Drill Hall at the Land Force Western Area Training Centre in Wainwright. Number 533 (Tommy Prince) PPCLI Cadet Corps operate in Winnipeg. Furthermore, the Canadian Forces established the Sergeant Tommy Prince Army Training Initiative (STPATI) in 2000 to increase the number of Aboriginal people serving in the infantry and related combat arms trades. Prince's own story reinforces the notion that Native soldiers are particularly suited to these fields, given their traditions, culture, and life experiences. In this program, Native volunteers receive specialized military indoctrination that takes into account Native views and values.[119]

Prince's name continues to attract media attention. In 2000, his war medals, which had been pawned or lost in a house fire, turned up at an auction in London, Ontario.[120] His family's desire to re-acquire them attracted national media attention. On 10 August, they "won" them back with a staggering bid of $75,000, backed by pledges from Native groups, the Royal Canadian Legion, and Veterans Affairs Minister Ron Duhamel.[121] In November 2001, his medals were placed on permanent display at the Manitoba Museum of Man and Nature. The following year, 25 years after his death, the French ambassador to Canada also presented the Prince family with a certificate recognizing the soldier's bravery in France during the Second World War.[122] He has been commemorated on a coin, a bronze plaque, three murals, and a stone memorial at the corner of Selkirk Avenue and Sergeant Tommy Prince Street in Winnipeg. A statue honouring Prince sits in a park in Scanterbury, on the Brokenhead Reserve, across from one of Chief Peguis — his great-grandfather.[123] He has been the subject of at least one play, and the Legislative Assembly of Manitoba unanimously passed a 2004 resolution honouring and recognizing Prince "for his contribution and sacrifice to both Canada and to the province of Manitoba."[124] He remains the best known Native soldier of the twentieth century.

Robert Hepenstall wrote that, during his first tour in Korea, "Prince belonged to the ten percent of the battalion who were really competent in battle. Prince was an excellent man in the field, but the demons that lurked within his personality rendered him useless in a garrison. Eventually, the demons would tear him apart and kill him; but not in a war. Some people are indestructible in war. Prince was one of them."[125] His individual exploits demonstrated daring and courage, and served as an inspiration to the men around him. "Soldiering was his life, the army his home," Peter Worthington offered. "The respect he got from comrades of all ranks was absolute — he was a living legend, esteemed by peers, deferred to by young recruits, a source of pride for officers. He was an army icon."[126] Perhaps so, but his record of leadership as an NCO in Korea was less cut and dry.

Prince's second tour proved that he was not indestructible. The stresses of battle, and his personal drive, took their toll. Lieutenant Robert Peacock later reflected that Prince "should have never gone back for the second tour in Korea. My personal view [was] that the man was worn out psychologically, and the [people] that sent him back, well, were they criminal? They probably thought they were doing him a favour."[127] Undoubtedly, Sergeant Prince would have agreed. "All my life I had wanted to do something to help my people recover their good name," Prince explained. "I wanted to show they were as good as any white man."[128] He would not let his people down. Prince also believed that he had an unpaid debt to his comrades who had died on the battlefields of Europe. "I didn't make Tommy Prince alone," he told a reporter in 1975. "My men made me. I left a lot of men over there. They are responsible for Tommy Prince's life."[129] He had self-imposed obligations and a reputation to maintain, commitments that eventually pushed him to the point of collapse.

Unfortunately, the trauma of war accompanied Prince on his postwar journey. In his poignant study on Native American veterans of the Vietnam War, Tom Holm reflected that:

> The veteran is expected to forget the battlefield and his comrades in arms and get on with the business of life. The battlefield, however, is not a thing that one easily forgets. If a veteran's life experiences were placed on a graph and measured in terms of his emotional responses to each one of them, combat would surely create a spike equaling and surpassing the peaks of most other meaningful experiences.

Indeed, Holm concluded that high rates of PTSD and alcoholism among Native veterans attest that the stresses of war cannot be simply forgotten at war's end.[130] Tommy Prince was a casualty of both. On the battlefields of Europe and Korea, he furthered his cause to restore Native pride and honour the only way he knew how — through courage, determination, and daring. To deny Prince his humanity by suppressing his psychological breakdown during his final tour, rather than discussing it openly, is unjust. His trauma is as revealing as his successes in helping to understand his difficult postwar life. Only by decoupling PTSD from "failure" can scholars and soldiers better come to terms with the physical and psychological impacts of combat on even the most courageous warriors. "He's a soldier's soldier and a man Canada can proudly claim," a reporter concluded in June 1945.[131] So he remains. Acknowledging that he was a casualty of war does not deny him the warrior status he earned and deserves. In the end, it affirms that Sergeant Tommy Prince was heroic but human.

NOTES

1. Thanks to Jennifer Arthur, Yale Belanger, Katharine McGowan, Alastair Neely, Scott Sheffield, WO Darcy R. Wanvig, and Jim Wood for sharing research and/or offering critical editorial comments.

2. Janice Summerby, "Prince of the Brigade" in *Native Soldiers, Foreign Battlefields* (Department of Veterans Affairs, 1993), accessed at *www.vac-acc.gc.ca/general/sub.cfm?source=history/other/native/prince*.

3. See, for example, Fred Gaffen, *Forgotten Soldiers* (Penticton, BC: Theytus Books, 1985); L. James Dempsey, *Warriors of the King: Prairie Indians in World War I* (Regina: Canadian Plains Research Centre, 1999); Royal Commission on Aboriginal Peoples (henceforth "RCAP"), *Final Report Volume 1: Looking Forward, Looking Back* (Ottawa: Canada Communication Group, 1996); Michael D. Stevenson, "The Mobilisation of Native Canadians During the Second World War," *Journal of the Canadian Historical Association* (1996), 205–226; R. Scott Sheffield, *Red Man's on the Warpath* (Vancouver: UBC Press, 2003).

4. See, for example, Summerby, *Native Soldiers;* RCAP, *Final Report;* Salim Karam, "Aboriginal Day at NDHQ," *The Maple Leaf* 5/25 (26 June 2002), 3. He is also featured on the cover of R.S. Sheffield, *A Search for Equity: A Study of the Treatment Accorded to First Nations Veterans and Dependents of the Second World War and Korea* (Ottawa: National Round Table on First Nations Veterans' Issues, 2001). On the "Indian at War," see R.S. Sheffield, *Red Man's on the Warpath.* Bill Twatio also called him "the ultimate native warrior" in "Bitter Legacy for Brave Native Soldiers: Out of Uniform They Were 'Just Another Poor Goddamn Indian,'" *Toronto Star*, 11 November 1994.

5. Prince has been the subject of a few biographies, the most thorough of which is D. Bruce Sealey and Peter Van De Vyvere, *Manitobans in Profile: Thomas George Prince* (Winnipeg: Peguis Publishers, 1981). This interesting, descriptive overview of Prince's life devotes little attention to his experiences in Korea and omits any reference to the troubles that Prince experienced during his second tour. The lack of references to source material also limits its usefulness. Also essential is the documentary film *Fallen Hero: The Tommy Prince Story*, director Audrey Mehler, 45 minutes. David Paperny Films Inc., 1999, videocassette. This is the best starting point to understand Prince's life and the impact of his experiences on family, friends, Native leaders, and comrades-in-arms. He is also the subject of a recent Historica minute. See "Tommy Prince," *www.histori.ca/minutes/*.

6. First Nations, Métis, and Inuit representatives hoped the pilgrimage to France and Belgium would draw attention to their grievances. See, for example, Michelle MacAfee, "Aboriginal Veterans Wrap Up Trip," Canadian Press, 2 November 2005. Some discussion became mired in a tangential debate about whether Prince actually was the "most decorat-

ed" First Nations soldier. See Peter Worthington, "Soldier Modest About Exploits: Canadians Don't Know Enough About Most-Decorated Native Vet," *Calgary Sun*, 13 November 2005, which rehashed his earlier article "The Best and the Bravest: Sgt. Tommy Prince Wasn't 'Canada's Most Decorated Aboriginal,'" *Toronto Sun*, 26 August 2001. Sergeant Charles Byce won a Military Medal and a Distinguished Conduct Medal during the Second World War, while Francis (Peggy) Pegahmagabow, an Ojibwa from Parry Sound, won the MM and two bars during the First World War. See Adrian Hayes, *Pegahmagabow: Legendary Warrior, Forgotten Hero* (Huntsville, ON: Fox Meadow Creations, 2003), 8.

7.   Summerby, *Native Soldiers*, 25; Chief Albert Edward Thompson, *Chief Peguis and His Descendants* (Winnipeg: Peguis Publishers, 1975); Special Joint Committee of the Senate and the House of Commons appointed to continue and complete the examination and consideration of the Indian Act, Minutes of Proceedings and Evidence (henceforth "SJC"), 1552.

8.   McKenzie Porter, "Warrior: Tommy Prince," *Maclean's* 65/17 (1 September 1952).

9.   Brian Cole, "Hero Condemns 'Punks' of Today," *Winnipeg Free Press*, 10 November 1976, 6; Sealey and Van de Vyvere, *Thomas George Prince*. Prince later blamed the Department of Indian Affairs for forcing him to leave school because his family did not have money.

10. "Sgt. Prince," *Winnipeg Free Press*, 25 June 1945, 3.

11. Prince had tried to enlist in the infantry on several occasions before he was accepted into the engineers, but had been rejected. He believed that this reflected racism, but his biographers aptly noted that "he was one of many unskilled men anxious to secure three meals a day and some excitement in their lives." Sealey and de Vyvere, *Thomas George Prince*, 3, 18–21. On government enlistment policies, see R.S. Sheffield, "'In the Same Manner as Other People …'" (M.A. thesis, University of Victoria, 1995), and "'Of Pure European Descent and of the White Race': Recruitment Policy and Aboriginal Canadians, 1939–1945," *Canadian Military History*, Vol. 5, No. 1 (Spring 1996), 8–15.

12. Porter, "Warrior: Tommy Prince"; Sealey and Van de Vyvere, *Thomas George Prince*, 19.

13. James A. Wood, "The Canadian Army and the First Special Service Force, 1942–1944" (M.A. thesis, University of New Brunswick, 2003), 1. The most accessible, short overviews are found in G.W.L. Nicholson, *Official History of the Canadian Army in the Second World War, Vol. II: The Canadians in Italy, 1943–1945* (Ottawa: Queen's Printer, 1967), 453–57, 666–71, and Stanley W. Dziuban, *Military Relations Between the United States and Canada, 1939–1945* (Washington: Office of the Chief of Military History, Department of the Army, 1959), 259–68. See also R.D. Burhans, *The First Special Service Force: A War History of the North Americans, 1942–1944* (Washington: Infantry Journal Press, 1947) and R.H. Adleman and G. Walton, *The Devil's Brigade* (Philadelphia: Chilton Books, 1966).

14. "1st Special Service Force HQ Located at Helena, Montana," *Globe and Mail*, 7 August 1942; "Troops Will Train in Both Countries, Ralston Explains," *Ibid.*, 7 August 1942; "U.S.-Canadian Super-Specialists Are Now in Training in Montana for Possible Action in Canada," *Toronto Daily Star*, 6 August 1942; "Clearing Aleutians of Japs May Be New Commando Job," *Hamilton Spectator*, 7 August 1942. The FSSF imposed age limits on officers (35) and other ranks (32), and required high standards of physical fitness.

15. Lennox interview in *Fallen Hero*.

16. "Name of 'Braves' May Be Selected for Combat Unit," *Hamilton Spectator*, 7 August 1942.

17. Wood, "Canadian Army," 44, 50, 51.

18. It did not come immediately. Peter Cottingham served with Prince in the FSSF and recalled a short refresher course in parachuting soon after their arrival in Montana. On their first jump, Prince apparently refused to bail out of the aircraft. "This was rather odd as Tom had already completed about a dozen or so jumps before this, and there was a rule that if someone failed to jump, they would be returned to their previous unit without any further consideration." The plane returned over the jump area, however, and Prince regained his composure. When he landed on the ground, "he had a very sheepish look on his face and his exact words were, 'I guess I am a chicken Indian.'" Cottingham noted that Prince "had just had a bad moment which he was quick to recover from, and he went on to prove to everyone that he was anything but 'a chicken Indian.'" Quoted in Sealey and de Vyvere, *Thomas George Prince*, 4.

19. Porter, "Warrior: Tommy Prince."

20. Sealey and de Vyvere, *Thomas George Prince*, 21.

21. Porter, "Warrior: Tommy Prince."

22. Alton Carroll, "Medicine Bags and Dog Tags: How the Military Influenced American Indian Traditions and How the Image of Indians Influenced the Military" (Ph.D. dissertation, Arizona State University, 2004), 15. Cherokee historian Tom Holm is weary of the stereotype that service was a desperate move by Native peoples to "legitimate" themselves and prove their worthiness to whites. Instead, in *Strong Hearts Wounded Souls: Native American Veterans of the Vietnam War* (Austin: University of Texas Press, 1996), 20, he describes military service as a continuation of family and tribal warrior traditions.

23. Porter, "Warrior: Tommy Prince."

24. "Clearing Aleutians of Japs May Be New Commando Job," *Hamilton Spectator*, 7 August 1942; Wood, "Canadian Army," 67; Alistair Neely, "First Special Service Force," accessed at *www.execulink.com/~kiska/FSSFHomepage.index.html*, 9 December 2005. Historian Galen Perras has systematically studied this campaign in *Stepping Stones to Nowhere: The Aleutian Islands, Alaska, and American Military Strategy, 1867–1945* (Vancouver: UBC Press, 2003), 136–57.

25. Porter, "Warrior: Tommy Prince." Others were similarly disappointed. See, for example, "Felt 'Let Down' on Kiska, Returned Buddies Say," *Globe and Mail*, 9 September 1943.

26. B.H. Reid, "Italian Campaign," in I.C.B. Dear, ed., *The Oxford Companion to World War II* (Oxford: Oxford University Press, 1995), 573–4. See also Dziuban, *Military Relations*, 266.

27. "Canadians Had Large Role in Unique Fighting Outfit," *Hamilton Spectator*, 29 June 1945. For a fuller treatment, see Burhans, *First Special Service Force*. See also Major S.C. Waters, "Anzio, the Right Flank, with Particular Reference to the Role of the 1st Special Service Force," *Canadian Army Journal* (August–September 1948), 18.

28. Nicholson, *Official History*, 455.

29. Porter, "Warrior: Tommy Prince."

30. "Canadians Had Large Role in Unique Fighting Outfit," *Hamilton Spectator*, 29 June 1945.

31. Quoted in Wood, "Canadian Army," 74. See also Nicholson, *Official History*, 455.

32. "Special Service Force Sees Heavy Action Near Nettuno," *Hamilton Spectator*, 11 February 1944.

33. Gilday interview in *Fallen Hero*. On Gilday, see "Obituaries — Thomas Gilday Led Elite Battalion," *Toronto Star*, 28 June 2001, B7.

34. Doris Small, "Thomas George Prince: October 1915–November 25, 1977," accessed at *web.mala.bc.ca/firstnations/doris/princet.htm*, 30 November 2005).

35. At night, Prince would set out alone or with a small patrol, crawl his way towards enemy lines, and estimate their numbers. "He would crawl out by day and watch the enemy runners dodging among the olive groves, and fix their defensive positions," McKenzie Porter later described. "Before every attack he snaked around the battalion front and came back with information on a track that would take the jeep ambulances, a wood that would shelter the radio truck, or a gulley that would cover the approach of a platoon." Armed with a sniper rifle he would set out as the solitary hunter, stalking enemy prey. "Once he went out hunting a German sniper who had been harassing his own battalion, engaged him in a movie-like shooting duel and brought him toppling down out of a tree like a big dead bird." Porter, "Warrior: Tommy Prince."

36. Dziuban, 266; Nicholson, *Official History*, 456. While at Anzio, the FSSF received their famous nickname, "The Devil's Brigade."

37. This famous episode is re-created based on the following sources: Porter, "Warrior: Tommy Prince;" *Reader's Digest, The Canadians at War 1939–45, Vol. 2* (Toronto: Reader's Digest Canada, 1969), 375; Sealey and Van de Vyvere, *Thomas George Prince;* Charmion Chaplin-Thomas, "Fourth Dimension: February 7, 1944," *The Maple Leaf*, 2 February 2005, 14; and Laura Neilson Bonikowsky, "Tommy Prince, Canadian Hero," *National*

Post, 9 November 2005, A23. Citation quoted in "Pte. Thomas Prince Citation Is Released," *Winnipeg Free Press*, 27 December 1944, 16 and Gaffen, *Forgotten Soldiers*, 56.

38. Quoted in Sealey and Van de Vyvere, *Thomas George Prince*

39. Nicholson, *Official History*, 457.

40. Dziuban, *Military Relations*, 266–7; Nicholson, *Official History*, 669–70.

41. Porter, "Warrior: Tommy Prince."

42. "U.S. Medals Given to 14 Canadians for Gallant Deeds," *Globe and Mail*, 26 February 1945; "Honored," *Winnipeg Free Press*, 2 March 1945; "Scanterbury Man Wins U.S. Medal," *Ibid.*, 21 March 1945. A rumour circulated after the war that the French commander also recommended Prince for the Croix de Guerre, but the courier was killed en route and the message never reached Charles de Gaulle. This translated into some newspaper articles suggesting that Prince actually won the French decoration, which is mistaken. See, for example, "The Patricias Salute Deeds of Tommy Prince," *Winnipeg Free Press*, 5 August 1975, 3.

43. Wood, "Canadian Army," 130.

44. I.C.B. Dear and Shelby Stanton, "USA," 5(f), in *Oxford Companion*, 1201; Dziuban, *Military Relations*, 267.

45. "U.S. Medals Given to 14 Canadians for Gallant Deeds," *Globe and Mail*, 26 February 1945, 9; Summerby, *Native Soldiers*.

46. SJC, 1552.

47. Small, "Thomas George Prince."

48. SJC, 1552.

49. On Native veterans' benefits see Sheffield, *A Search for Equity*. Immediately after he returned to Canada, Prince told reporters that his plans for civilian life tended towards engineering work, and that "he wouldn't mind working on the Alaska project." "Sgt. Prince," *Winnipeg Free Press*, 25 June 1945, 3.

50. "Indians Find Champion in Indian World War Hero," *Winnipeg Tribune*, 7 December 1946, 17. Bruce Larsen, painted a similar image of Prince on the "warpath" to Ottawa in "Indian War Hero Heads New Battle," *Ibid.*, 4 December 1946, 1, 5: "Sgt. Tommy Prince, the Scanterbury Indian, who spread terror through German and Italian troops in the recent war with his savage attacks and deadly sniping, is now leading fellow treaty Indians down another warpath. They are fighting for many reforms for the Canadian Indian." See also "Bemedalled Warrior Leads Fight for Indian Rights," *The Indian Missionary Record* (April 1946), 6; "Wants Treaty Rights Restored: Tom Prince Appeals for Fellow Indians," *Winnipeg Tribune*, 5 June 1946; "New Champion of the Indian," *Ibid.*, 7 December 1946, 6.

51. On the Manitoba Indian Association (MIA) and the Standing Joint Committee, see Yale Belanger, "Seeking a Seat at the Table: A Brief History of Indian Organizing in Canada, 1870–1951" (Ph.D. thesis, Trent University, 2005), Chapter 6. For an example of a national newspaper

article highlighting his military background, see "Manitoba Indians Ask Treaty Rights Lost to Province," *Globe and Mail*, 6 June 1947, 12.

52.   "New Champion of the Indian," *Winnipeg Tribune*, 7 December 1946, 6. Prince supported Tootoosis and claimed that he was "all in favour of national unity." For Prince, a united Indian front would accomplish two goals. First, by working in one national organization, "[W]e would understand each other much better;" and second, all written briefs submitted to the federal government for consideration "will be much stronger." He also stressed that "we must work too and compromise with the government concerning our treaties," adding "we will find after we compromise with the government the Indians will have better living in the future." Standing Joint Committee, Minutes of Proceedings and Evidence, No. 30 (henceforth "SJC"), 1581, quoted in Belanger, "Seeking a Seat," 171.

53.   SJC, 1585–86, 1591. The Natives had "trusted the white man to carry out these [treaty] promises," Prince explained. "They were very glad then to offer these terms, but today we find it different. How can I walk along the street, stick out my chest and say, 'I trust the next man, the next man trusts me,' when I could not get these terms?" As Prince saw it, the committee's purpose was to reach a conclusion "that will really bind the white man and red man together so that they can trust each other and we can walk side by side and face this world having faith and confidence in one another. I would have your confidence and you would have mine." SJC, 1508–09.

54.   Prince also encouraged the committee to "go out to the province of Manitoba and … look over each individual reserve and I believe you would see our point of view and try to better the living conditions of our people." SJC, 1568, 1637, 1653.

55.   SJC, 1569–70, 1597–98.

56.   SJC, 1581. On inequalities in veterans benefits see Canada, Senate, *The Aboriginal Soldier After the Wars*, Ninth Report of the Standing Senate Committee on Aboriginal Peoples, March 1995; RCAP, *Final Report v.1;* and Sheffield, *Search for Equity*.

57.   SJC, 1658. Others foresaw a future for Prince as a Native activist. An editorial in the *Winnipeg Tribune*, entitled "New Champion of the Indian," suggested that "given a few more leaders like Tommy Prince, the Indian bands in Canada would unite in the fight for more consideration and improved facilities." 7 December 1946, 6.

58.   Sealey and de Vyvere, *Thomas George Prince*, 28–9.

59.   "'Recruit' Prince Decorated in '44 Has Another Go," *Winnipeg Free Press*, 16 August 1950; "I Owed Something to My Friends," *Winnipeg Sun*, 28 November 1977. Recruiting ads for the CASF (later renamed the 25th Canadian Infantry Brigade Group) first appeared in the nation's newspapers on 8 August. Brent Watson, "Recipe for Victory: The Fight for Hill 677 During the Battle of the Kap'yong River, 24–25 April 1951,"

Canadian Military History (Spring 2000), 7–8. Like 75 percent of CASF soldiers, Prince had previous military service and, at 34, was older than the Active Force average. On enlistments more generally, see Brent Byron Watson, *Far Eastern Tour: The Canadian Infantry in Korea, 1950–1953* (Kingston and Montreal: McGill-Queen's University Press, 2002), 13–14.

60. 2 PPCLI War Diary, courtesy of Warrant Officer Darcy Wanvig. Prince was injured and admitted into Calgary Military Hospital on 17 September 1950, but there is no detail on the injury.

61. Prince quoted in Granatstein and Bercuson, *War and Peacekeeping*, 105.

62. Watson, *Far Eastern Tour*, 142.

63. Hepenstall, *Find the Dragon*, 68.

64. Johnson quoted in Watson, *Far Eastern Tour*, 151.

65. Thorsen quoted in Hepenstall, *Find the Dragon*, 82.

66. Munro quoted in *Ibid.*, 317.

67. Watson, "Recipe for Victory," 7–24, is an accessible starting point to understand the Kap'yong battle. See also DHH, File 145.2P7013(D5), "2 PPCLI Action Kap'yong Area;" H.F. Wood, *Strange Battleground: The Operations in Korea and Their Effects on the Defence Policy of Canada* (Ottawa: Queen's Printer, 1966); and Colonel James R. Stone and Jacques Castonguay, *Korea 1951: Two Canadian Battles* (Ottawa: The Canadian War Museum, 1988).

68. Porter, "Warrior: Tommy Prince."

69. Hepenstall, *Find the Dragon*, 93.

70. See Michelle Fowler, "'For Extraordinary Heroism and Outstanding Performance': Kap'yong, 2 PPCLI and the Controversy Surrounding the U.S. Presidential Unit Citation," *Canadian Military History* 13/4 (Autumn 2004), 19–28.

71. Hepenstall, *Find the Dragon*, 112.

72. *Ibid.*, 52.

73. Porter, "Warrior: Tommy Prince."

74. Hepenstall, *Find the Dragon*, 311.

75. Porter, "Warrior: Tommy Prince."

76. *Ibid.*

77. "Indian Veterans Remember: Allan Bird SL4779," *Saskatchewan Indian* (October 1989), 5. See also "Back to War," *Winnipeg Free Press*, 14 October 1952.

78. Hepenstall, *Find the Dragon*, 312. On the Prince-Buxton fight, see also R.S. Peacock, *Kim-chi, Asahi and Rum: A Platoon Commander Remembers Korea, 1952–1953* (Toronto: Lugus Publishing, 1994), 66.

79. Quoted in Sealey and Van de Vyvere, *Thomas George Prince*, 7. Prince felt that some members of his platoon were anti-Native. At the same time his mates remembered that the sergeant "never hesitated in making disparaging remarks against whites; when someone took an opportunity to get back at him, he did not like it." One such incident occurred as Prince prepared to take out a patrol and one of his men, who was Métis (mixed Native and non-Native descent), fell down and

could not get up. After Prince berated him and ordered him to kitchen duty, the man jumped up and ran down the hill. One of the patrol members snickered "There goes a good Indian." An angry Prince retorted, "That's the white part, running down the hill." Quoted in Hepenstall, *Find the Dragon*, 113.

80. Peacock, *Kim-chi, Asahi and Rum*, 26–27; William Johnston, *A War of Patrols: Canadian Army Operations in Korea* (Vancouver: UBC Press, 2003), 331–32; David Bercuson, *Blood on the Hills: The Canadian Army in the Korean War* (Toronto: University of Toronto Press, 1999), 211; C.P. Stacey, *Canada's Army in Korea: The United Nations Operations, 1950–53, and Their Aftermath* (Ottawa: Queen's Printer, 1956).

81. Bercuson, *Blood on the Hills*, 208. C.P. Stacey explained that "the 29th Brigade, on the left of the 28th, held positions on either side of the Sami-chon. Flowing eastward into this river about 5,000 yards above its junction with the Imjin was an unnamed stream; its valley was dominated by a crest-line which, running through a feature known as "the Hook," continued southeastward for a further 1,500 yards to Hill 146. The 1st Black Watch was guarding this line with one company on the Hook, another on 146, a third company in between, and the fourth on Hill 121 (south of the Hook). Standing two and a half miles north of Sanggorangpo, the Hook dominated much of our rear areas, for which reason it was a favourite objective of enemy attacks." Historical Section, General Staff, Army Headquarters, *Canada's Army in Korea: The United Nations Operations, 1950–53, and Their Aftermath — A Short Official Account* (Ottawa: Queen's Printer, 1956), 66.

82. Johnston, *War of Patrols*, 329.

83. Summerby, *Native Soldiers;* "Manitoban War Hero Wounded," *Winnipeg Free Press*, 25 November 1952. 1. "C" Company remained on the Hook until 22 November, and "B" Company continued to hold Hill 146 until 24 November. The battalion spent the rest of the month in training and in preparation for the 25th Brigade's return to the line. Historical Section, *Canada's Army in Korea*, 66.

84. Petit interview in *Fallen Hero*.

85. Peacock interview in *Ibid.*

86. Johnston, *War of Patrols*, 335.

87. Peacock, *Kim-chi, Asahi and Rum*, 79–80; PPCLI Museum and Archives, 3 PPCLI Operations Log, 24 December 1952, sheet no. 2; Hepenstall, *Find the Dragon*, 312–13. The war diary for December encapsulates this episode with a single sentence: "The ambush party had one man killed by enemy mortar fire while they were on their way in." See 3 PPCLI War Diary, 24 December 1952. No one was actually killed, as the 3 PPCLI operations log confirms.

88. Peacock, *Kim-chi, Asahi and Rum*, 80. Allan Bird, a First Nations soldier who served with Prince in Korea, reflected that "Prince got shell shock" after he was hit by shells on the patrol. Bird was mistaken on some details

(suggesting that Prince had left three men in the field, who were killed), as was the 3 PPCLI war diary. Nevertheless, he captured the essence of what happened to his comrade in late December 1952, and ended by explaining that "Sergeant Prince was sent home with shell shock." "Indian Veterans Remember: Allan Bird SL4779," *Saskatchewan Indian* (October 1989), 5.

89. Ardelian interview in *Fallen Hero*.

90. Although the Commonwealth Division recorded relatively few neuropsychiatric casualties from mid-1952 to 1953, Prince hardly resembled those cases attributed to "acute reaction to battle stress by immature and poorly motivated individuals." Johnston, *War of Patrols*, 336; Bill Rawling, *Death Their Enemy: Canadian Medical Practitioners and War* (Ottawa, 2000), 252. Johnston noted a casualty to battle casualty ratio of less than 2 percent, compared to ratios near 25 percent in intense periods of fighting during the Second World War.

91. Allan Young, *The Harmony of Illusions: Inventing Post-Traumatic Stress Disorder* (Princeton: Princeton University Press, 1995), 3–5; A. Kardiner, *The Traumatic Neuroses of War,* Psychosomatic Medicine Monograph II-III (Washington: National Research Council, 1941); Terry Copp and Bill McAndrew, *Battle Exhaustion: Soldiers and Psychiatrists in the Canadian Army, 1939–1945* (Montreal and Kingston: McGill-Queen's University Press, 1990), 43. The American Psychiatric Association accepted PTSD — including "Vietnam veterans' syndrome" — as a medical diagnosis in its 1980 *Diagnostic and Statistical Manual of Mental Disorders* (DSM). It was a controversial step: PTSD is the "only psychiatric illness in which the cause is clearly acknowledged as originating outside the individual rather than inside as an inherent weakness or flaw." Sarah Jane Growe, "PTSD," *Toronto Star*, 24 September 2000.

92. DND/CF Backgrounder "Post-Traumatic Stress Disorder (PTSD)," BG-04.036, 15 November 2004. The Canadian Forces officially define an Operational Stress Injury (OSI) as "any persistent psychological difficulty — including anxiety, depression and post-traumatic stress disorder (PTSD) — resulting from operational duties performed by the men and women of the CF." Official statements stress that these injuries are not signs of cowardice nor mental weakness: They strike service personnel indiscriminately, and are legitimate medical conditions. They can be as psychologically dehabilitating as a physical injury, but are often more difficult to discern. "The effects of an OSI can surface immediately after the operational stress or trauma," the OSI Social Support program explains, "or the symptoms may appear many years later…. Sadly, an undiagnosed OSI often has an impact on many facets of a CFs member's or veteran's life, and on the lives of the entire family." Common effects include increased irritability, social isolation, sleep difficulties, and hyper-vigilance. OSISS program, "The reality of operational stress injuries," *CF Personnel Newsletter* 10/05 (19 October 2005). Tommy

Prince experienced many of these symptoms after he returned home. His life deteriorated, his family fell apart, and he sought refuge in the bottle.

93. Copp and McAndrew, *Battle Exhaustion*, 153.
94. Graham Richards, *Mental Machinery: The Origins and Consequences of Psychological Ideas* (Baltimore; Johns Hopkins Press, 1992), 159–61; Mary Warnock, *Memory* (London: Faber and Faber, 1987), 57–60; Young, *Harmony of Illusions*, 4.
95. See chart in Young, *Harmony of Illusions*, 23.
96. To be effective, treatment in a clinical milieu must enable "patients to confront their traumatic memories and lengthen the periods during which memory content is processed," and patients must receive rational, realistic "cognitive schemes to replace their old self-defeating ones." Young, *Harmony of Illusions*, 8–9. Unfortunately, Prince did not have the peer and social support now available to veterans suffering from operational stress injuries. Support networks ensure that returned soldiers do not have to face psychological injuries alone. Comradeship is critical in the field, and mutual empathy and commitment is equally important at home. Today, the military recognizes that PTSD is best treated early and has implemented an Enhanced Post-deployment Screening Process. This screening process occurs three to six months after return from deployment and consists of a set of standard health questionnaires (including one on PTSD symptoms) followed by an in-depth interview with a mental health professional. CF members who develop PTSD and other operational stress injuries receive care from interdisciplinary teams including chaplains, psychiatrists, psychologists, mental health nurses, social workers and addictions specialists. See OSISS program, "The reality of operational stress injuries"; DND/CF Backgrounder "Post-Traumatic Stress Disorder (PTSD)," BG-04.036, 15 November 2004.
97. This episode is not disclosed in most sources, including Sealey and de Vyvere, *Thomas George Prince*; Summerby, *Native Soldiers;* and all newspaper tributes.
98. Roméo A. Dallaire with Brent Beardsley, *Shake Hands with the Devil: The Failure of Humanity in Rwanda* (Toronto: Random House Canada, 2003); CBC Archives, "The Ghosts of Rwanda," 11 June 2000, accessed at *archives.cbc.ca.*
99. Growe, "PTSD." For a discussion of another decorated Native veteran who likely suffered from PTSD, see Janice (Byce) Phillips, "Special Place Required" (letter to the editor), *Toronto Sun*, 19 November 2005. Journalist Sarah Jane Growe quoted "U.S. Department of Veterans' Affairs reports that 30.9 per cent of the 3,140,000 men who served in the Vietnam War have had full-blown PTSD at some point in their lives. A 1990 study showed that, 20 years after the war, 15.9 per cent of those veterans, about 500,000 men, still suffered from full-blown PTSD and another 11.1 per cent from partial PTSD. One of four Vietnam-era combat veterans was arrested within two years of discharge, according to

studies, and 200,000 are thought to be addicted to drugs or alcohol, an associated feature of PTSD. Their divorce rate is twice that of the general population and their suicide rate is 23 per cent higher." This undoubtedly contributed to Vietnam veterans' aversion to war. On the latter phenomenon, see Andrew E. Hunt, *The Turning: A History of Vietnam Veterans Against the War* (New York and London: New York University Press, 1999).

100. DND/CF Backgrounder "Post-Traumatic Stress Disorder (PTSD)," BG-04.036, 15 November 2004.
101. "You Are Not Alone," *Salute* (Veterans Affairs Canada, Fall 2005).
102. Sealey and De Vyvere, *Thomas George Prince*, 42, 44.
103. "War Hero Tommy Prince Saves a City Man's Life," *Winnipeg Free Press*, 21 June 1955, 1, 4; "I Owed Something to My Friends," *Winnipeg Sun*, 28 November 1977.
104. "You Can't Eat Medals," *The Native Voice* (June 1950), 4.
105. Canada, Senate, *The Aboriginal Soldier After the Wars: Report of the Standing Committee on Aboriginal People* (Ottawa, 1995), 13.
106. Sealey and De Vyvere, *Thomas George Prince*, 43.
107. See Lloyd Dohla, "Thomas Prince: Canada's Forgotten Aboriginal War Hero," *First Nations Drum* (Fall 2002), accessed at *www.firstnationsdrum.com/Fall2002/HisPrince.htm.*
108. Quoted in Sealey and De Vyvere, *Thomas George Prince*, 45.
109. *Ibid.*, 44, 46. Allan Young outlined the three ways that PTSD patients respond to the cognitive dissonance originating in traumatic experiences. Based on his schema, Prince appears to have tried to empty his memories of their salience and emotional power through generalized emotional numbing (self-dosing with alcohol). This activity generates cyclical processing that metabolizes the memory in an individual's inactive memory, but continues to create a high level of anxiety because the memory cannot be buried: "it lives on for decades, a source of suffering and socially and psychologically maladaptive behavior." *Harmony of Illusions*, 8–9.
110. Cole, "Hero Condemns 'Punks' of Today," 6; "I Owed Something to My Friends," *Winnipeg Sun*, 28 November 1977.
111. Petit interview in *Fallen Hero*.
112. Cole, "Hero Condemns 'Punks' of Today," 6; Sealey and Van de Vyvere, *Thomas George Prince*, 6–7.
113. "The Patricias Salute Deeds of Tommy Prince," *Winnipeg Free Press*, 5 August 1975; "Indian War Hero Tommy Prince Dies," PPCLI Museum and Archives clipping file. His name was also put forward to participate in the opening of the Pan-American Games. See "Beat of the City," *Winnipeg Free Press*, 27 October 1966, 3.
114. "Pauper's Burial for War Hero," PPCLI Museum and Archives clipping file; Brian Cole, "Hero Condemns 'Punks' of Today," *Winnipeg Free Press*, 10 November 1976, 1, 6. The Manitoba Indian Brotherhood also hon-

oured Prince for his contributions in late 1976. See "MIB Conference Opens," *Winnipeg Free Press*, 7 December 1976, 2.

115. Cole, "Hero Condemns 'Punks' of Today," 6; "Pauper's Burial for War Hero," PPCLI Museum and Archives clipping file. Allan Young explains that "PTSD is a disease of time. The disorder's distinctive pathology is that it permits the past (memory) to relive itself in the present, in the form of intrusive images and thoughts and in the patient's compulsion to replay old events." Young, *Harmony of Illusions*, 7.

116. "'A Hell of a Warrior' Buried with Indian, Military Honors," PPCLI Museum and Archives clipping file; and "Crowds Flock to See Prince Laid to Rest," *Winnipeg Free Press*, 1 December 1977, 3. On his funeral and obituary tributes, see also "Hero" and "Deaths" *Winnipeg Free Press*, 28 November 1977, 7, 28; "Hero's Burial for Prince," *Ibid.*, 29 November 1977, 1, 4; "Full Honors Wednesday for Prince," *Ibid.*, 29 November 1977; "Prince Honors Urged," *Ibid.*, 30 November 1977; "Tommy Prince," *Winnipeg Tribune*, 1 December 1977.

117. Sealey and de Vyvere, *Thomas George Prince*, 6.

118. "'A Hell of a Warrior.'"

119. Andrew Iarocci, *Canadian Forces Base Petawawa: The First Century, 1905–2005* (Waterloo: Laurier Centre for Military and Strategic Disarmament Studies, 2005), 48; "Bold Eagle: Youth Development Combined with Traditional Culture," *Ogimaakaan* (2000), 22 and 25; PPCLI, *History of the Regiment*, 2–16 and 18; Lieutenant-General Claude Couture, ADM(HR-Mil) to ADM (IE), 27 October 2003, DND File 1000–11 (DMGIEE 3).

120. "Lost and Found," *The Beaver* (October/November 2001), 4.

121. On Prince's medals, see "Dealer Set to Auction Medals of War Hero Tommy Prince," *London Free Press*, 11 February 1997, A6; "Canada's Most-Decorated Aboriginal War Veteran's Medals Up for Auction," *North Bay Nugget*, 24 July 2001, A8; "Medals of Famous Native Veteran to Be Auctioned," *Sarnia Observer*, 24 July 2001, A2; "War Hero's Medals for Sale," *Toronto Star*, 25 July 2001; "Regional Report," *Windsor Star*, 25 July 2001, B1; "Ottawa Joins Battle to Get War Hero's Medals Back," *Winnipeg Free Press*, 26 July 2001; "Veteran's Valour Shouldn't Be Forgotten," *Orillia Packet and Times*, 2 August 2001, 6; "War Hero's Medals on Sale Today," *Edmonton Journal*, 9 August 2001, D10; "Group Ready to Bid On Medals," *Barrier Examiner*, 9 August 2001, A8; "Group Hopes to Bring Hero's Medals Home," *Kingston Whig-Standard*, 9 August 2001, 10; "Native War Hero's Medals Up for Auction," *Niagara Falls Review*, 9 August 2001, A8; "Native Hero's Medals Auctioned," *St. John's Telegram*, 9 August 2001, A10; "Native Determined to Buy Back War Medals," *Vancouver Sun*, 9 August 2001, A4; "Regional Report," *Windsor Star*, 9 August 2001, B1, 10 August 2001, B1; "Family Gets Long-Lost Medals of Native Hero," *Edmonton Journal*, 10 August 2001, A6; "War Hero's Family Wins Medals: Most-Decorated Aboriginal," *Halifax Daily News*, 10

August 2001, 12; "London: Family Wins War Hero's Medals," *Kingston Whig-Standard*, 10 August 2001, 9; "Aboriginal War Hero's Kin Buy Back Medals," *Montreal Gazette*, 10 August 2001, A9; "War Hero's Medals Back with Family," *Niagara Falls Review*, 10 August 2001, A12; "Family Pays $75,000 for Aboriginal War Hero's Medals," *Welland Tribune*, 10 August 2001, A2; "Manitoba: Native War Hero's Family Buys Medals at Auction," *Ottawa Citizen*, 10 August 2001, A7; "Medals Coming Home! Stunning Bid Returns Hero's War Honours," *Winnipeg Free Press*, 10 August 2001; "Tommy Prince's Medals Fetch $75,000: Decorations Going Back Home to Winnipeg After Family's Successful Bid," *Vancouver Sun*, 11 August 2001, A6; "War Hero's Medals Back in Manitoba," *Legion Magazine* (November/December 2001), 65.

122. From CBC news archives: "Prince Medals Return to Province," 5 November 2001; "War Hero's Memorial to Be Unveiled," 2 September 2002; "French Government to Honour Prince," 22 November 2002; various articles accessed at *www.winnipeg.cbc.ca*.

123. "Coins," *Winnipeg Free Press*, 10 March 1978; "Sgt Prince Honored," *Ibid.*, 20 April 1978; Legislative Assembly of Manitoba, 13 May 2004, 2080; "Monument to Prince Planned," *Winnipeg Free Press*, 17 September 1989; "Not to Be Forgotten," *Winnipeg Free Press*, 18 December 1988; "Tommy Prince Statue Unveiling Set," *Winnipeg Free Press*, 5 November 1989; "What About Tommy Prince as a Name for New City Avenue?," *Los Angeles Times*, 31 August 1986, 8; "What's Stopping Us from Honouring Prince?," *Winnipeg Free Press*, 25 October 1987, NT/5; "War Hero's Name Rejected Again," *Ibid.*, 31 December 1989; "Street Renamed," *Ibid.*, 3 January 1990; "Prince Honor Slated," *Ibid.*, 24 May 1990; "Winnipeg Honours War Hero," *Legion Magazine* (January/February 2002), 56.

124. Vit Wagner, "Indian War Hero's Story Told," *Toronto Star*, 30 November 1995; Legislative Assembly of Manitoba, 13 May 2004, 2080–89. The Manitoba Indian Brotherhood also established an educational trust fund in Prince's name. See "Prince's Name on Trust Fund," *Winnipeg Free Press*, 10 April 1978, 36.

125. Hepenstall, *Find the Dragon*, 66.

126. Peter Worthington, "Soldier Modest About Exploits: Canadians Don't Know Enough About Most-Decorated Native Vet," *Calgary Sun*, 13 November 2005.

127. Peacock interview in *Fallen Hero*.

128. Quoted in Bonikowsky, "Tommy Prince, Canadian Hero."

129. "The Patricias Salute Deeds of Tommy Prince," *Winnipeg Free Press*, 5 August 1975, 3.

130. Holm, *Strong Hearts Wounded Souls*, 7.

131. "More About Sgt. Prince," *Winnipeg Free Press*, 25 June 1945, 3.

CHAPTER 5

When Leadership Really Mattered:
Bert Hoffmeister and Morale During the
Battle of Ortona, December 1943

by Douglas E. Delaney

> During a sticky battle, morale is as important, if not
> more important, than good tactics. On the scale of 1 to
> 10, morale will go from 4 to 9 just by the appearance of
> a senior commander in the line when and where the
> bullets are flying.[2]
>
> — Colonel S.W. (Syd) Thomson,
> Commanding Officer, Seaforth Highlanders of Canada

Sometimes it takes more than good tactics. Sometimes morale, the
product of good leadership, is what wins battles. Napoleon
Bonaparte thought morale even more important than weapons, numbers, and tactics combined: "The moral is to the physical as three is to
one."[3] Nearly a century-and-a-half after Napoleon's victories and final
defeat and in spite of dizzying developments in weaponry and tactics,
Field Marshal Viscount Montgomery of Alamein thought the same:
"The morale of the soldier is the greatest single factor in war."[4] Canadian
soldiers who served under Montgomery learned this too, nowhere more
acutely than at the Italian town of Ortona in December 1943. The slow
and bloody struggle for the town and its little port strained the morale
of the soldiers of the 2nd Canadian Infantry Brigade (2 CIB), and tested the leadership abilities of the officers and non-commissioned officers
(NCOs) who led them. It especially tested mettle of the brigade's new
commander, Brigadier Bert Hoffmeister.

The battle of Ortona came at the end of the Eighth Army's gruelling
Adriatic offensive, that had started with the crossing of the Sangro River
on 24 November. By the time Hoffmeister's brigade entered the town on
20 December, nearly a month's worth of hard slogging had ground the

offensive to a crawl and Montgomery, the Eighth Army commander at the time, had modified his original goal of breaking through to Rome to one of simply making it to the Pescara River before a winter break to rest, recover, and rebuild for a renewed offensive in the spring. Ortona, boasting a functioning port and serving as a road and rail hub, was deemed an important part of that plan. The task of taking the town fell to the commander of the 1st Canadian Division (1 CID), Major-General Chris Vokes, who in turn passed it on to Hoffmeister's brigade:

> At the time I was given my orders for Ortona, it [the town] was represented to me as being a vital spot that would play a most important role in Eighth Army communications and supply, in that there was a rail center and a port where ships could operate, and that it was most important in the administrative scheme of things. I never questioned it at any time. I was given my orders and we got on with it.[5]

Unfortunately, Ortona never turned into the administrative centre that division and corps staffs had hoped it would become. Eight days of fighting eventually reduced the town and its facilities to rubble. What was left of the town hardly justified the cost.

The terrible contest for the town also caught Canadian and British staffs by surprise. After much brutal fighting to push the Germans off the Sangro and Moro rivers, and after breaching the defences of a topographical feature south of Ortona called the "Gully," intelligence staffs, from army down to brigade, believed the Germans would have to withdraw to the next defensible river line, the Arielli, five kilometres

Library and Archives Canada PA-132779

Then Lieutenant-Colonel B.M. Hoffmeister, commanding officer of the Seaforth Highlanders, during the Sicilian campaign, August 1943.

north of the town. On 18 December, Hoffmeister received the following intelligence summary from 5th British Corps:

> ARIELLI however is strongly held as is ORSOGNA, both places by parachutists. Indeed the parachutists having temporarily stopped the gaps at various points along the front are now holding key positions in order to cover the withdrawal of formations which might not otherwise be able to extricate themselves.[6]

Soldiers assigned to covering withdrawals do not normally stay in place long, just long enough to let the retiring force pass through. Accordingly, intelligence staffs anticipated that the soldiers of the German 1st Parachute Division would withdraw to positions north of Ortona. They were dead wrong. By 21 December, the German paratroopers, part of a fresh division, had taken over the coastal sector. They stayed and they fought viciously to hold on to the town. Had anyone in Eighth Army guessed right, they might have thought about cutting the town off before assaulting it, but they did not.[7] Not cutting it off meant that Hoffmeister's brigade attacked an enemy that was both determined to fight and free to reinforce and relieve troops from the north. To make matters worse, foul weather prevented the Desert Air Force from bombing enemy concentrations north of Ortona.[8] This battle turned out to be way tougher than anyone anticipated.

Despite the brutality of a street-fight, from a purely tactical perspective, it is actually "very simple" for a commander to plan. Syd Thomson, one of Hoffmeister's subordinate commanders during the battle described it as "probably the simplest of any kind of operation, town-fighting … because the [terrain] features were sitting right there on the map in front of you, or the [air] photos, and we could say we own this house and not that one. Next day we'd decide to take this one or that street, and so on."[9]

Roads and railways, houses, and hospitals: All these things make it easy to mark boundaries, carve up the terrain into sub-unit sectors, and parcel out the objectives, which is what Hoffmeister did on 20–21 December. He chose the most obvious landmark in the town — the Ortona-Orsogna lateral, which ran roughly north-south — and assigned the western half to the Seaforth Highlanders of Canada, leaving the Edmontons to clear the eastern portion of the town. He kept his third infantry battalion, the Princess Patricia's Canadian Light Infantry (PPCLI), in reserve. Those decisions were easy. From the time he issued orders, his principal concerns were when he should commit his reserve and how to keep the forward troops armed and fed — not the types of tasks that tax a commander's intellect.

The real difficulty for an attacker in a street-fight lies in the execution, for a number of reasons. First among them, is the advantage an urban battlefield offers skilled defenders. At Ortona, the soldiers of the 1st German Parachute Division got to choose where to defend and where to kill. They placed obstacles on obvious approaches and covered them with machine gun and anti-tank fire. An after action report prepared by the 1st Canadian Division staff described the challenge the attackers faced at Ortona:

> All roads, except those leading into the pre-selected "killing grounds," were blocked by demolished houses which formed admirable barricades. These piles of rubble were in such a position that they could be covered [by machine gun fire] from above and from the rear, as well as from the front.... The rubble would normally be liberally sowed with mines and booby traps.... The main tank approaches, naturally limited to streets, were covered by A Tk [anti-tank] guns sited to fire at short range.[10]

Not knowing which house was booby-trapped or which window would spit out machine-gun fire made attacking a slow and costly business: "Except under the best conditions troops did not work along the streets, but worked their way from house to house. In some cases 'mouse-holing' [blowing holes through walls of connected buildings] was necessary, which generally being done by hand, took some time."[11] In all, it took the soldiers of 2 CIB eight days of incessant fighting to blast their way through a mere 1,100 meters of defended town.

Ortona was less one well-orchestrated effort than a series of isolated engagements fought in "fours and fives."[12] The building-to-building, room-to-room nature of the fighting meant that a soldier seldom saw more than three or four of his comrades, a circumstance that naturally gave rise to questions like "Are we the only ones here?" or "Are we in danger of being cut-off?" And fallen comrades were a constant reminder of the possibility of being ripped open with bullets or dismembered by a booby trap. The consequent and pervasive "tension and nervousness of Ortona" took its toll.[13] In a little over a week of fighting at Ortona, 2

Major-General C. Vokes discusses the Moro River crossing operations with Brigadier Hoffmeister and Brigadier Wyman, 8 December 1943.

CIB sustained a total of 305 killed, missing or wounded.[14] In fact, since the brigade had started fighting at the Moro River in early December, the battalions of Hoffmeister's brigade had lost 50 percent of their rifle company strength.[15]

Those kinds of odds make riflemen edgy. Indeed, battle exhaustion casualties accounted for approximately 20 percent of the brigade's casualty count for the month of December, a number that spiked during the Ortona fighting.[16] It took tremendous leadership skill to keep these "fours and fives" fighting. Jim Stone, who led his company of Edmontons through the streets, alleys, and mouseholes of Ortona acknowledged the important role leadership plays at this level:

> Street-fighting is won by the men, not by the weapons — the men actually in contact with the enemy, mostly commanded by junior NCOs. People have to be really well-trained if you're going to be successful. It's these junior NCOs who take five or six men into dangerous places [that] keep up the momentum of whatever attack you're making.[17]

But even leaders — from corporal to colonel — need to be led. People who have to stick their heads up to "take five or six men into dangerous places" need to know that they are not the only ones exposing themselves, especially when the risks are so high. At Ortona, NCOs and junior officers suffered a disproportionately-high percentage of the casualties, which is significant because, if they had given in to fear and doubt, the attack would definitely have foundered. Hoffmeister understood the need to show all ranks under him that they were not alone: "[A commander] has to be prepared to go forward and be seen by the troops, under shellfire, and indicate that you know what they're putting up with and that you're not afraid to expose yourself a bit when necessary."[18] Ortona gave him ample opportunity to demonstrate his ability to do this and affect morale. The nature of the street-fighting demanded it.

Hoffmeister had fought many actions as both a battalion and a brigade commander since landing in Sicily in July 1943, but Ortona was like nothing he had faced to that point. There was only so much that he, as a brigade commander could do to influence the battle. This was no battle for the massed use of firepower that he had learned fighting in Montgomery's Eighth Army.[19] In a November 1943 officer training session, he described his ideal sequence for an attack as starting with air bombardment, followed by air strafing, followed by an artillery barrage, followed by the machine gun, mortar, and anti-tank fire of the brigade support group, followed closely by infantry assault. He further emphasized that an attacking force "must not move beyond the range of its [supporting] arms," most importantly, its artillery.

The problem was that this approach was not conducive to fighting in built-up areas. Bombardment did little to destroy or neutralize the defenders; it only created more rubble, enhancing the obstacles and making vehicle movement more difficult. Ortona was no battle of manoeuvre either. Hoffmeister did not have the troops to assault the town *and* cut it off; even his boss, Chris Vokes, had difficulty mustering the strength to drive a force west of the town to sever the main German supply route from the north. Instead, Hoffmeister's battalions had to fight a decentralized battle, where the main brunt of fire support came in the form of single tanks inching forward to blast away at enemy anti-tank guns as "fours and fives" of infantry soldiers moved from house to house, rooting the enemy out of their strong points.

The nature of the coming street-fight had not been obvious to Hoffmeister when he first assaulted Ortona with the support of a tank regiment (The Three Rivers Regiment), an anti-tank battery, and the full weight of divisional artillery on 20 December. He had come at the town from two directions: The main attack came from the Loyal Edmonton Regiment, which advanced closely behind a timed artillery barrage, from the southwest.[20] The Seaforths, who had relieved the Hastings and Prince Edward Regiment of 1 CIB along the coastal road south of Ortona, drove towards the town from the south. Concurrent with these actions, the PPCLI had moved to the north side of the Gully to protect the brigade's left flank from enemy counterattack.

Throughout the fighting, Hoffmeister kept a grip on things from his tactical headquarters. At first, he perched himself on a high feature "about 2000 yards short [south] of Ortona," a position that gave him a "marvelous view" of the battle.[21] He could see the Edmontons and the Seaforths converging on the town; and at one point, he intervened to prevent the units from firing on each other as they simultaneously reached southern approaches.[22] But soon after the battalions had slipped into the town and out of sight, Hoffmeister moved his tactical headquarters to the outskirts of Ortona.[23] Because the buildings and rubble of the town limited fields of observation to a 100 metres, less in many instances, no single position could give Hoffmeister the view he needed to get an adequate feel for the battle. So he had to move forward and often. The 2 CIB Intelligence officer described Hoffmeister's routine: "During the morning the Brigadier breezed into town, right up to the forward troops and very nearly got hit. He did this every morning during the ORTONA fighting."[24] A dangerous way of doing business, but it suited the tactical situation.

It suited the tactical situation in two main respects: It gave him control (what little could be achieved) and, perhaps most important, it helped morale. As one of Hoffmeister's radio operators remembered: "He knew instinctively … that his presence would inspire confidence in the troops. And he wanted to know what the hell was going on!"[25] For control, he could talk to the troops in contact with enemy, get a feel for their battle, and determine what they needed to fight it. Given the difficulties of communicating by wireless or land-line in the broken ground of an urban environment, face-to-face communication was the main way of passing on direction: "There really wasn't much for orders at Ortona. They were verbal or by runner."[26] But the residual effect of his forward forays had, perhaps, even more impact on the battle. His being seen up forward affected soldiers: "You just felt … he's there. I guess I should be too."[27] With soldiers of all ranks quickly calculating the odds of getting killed or wounded, that mattered. Hoffmeister's example filtered down the chain of command too. Subordinate officers like Jim

Photographer Lieutenant T. Rowe, Library and Archives Canada PA-116852

Soldiers from "B" Company, The Loyal Edmonton Regiment, advancing through Ortona, 21 December 1943.

Stone recognized the importance of a commander's presence to the soldiers doing the fighting:

> My presence was useful.... I demonstrated a certain lack of concern for the enemy shots that were flying around. And it made people wonder, "what am I doing hanging back when he'll go?" And that, I think, is the point of why you need — it sounds a bit egotistical — but BOLD leaders in towns.[28]

Maintaining morale was no easy feat with soldiers who were scared and dead-tired. Jock Gibson, a rifle company sergeant-major with the Seaforth Highlanders came across Hoffmeister while delivering ammunition to a platoon on the front line: "I just couldn't believe my eyes — seeing a brigadier in the middle of a battle."[29] Hoffmeister had ventured ahead of the Seaforth battalion headquarters to get a better appreciation of what was happening. The Seaforths were his old regiment and Hoffmeister knew Gibson, who had been his piper in "B" Company three years earlier. After several days that were long on battle, but short on sleep, Gibson looked understandably haggard. Hoffmeister smiled and quipped: "You didn't shave today, did you Jock?" Gibson returned the smile and responded, "No Sir, I've been a bit busy."[30] Not much else was said. Not much else had to be said. In the middle of much mayhem, two tired men had shared a bit of soldier's sarcasm, something that gave Gibson's morale a much-needed boost. Instead of sitting in his command post and fretting about things he could not control, like the room-to-room fight, Hoffmeister focused his efforts on shoring up morale in what had quickly become a grinder of a battle. Syd Thomson remembered how one particular visit from the brigadier affected him:

> On this particular day, Bert came into Ortona and said, "Great show, Syd, terrific show, you are doing great." He patted me on the back when all I wanted to say was "For Christ's sake Bert, can't I have a rest[?]" There was no way I could say that to him. He was so great that way…. I was so impressed with the way he inspired and put so much spirit into people. You couldn't say no to him.[31]

This was a commander who understood people.

He also understood their fears. Three days into the battle, he visited a field hospital at San Vito Chietino.[32] Medics and army surgeons in an abandoned school were working tirelessly to repair the wounded that had literally piled up in the corridors following the first few gruelling days of battle. Hoffmeister understood how hard the medical staff had been working to care for his soldiers, but the sight of it all unsettled him. It was not just the number of wounded that saddened him, it was also the state of those that had already been treated: "They still had the original blood from their wounds on their faces and their hands." Most people, given the circumstances, might not have thought this important; the priority was treating the wounds and that had been done. But Hoffmeister understood that a wounded soldier not only needed medical treatment for his injuries, he needed to feel that he had not been abandoned. He needed to be washed, spoken to, and reassured, and that was clearly beyond the capabilities of the overburdened medical staff. Hoffmeister also knew that the soldiers still fighting needed to believe that they would be well looked after, if ever they fell.

After discussing the issue with one of the surgeons, Hoffmeister sent a request through the medical chain of command for nursing volunteers who could provide comfort for the wounded. In spite of regulations that precluded women from duty that close to the front, the next day, a contingent of British nursing sisters — there was no shortage of volunteers — arrived at San Vito Chietino, only six kilometres behind the fighting troops. "[W]orking under shell fire and within range of long-range German mortars,"[33] they provided the essential comfort that Hoffmeister knew had been lacking.

Not knowing what was happening also weighs on a soldier's morale. Hoffmeister understood that; he had long believed that keeping people informed could mitigate the fear of the unknown and feelings of isolation. He rarely "scaled back" orders to give people only what they "require[d] to know to carry out [their] task."[34] What they needed, as far as Hoffmeister was concerned, was enough information to make them comfortable with what was happening. And generally, that meant passing on pretty much everything he knew. Doing that was not easy at Ortona, but Hoffmeister did his best.

The 2 CIB Intelligence Log records the passage of many situation reports from Hoffmeister's headquarters on current enemy identifications and dispositions, the movement of civilians, and the progress of flanking formations.[35] Early in the fighting, for instance, the following message went to all units in the brigade group: "Bde Comd directs [that] all ranks be warned of German TELLER MINES and BOOBY TRAPS in rubble in and around ORTONA."[36] Four days into the battle, a situation report also advised the battalions of 1 CIB's attempt to outflank Ortona to the west. It is impossible to determine how much of the information made it to individual soldiers, but, based on Hoffmeister's well-established practice of passing as much information as possible, to as low a level as possible, the intent was clear: he wanted to assure his subordinates that he was on top of things, and that those above him were as well.

Hoffmeister also looked beyond the battle — to the longer-term impact it could have on morale. Victories, however difficult, are the lifeblood of morale. People think twice about giving their all when all they have is a string of defeats behind them. This is why Hoffmeister opted to continue the battle for Ortona, even after Vokes had offered to call it off, mid-way through.[37] His brigade had fought hard and suffered

Photographer Laurie Audrain, Library and Archives Canada PA-115149

Sergeant Charles Lord (foreground) and Private Richard Greaves of "A" Company, PPCLI, man their positions near Ortona.

much, so this was no easy decision for Hoffmeister. He had to choose between sending even more men to the hospital at San Vito in the hope of achieving victory or conceding defeat and admitting that those who had fallen to that point had done so in vain:

> Chris Vokes asked me if I would like to quit, and I said "absolutely not, to quit at this time would be letting the brigade down and the effect on the morale of the brigade would be such that it would be just shocking." Furthermore the objective was represented to me as being extremely important, one that Eighth Army just must have, and I said nothing has changed as far as 2nd Brigade is concerned[;] we'll see it through, which we did.[38]

It was the right decision, but a painful one.

The battle for Ortona proper ended on 28 December. Early that morning, after patrols reported that the enemy had vacated the town,

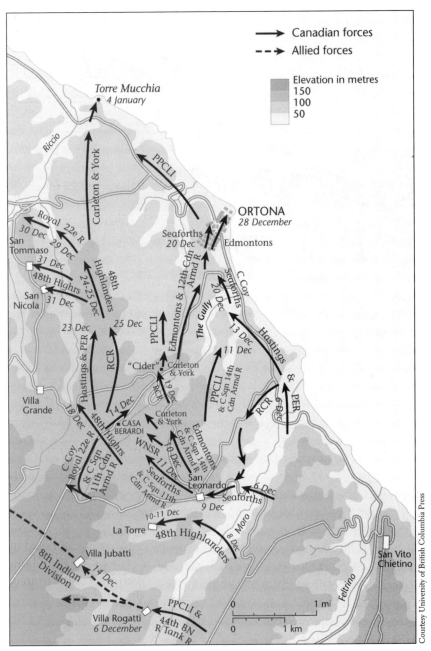

Canadian forces
Allied forces

Elevation in metres
150
100
50

Torre Mucchia
4 January

Riccio

ORTONA
28 December

Carleton & York

PPCLI

Royal 22e R
30 Dec
29 Dec
San Tommaso
31 Dec
48th Highlanders
48th Highs
San Nicola
31 Dec
24-25 Dec

Seaforths
20 Dec

Edmontons

C Coy
Seaforths

Edmontons & 12th Cdn Armd R

The Gully
20 Dec
13 Dec
11 Dec

Hastings

23 Dec
25 Dec
PPCLI
RCR

"Cider" • Carleton & York

PPCLI
& C Sqn 14th
Cdn Armd R

RCR

RCR
9 Dec

9 Dec

PER

Villa Grande

14 Dec

18 Dec

48th Highs

Carleton & York

CASA BERARDI

Carleton & York
WNSR
Edmontons
& C Sqn 14th
Cdn Armd R
9 Dec

C Coy
Royal 22e R
& C Sqn
11th Cdn
Armd R

Seaforths
& C Sqn 11th
Cdn Armd R
11 Dec

San Leonardo

6 Dec
Seaforths

9 Dec

Moro
8 Dec

10-11 Dec
La Torre
48th Highlanders

Villa Jubatti

8th Indian Division
14 Dec

San Vito
Chietino

Villa Rogatti
6 December

PPCLI &
44th BN
R Tank R

Feltrino

0   1 mi
0   1 km

Courtesy of University of British Columbia Press

The Battle for Ortona.

Hoffmeister cancelled his plan to pass the PPCLI through the dwindling ranks of the Loyal Edmonton Regiment.[39] Instead, he moved the PPCLI around the left flank to cut the coastal road north of Ortona. By this time, 1 CIB was preparing to attack San Nicola and San Tommaso, and Vokes was developing plans to send 3 CIB through 1 CIB towards Torre Mucchia on the coast.[40] These actions essentially closed the Adriatic offensive. The weather was too bad, the casualties too many, and the gains too few to continue.[41] A month's worth of fighting and dying was finally at an end.

It is difficult to imagine the Battle of Ortona without Hoffmeister. It is impossible to say whether it would have ground to a successful conclusion without him, but it is clear that he thought hard about the morale of his troops and he did everything he could to keep them fighting. Mostly, that meant being seen and sharing risks. There was not a whole lot else he could do for them. With the broken terrain of the town, with the room-to-room nature of the battle, with his ability to mass firepower rendered almost useless, with the Desert Air Force grounded because of bad weather; he could not do much to help them — except to be seen. When soldiers see the boss, they can at least feel that they are not alone or unappreciated or dying for nothing. And Hoffmeister's soldiers kept fighting.

On Christmas day, the Seaforth Highlanders held a remarkable Christmas dinner in the church of Santa Maria di Constantinopoli, barely 700 metres from the front line of the fighting troops. Companies were brought back in rotation for some turkey, some minced pie and one bottle of beer per man. Amid the "deathly chatter of machine guns," the "rumbling of falling buildings" and the "roar of guns," they ate their meals with gratitude and sang Christmas carols in defiance.[42] Hoffmeister, who had been the commanding officer of the Seaforths only three months earlier, was invited to attend, which he did in the company of the Seaforth commanding officer, Syd Thomson. The padre of the regiment noted in his diary that, during the "C" Company dinner, the troops "cheered" both Hoffmeister and Thomson, shortly after the two men entered the church. At the fever pitch of the battle, and after having endured so much, they cheered the two men who had led them into that little urban hell. That says something.

NOTES

1. This article is based largely on Douglas E. Delaney, *The Soldiers' General: Bert Hoffmeister at War* (Vancouver: UBC Press, 2005), Chapter 6.
2. Royal Military College of Canada (henceforth RMC), William J. McAndrew Collection (henceforth McAndrew Collection), Colonel S.W. Thomson, interview with William J. McAndrew, Sydney, b.c., 6 April 1980, 2.
3. Accessed at *www.military-quotes.com/Napoleon.htm*, 24 August 2005.
4. Accessed at *www.military-quotes.com/database/m.htm*, 24 August 2005.
5. RMC, McAndrew Collection, Interview with General B.M. Hoffmeister by W. McAndrew and B. Greenhous, 1980 (henceforth McAndrew/Greenhous-Hoffmeister Interview), 68.
6. Library and Archives Canada (LAC), Record Group [RG] 24, Vol. 10776, File 224B5.023 (D1), Intelligence Summaries 5 (British) Corps, 5 Corps Intelligence Summary, No. 256 (for period ending 2300 hrs 18 December 43).
7. Brereton Greenhous, "Would it not have been better to bypass Ortona completely …?" *Canadian Defence Quarterly* (April 1989) 51–55. For more criticism of Vokes' generalship see Michael Cessford, "Hard in the Attack: the Canadian Army in Sicily and Italy, July 1943-June 1944," unpublished Ph.D. dissertation, Carleton University, 1996, 256–258; and Mark Zuehlke, *Ortona: Canada's Epic World War II Battle* (Toronto: Stoddart, 1999), 377–380.
8. LAC, RG 24, Vol. 10982, Dewar Account.
9. Extracts from an Interview with Brigadier S.W. Thomson, dated 15 July, 1960, at Victoria, b.c. Reprinted in Robert L. McDougall, *A Narrative of War: From the Beaches of Sicily to the Hitler Line with the Seaforth Highlanders of Canada, 1943–1944* (Ottawa: The Golden Dog Press, 1996) 156.
10. LHCMA, Allfrey Papers, 4/8. "ORTONA." Report by H.Q. 1 CDN INF DIV, 16 February 1944: 2–3.
11. *Ibid.*, 5.
12. MacLeod Collection, Canadians in Italy, WWII, Vol. 8, Interview with Major Stewart Lynch, Seaforth Highlanders (n.d.). Lynch was a rifle platoon commander with the Seaforth Highlanders of Canada during the battle for Ortona.
13. *Ibid.*
14. LAC, RG 24, Vol. 14074, WD 2 CIB, Reports of "Approximate Fighting Strength," 20–29 December 43.
15. Archives of the Seaforth Highlanders of Canada [henceforth ASHC], Personal Diaries, Memoirs, Interviews, Accounts [henceforth PDMIA], Major-General C. Vokes, "Narrative: Crossing MORO R [River] and subsequent operations including capture of ORTONA," [henceforth Vokes Moro Narrative] 14 May 44.
16. The casualty breakdown for the units of 2 CIB during the period 28 November 1943 to 12 February 1944 were as follows: Princess Patricia's Canadian Light Infantry — 241 total casualties (23.2 percent battle

exhaustion); Seaforth Highlanders — 261 total casualties (22.5 percent battle exhaustion); Loyal Edmonton Regiment — 224 total casualties (16.9 percent) battle exhaustion. See Terry Copp and Bill McAndrew, *Battle Exhaustion: Soldiers and Psychiatrists in the Canadian Army, 1939–1945* (Montreal and Kingston: McGill-Queen's University Press, 1990), 58.

17. MacLeod Collection, Canadians in Italy, WWII, Vol. 7, Interview with Jim Stone (n.d).

18. RMC, McAndrew Collection, Hoffmeister/Greenhous-McAndrew Interview, 141.

19. ASHC, PDMIA, Diary of Captain W.H. Melhuish, Brigadier Hoffmeister lecture.

20. For the barrage plan on 20 December, see LAC, RG 24, Vol. 14074, WD 2 CIB, Appendix 23, Barrage Trace, 20 December 43. On the part played by the Loyal Edmonton Regiment during the battle of Ortona, see Shaun R.G. Brown, "'The Rock of Accomplishment' The Loyal Edmonton Regiment at Ortona." *Canadian Military History*, Vol. 2, No. 2 (Autumn 1993): 11–22.

21. The description of the view from Hoffmeister's tactical headquarters was Allfrey's. LHCMA, Allfrey Papers, 4/1, Diaries, 20 December 43.

22. LAC, RG 24, Vol. 14074, 2 CIB WD, Intelligence Log, entries for 1411 hrs, 1415 hrs, 20 December 1943.

23. The main brigade headquarters later moved to the location vacated by the tactical headquarters.

24. LAC, RG 24, Vol. 10982, Dewar Account.

25. Interview with Denis Meade, 6 December 2000.

26. Telephone Interview with Colonel Syd Thomson, 10 December 2000.

27. Meade Interview.

28. MacLeod Collection, Stone Interview.

29. MacLeod Collection, MacLeod Interviews, Vol. 6, Interview with Jock Gibson.

30. Interview with Jock Gibson, Langley, b.c., 9 December 2000.

31. RMC, McAndrew Collection, Thomson-McAndrew Interview.

32. The details of the visit, based on an interview with Hoffmeister, are recounted in Zuehlke, *Ortona*, 290–291.

33. Hoffmeister, quoted in *Ibid*.

34. War office (UK), *Operations Military Training Pamphlet, No. 2, Part III — Appreciations, Orders Intercommunications and Movements — 1939* (Ottawa: King's Printer, 1941), 6.

35. LAC, RG 24, WD 2 CIB, Intelligence Log December 1943. For reports on the enemy situation, see entries 1925 hrs, 20 December 43, 1425 hrs, 23 December 43, 2300 hrs, 27 December 43. On 1 CIB actions, see the entry for 1050 hrs 24 December 43. On restricting the movement of civilians, see the entry 0950 hrs, 21 December 43.

36. LAC, RG 24, Vol. 14074, WD 2 CIB, Intelligence Log, entry for 1450 hrs, 22 December 43.

37. RMC, McAndrew Collection, McAndrew/Greenhous-Hoffmeister Interview, 70.
38. *Ibid.*
39. LAC, RG 24, Vol. 14074, WD 2 CIB, Intelligence Log, entries 0800 hrs and 0940 hrs, 28 December 43. See also LAC, RG 24, Vol. 10982, Dewar Account.
40. ASHC, PDMIA, Vokes Moro Account. See also LHCMA, Allfrey Papers, 4/2, 27th, 28th December 43.
41. Lieutenant-Colonel G.W.L. Nicholson, *Official History of the Canadian Army in the Second World War, Volume II, The Canadians in Italy 1943–1945* (Ottawa: Queen's Printer, 1966), 338.
42. ASHC, PDMIA, Diary of Major Durnford, 25 December 43.

CHAPTER 6

Four Gallant Airmen: Clifford MacKay McEwen, Raymond Collishaw, Leonard Joseph Birchall, and Robert Wendell McNair

by David L. Bashow

W hat elements have historically defined outstanding air leadership in combat conditions? They are surprisingly difficult to categorize, to qualify, and to quantify, due in no small measure to the frequently isolated and variable circumstances of aerial warfare. A successful air leader has to be a chameleon, to be many things to many people, depending on personalities, service needs, combat conditions, and a host of other variables. However, first and foremost, an effective air leader must lead by example, and must not only be prepared to personally go in harm's way, but must do so in a manner that inspires confidence and a willingness in others to engage the enemy. Frequently, that appears to involve a somewhat-indefinable sense of *savoir faire*, that is, the ability to act suitably in *any* situation. Bill Grierson, a distinguished and highly decorated Second World War Royal Canadian Air Force (RCAF) airman who eventually served as the navigation leader of 35 (Royal Air Force [RAF]) Squadron in Bomber Command, offered the following with respect to his commanding officer, Wing Commander Jimmy Marks:

> In my now long forgotten book, *We Band of Brothers*, I say that if Jimmy had asked all to lie on the ground and let him walk over us, we would not have asked why. Such is the magical quality of true leadership. I have yet to encounter an explanation of how such magical leadership could apply within Bomber Command, when each plane flew utterly alone in the dark, deadly skies over Europe. I will not attempt an explanation, but I will offer an example. Losses in Bomber Command in my time (October 1941 to March 1943) averaged a remorseless 5

percent per raid. Send out 20 crews, night after night, and one crew would not return. Yet under command of Jimmy Marks, we had an unbelievable run of 100 sorties without a crew loss. How could an inspirational leader have such an effect when each crew flew alone in radio silence through the dark skies of wartime Europe? ... When one of our 35 Squadron RAF captains, Hank Malkin, was congratulated for landing his Halifax with just the two engines on one side remaining, his tires shot away, and with two wounded crew members, he replied, "But Jimmy expects us to bring his planes home."
— Squadron Leader W.R.F. Grierson-Jackson, DFC, AFC, MiD[1]

While the foregoing leadership example pertains to an Englishman and a very gallant one at that, fortunately, Canada possessed many men such as Jimmy Marks. They were distinguished warriors who also proved able to motivate and inspire subordinates and peers alike, through self-less personal example, exceptional dedication, and a pronounced concern for the welfare of their charges.

If the rather draconian, British-initiated "Lack of Moral Fibre" (LMF) policy, crafted to deal with psychological battle casualties in the RAF, and, consequently, the RCAF during the Second World War was the mailed fist of encouragement, inspirational leadership was the velvet glove. While many Canadian airmen showed such leadership, the four brave souls highlighted in this chapter title, coming from different backgrounds and serving in very different wartime environments

National Aviation Museum 26306

Clifford M. "Black Mike" McEwen in full dress uniform after the war, 1918.

and operational circumstances, were all exceptional in this regard during their remarkable careers. The individual fibres of their contributions are inextricably woven into a rich tapestry of a legacy, a proud air force history, from which all serving members, veterans, and Canadian citizens can draw pride and inspiration. Here are their stories.

CLIFFORD MACKAY McEWEN

Clifford M. "Black Mike" McEwen, so-named, not for any sinister reason, but for his ability to tan easily and darkly, was an inspirational warrior chieftain in every sense of the word. Born in Griswold, Manitoba on 2 July 1896, he was educated in Moose Jaw and at the University of Saskatchewan, while making his home in Radisson, Saskatchewan.

Mike McEwen enrolled in Western University's 196th Battalion of the Canadian Expeditionary Force (CEF) on 24 March 1916, just months short of his 20th birthday. After service in England with the 196th Battalion, and then the 15th Reserve Battalion, McEwen was commissioned a second-lieutenant on 28 April 1917, and transferred to the Royal Flying Corps (RFC) in June. Following pilot training, he was posted to No. 28 Squadron, and eventually the Italian front, in October 1917, where he proved to be a stellar fighter pilot. There, he fell under the influence of the flamboyant and highly successful Canadian ace, Major William George "Billy" Barker, who was at the time a flight commander in the neighboring No. 66 Squadron. In Italy, the unparalleled king of audacity was Bill Barker. His exploits were the stuff of legends. One such event occurred in June 1918, when Barker, supposedly accompanied by Lieutenant Gerald Alfred Birks of Montreal and Lieutenant Clifford Mackay McEwen of Griswold, Manitoba, dropped the following challenge on Godega airfield:

> Major W.G. Barker and the officers under his Command present their compliments to Captain Bronmoski, 41 Reconnaissance, Portobouffole, Ritter von Fiala, 51 Pursuit, Garjarine, Captain Navratil, 3rd Company, and the pilots under their command and request the pleasure and honour of meeting in the air. In order to save Captain Bronmoski, Ritter von Fiala, and Captain Navratil, and gentlemen of his party the inconvenience of searching for them, Major Barker

and his Officers will bomb Godigo [*sic*] aerodrome at
10:00 a.m. daily, weather permitting, for the ensuing
two weeks.[2]

There is no record that the Austrians responded in any manner to
this challenge. Perhaps more to the point, there is no conclusive evidence to suggest this challenge was ever actually issued, although it
would not have been out of character with Barker's well-documented
audacity. In fact, McEwen was serving with 28 Squadron at this time,
although it was not unusual to mix pilots on operations from neigh-
bouring units. This story, perhaps at least partially apocryphal, has
become "an enduring legend."[3]

But whether the story was apocryphal or not, Mike McEwen was a
very successful First World War scout pilot. No. 28 Squadron, equipped
with Sopwith Camels,

> served briefly in France before being sent to Italy.
> There, over Liential, on December 30 (1917),
> McEwen shared in the destruction of an observation
> balloon and next day shot down his first plane, an
> Austrian-piloted Albatros. As he gained experience,
> he and his comrades became increasingly frustrated
> with the close support tactics used to escort
> bombers. Instead of waiting for the enemy, they
> evolved a strategy of breaking up enemy formations
> before they could make their attack. With this
> method, the squadron's and McEwen's own tally of
> Austrian planes began to mount. A successful
> demonstration of this theory occurred on 19 June
> 1918, when, with two others, McEwen put a forma-
> tion of Bergs to flight before they could reach the
> bombers. Downing one in the process, McEwen
> found himself alone among five enemy planes and
> made his escape by flying low through the narrow
> Astico Valley ...[4]

A skilful and fearless officer, McEwen would score 27 victories dur-
ing his nine-month tour in Italy, winning a Military Cross (MC), the
Distinguished Flying Cross (DFC) and Bar, [second award] and the
Italian Bronze Medal for Valour in the process. The citation for the Bar

to his DFC, gazetted on 3 November 1918, speaks volumes about his fighting spirit:

> A brilliant and courageous pilot, who has personally destroyed [at the time of the recommendation] twenty enemy machines. Exhibiting entire disregard of personal danger, he never hesitates to engage the enemy, however superior in numbers, and never fails to inflict serious casualties. His fine fighting spirit and skilful leadership inspired all who flew with him.[5]

This documented score did not capture McEwen's final tally, nor did the system recognize one of his victories until much later. On 18 February 1918, McEwen, Barker, and the rest of "C" Flight from 28 Squadron were on an offensive patrol at 15,000 feet above the town of Rustigno. To quote the words of McEwen's combat report:

> My engine began to run badly. I left the patrol and flew back towards the lines, heading southeast. My engine picked up and on re-crossing the lines to rejoin the patrol, I spotted an EA below me. I got in several bursts and the EA did not offer to avoid me and went down out of control. As my goggles frosted up, I could only follow him down to 4000 feet. I last saw him out of control over Rustigno.[6]

Since the frosted goggles had prevented McEwen from witnessing the enemy aircraft's impact, he was officially credited with only an "out-of-control" category victory. Years later, this claim was upgraded to "destroyed" when the tangled remains of the appropriate aircraft were found in the proper vicinity.[7]

On 1 May 1919, McEwen was repatriated to Canada. Between the wars, he remained in the fledgling RCAF, serving on the Air Board and becoming very active in the RCAF's early aerial survey work. He attended the RAF Staff School in 1930, and then went on to command RCAF Station Trenton, which would eventually become a focal point of the British Commonwealth Air Training Plan. During the early years of the Second World War, he commanded, in succession, No. 1 Training Command in Toronto, No. 3 Training Command in Montreal, and No. 1 Group Headquarters in St. John's, Newfoundland. Posted to England in 1942 as an air commodore, he eventually became the commanding officer of two bomber stations, comprising collectively No. 62 Base at Linton in Yorkshire, for which he was subsequently awarded a Mention in Dispatches:

> This officer was appointed Base Commander at No. 62 Operational Base in June 1943; since then five squadrons have either formed or converted after movement into the base, the three Lancaster II squadrons already being units in the base. Air Commodore McEwen has by his untiring efforts and leadership brought the base to a very high level of operational efficiency. His ability and zeal have been worthy of the highest praise.[8]

However, all his prior exemplary military accomplishments would pale in comparison to the inspirational leadership he provided as the Air Officer Commanding (AOC) of No. 6 Group Bomber Command from February 1944 until the cessation of hostilities in Europe. This was no mean feat, as the performance of the group during the first year of its existence (January 1943 — January 1944), while under the command of its first AOC, Air Vice-Marshal George Brookes, had been something less than stellar. Although this proved to be a trying time for all the combatant groups within Bomber Command, and though some of early criticism levied upon the Canadian formation was either unwarranted or exaggerated, 6 Group was exhibiting some legitimate training, tactical, and morale shortcomings. Combat losses resulting from the operational tempo of the bombing campaign at the time were dreadful, and 6 Group was a formation in shock and feeling sorry for itself. In short, it was a unit in need of tough love. Perhaps the most difficult problems to overcome were the significant morale problems generated by the losses themselves, particularly those experienced during the arduous 2nd Battle of the Ruhr in the spring of 1943, and the Berlin series of raids of the following winter.

Nonetheless, in February 1944, Mike McEwen succeeded George Brookes as AOC, and the fortunes of the group changed dramatically from that time. A dynamic, capable leader who had proved his mettle in the Great War, McEwen was an unrepentant advocate of arduous, realistic, and demanding training, as well as stern discipline. No armchair commander, McEwen led fearlessly from the front, accompanying his crews on their toughest missions and against the explicit orders of Sir

Arthur Harris, Bomber Command's helmsman. Knowing that their commander fully appreciated and shared their dangers, 6 Group crew performance soon became as good as any in Bomber Command, and better than most. "McEwen's presence was soon taken for granted — he even became a good luck symbol. As the men saw it, when the man with the moustache was along, things were going to be fine. They felt drawn to this colourful airman who wanted to share their danger, and when ordered not to, could not sleep while his men were on a raid."[9] Howard Ripstein, a wartime mid-upper gunner with 426 *Thunderbird* Squadron, recalls McEwen's leadership style:

> As Air Officer Commanding 6 Group, Black Mike's credo was leadership by example, albeit, in his case, illegal when he flew on operations, usually dressed in a sergeant's uniform. Despite an almost total ban by the highest of authorities, "Bomber" Harris winked at McEwen's actions ... However, what he was doing soon became known throughout 6 Group and beyond. Group Captain (Retired) Bill Swetman, DSO, DFC, a wartime commanding officer of the Thunderbirds, vividly recalls such a flight when flying on the last trip of his second tour of operations. At the last possible moment, Sergeant-Pilot McEwen was driven up to Swetman's Lancaster Mark II on the Linton-on-Ouse tarmac, and the AOC climbed aboard.
>
> This trip was particularly interesting, as many bombers were flying raggedly with their navigation lights on. Navigation lights to this point had been normally turned on for take-off, and then extinguished no later than crossing the English coast outbound until established for landing upon recovery. Black Mike soon modified the policy by making the requirement for "lights out" operations considerably broader. How? He threatened to send up fighters to shoot offenders down, and this threat was confirmed to me by Bill Swetman. On the ground as well as in the air, he was a stickler for discipline, standards and training — and more training. Still, he was fully aware of the stress endured by his air and ground crews. Within reason, his office door at Allerton Hall, the Group's headquarters, was always

open to any of the Group's men and women who wanted to see him.

Black Mike never slept when 6 Group was operational. He attended as many debriefings, then known as "interrogations," as he could, informally chatting with the returned, tired crews, many of whom became his close friends after the war.[10]

One element of the morale issue centred upon the need for recognition of outstanding performance. Air Vice-Marshal Brookes does not appear to have assigned any great priority to obtaining decorations for the personnel under his command. However, the same could not be said for Mike McEwen. He was attuned to the value and necessity of recognition for his people, both the warriors and the supporting crews, and in July 1944, he forcefully instructed his base commanders to increase the number of award submissions. The thrust of his initiatives were reflected in the following letter from Group Captain Johnnie Fauquier, then the commanding officer of No. 62 "Beaver" Base at Linton, to the commanding officers of 408, 415, 420, 425, 426, and 432 Squadrons:

> Headquarters No. 6 (RCAF) Group has expressed a desire that the numbers of recommendations submitted from this Base for Non-Immediate awards be increased, pointing out that the recommendations submitted by other Groups in Bomber Command are greatly in excess of this Group, regardless of the fact that this Group is reputed to be one of the most efficient from an operational standpoint. In view of this it is considered that the Group is not receiving an equitable share of honours and awards, due largely to the small number of recommendations submitted ... In order that this situation may be improved it is requested that each squadron submit a minimum of ten recommendations for Non-Immediate awards monthly. This is in no way to change existing instructions relative to recommendations for Immediate awards.[11]

This clarion call for action from "Black Mike" McEwen had the desired effect, and from the summer of 1944 onward, honours for the personnel of 6 Group were much more forthcoming. This resulted in better group morale, and probably factored into the outstanding performance record of 6 Group during the last year of the war.

In fact, under McEwen's able stewardship, 6 Group's performance during the last year of the European war was unsurpassed throughout Bomber Command. At the same time, the group's combat loss rate had become the lowest in the command, even though its planes had to cover more distance than anyone else to reach enemy targets from its northerly Yorkshire bases. Sir Arthur Harris thought so highly of McEwen's performance at the helm of 6 Group that he lobbied forcefully, eloquently, and extensively to get him a knighthood for his wartime contributions. However, Canadian regulations forbade the acceptance of such chivalric distinctions, so Harris's initiatives were for naught. In the end, Harris was reluctantly forced to award McEwen a lesser but still highly significant order. Accordingly, "Black Mike" was made a Companion of the Order of the Bath in the 1945 New Year's Day Honours List, and King George VI duly bestowed the decoration upon him on 2 February 1945 at Buckingham Palace.

This decoration from the British was far from his only recognition. The Allied bomber offensive had been a truly international effort, and other nations soon recognized McEwen's forceful and dynamic leadership. The French made him an Officer in the Legion of Honour, singling out for special mention the operational efforts of 6 Group during the invasion of Normandy and the subsequent liberation of France. The Americans, as the other principal partner in the Combined Bomber Offensive (CBO), were even more effusive in their praise, appointing him a Commander of the Legion of Merit in June 1945:

> Air Vice-Marshal McEwen has served overseas since late 1942 at RCAF Headquarters and as Air Officer Commanding No. 6 RCAF Bomber Group of RAF Bomber Command. His outstanding achievements on the headquarters staff and as the operational commander of the Canadian bomber group, in planning and executing the RCAF's part in the close cooperation which has existed between the USAAF [United States Army Air Force] and the British air services, and his success in advancing cordial relations between these services have been outstanding characteristics of his fine work. These achievements are a reflection of his effective association with the

United States forces in his previous position of Air Officer Commanding No. 1 Group, Eastern Air Command, whose cooperation between the services was the foundation of their success.[12]

The European war now over, "Black Mike" was appointed commander of the bomber group within Tiger Force, the new operational command tasked to deploy to the Pacific theatre to help the war effort there. However, the two atomic drops on Hiroshima and Nagasaki in August 1945 rendered the planned deployment unnecessary.

Mike McEwen hung up his uniform for the last time in April 1946, after 30 years of exceptionally distinguished service. But he remained in close contact with many of his wartime charges and companions throughout the rest of his life. In retirement, he continued to champion veterans' causes and to contribute to the development of aviation in Canada, serving with distinction as national vice-president of the Canadian Legion, vice-president of the Dominion Council of the Last Post, and as a director of Trans Canada Airlines, the forerunner of present-day Air Canada. He passed away during Canada's centennial year, 1967, leaving a formidable legacy of service to the nation.

RAYMOND COLLISHAW

Raymond "Collie" Collishaw was born in Nanaimo, British Columbia, on 22 November 1893, the son of an itinerant miner who had stopped his wanderings in Nanaimo to earn some money in the coal mines so he could continue prospecting gold in California. Dropping out of school at age 15, Collishaw joined the Canadian Fisheries Protection Services. After a 1911 cruise on the *Alcedo* into the Arctic Circle in search of the ill-fated Stefansson expedition, he went on to serve for seven years on Canada's west coast, eventually rising to first officer aboard one of the standard coastal patrol vessels.

When war broke out in 1914, he tried to enlist in the Royal Canadian Navy (RCN), but hearing nothing from them, decided to apply to the Royal Naval Air Service. Eventually, he was accepted as a probationary flight sub-lieutenant, and was informed that he would become a full flight sub-lieutenant upon successfully completing a flight-training course … at his own expense, a custom during the early war years. However, Collishaw and many of his colleagues were destitute and could not afford the necessary training. Accordingly, the Royal Navy eventually shipped them to Britain and the naval air station at Redcar for some very primitive flight training. Collishaw worked hard, benefiting from the excellent tutelage of John Alcock, who, with Arthur Brown, would later make the first non-stop flight across the Atlantic. His training was not without colour, however. At one point, while attempting to deliver a note from a chum to a local girl, he crashed into a row of outhouses, destroying his aircraft, and covering himself with excrement and toilet paper. While exploits of this nature are the stuff of legends, neither the young lady, nor Collishaw's superiors were impressed. Nonetheless, by the summer of 1916, he was considered a better-than-average pilot, and received his wings.

He was posted to No. 3 Naval Wing on the continent, a bomber wing flying Sopwith 1 1/2 strutters on long range bombing sorties and other duties from Luxeuil-les-Bains, France. He destroyed his first two enemy aircraft over Luneville on 25 October. He was shot down on 27 December,[13] however, he survived uninjured, and was posted to 3 Naval (N) Squadron flying the diminutive Sopwith Pups, which he would use to score a brace of victories.

Collishaw later questioned the wisdom of Major-General Hugh Trenchard, commander of the Royal Flying Corps in France, criticizing his unrelenting call for offensive action behind enemy lines in the face of heavy Allied aircraft losses in 1916 (which paled in comparison to those that would be incurred a year later):

Department of National Defence PMR-71788

Raymond "Collie" Collishaw in the cockpit of his fighter aircraft, 1917.

While his conception gave lip service to the principle of war to sustain an offensive attitude, it conflicted sharply with the major principle of war, "to be the strongest at the vital phase." The general result of this policy was that all the enemy had to do was to count the number of aircraft on patrol and then to send up superior force to overwhelm them. The air war between the contending fighters gradually developed in 1917 and 1918 into a war of attrition. No one can deny that it was the persistent policy of sending out small forces of British fighters to be overwhelmed by numerically superior hostile forces, that contributed in a major manner to the heavy casualties suffered by British fighter squadrons in France. In practice, there was almost a complete lack of imagination in RFC operational control and the operation orders usually resolved themselves into an offensive patrol to endurance, at dawn and dusk. This process went on for years, as a kind of fixed idea. The German fighter control authorities were, of course, fully informed of this inflexible rule, and numerous German autobiographies have since provided plenty of evidence that advantage was taken of RFC inflexibility of purpose, to send up numerically superior forces to overwhelm the patrols.[14]

In April 1917, Collishaw was again posted to the newly-formed 10 Naval Squadron, equipped with Sopwith Triplanes. This little scout aircraft was even more agile than the Pup, and with its three wings, it had a better rate of climb, better flight visibility above, and a very small turning radius. Although Collishaw went on to score many of his aerial victories in this aircraft, he believed it was not without its shortcomings:

> Looking back on triplane history, I now realize that the Sopwith Triplane was considerably underpowered and had it been fitted with more power, the resultant story would have been quite different. Increased horsepowered engines were available, but they were used later in new types, particularly the Sopwith Camel.
>
> Actually, there were three types of Sopwith Triplanes used in the Naval squadrons operating with the army in France. Sopwith sublet the manufacturing contract to

two other firms. These firms produced faulty aircraft with skimpy-sized flying and landing wires; also cross-bracing wires in the undercarriage. There were also two different types of engines used; an English model and a French model, of which the French engine was far superior. It was the bad material types that caused all the trouble and ended the careers of the triplanes.[15]

Nonetheless, Raymond Collishaw soon became an outstanding exponent of the Sopwith Triplane. When he had served in 3 (N) Squadron, his flight had the cowlings of their Pups painted black to distinguish them from others in the air. Now as a flight commander in 10 (N) Squadron, he extended the practice to the Triplanes, and the famous "Black Flight" was born. Owing to British reticence in publicly acknowledging its heroes, the exploits of this remarkable and charismatic group did not become widely known until much later. Collishaw and his four colleagues — John Edward Sharnan of Oak Lake, Manitoba, Ellis Vair Reid of Belleville, Ontario, William Melville Alexander of Toronto, and Gerald Ewart Nash of Stoney Creek, Ontario — flew highly distinctive Triplanes into battle. However, these aircraft were not entirely black, as they have frequently been misrepresented. In Mel Alexander's words:

> I can't tell you why Collie named it the Black Flight, but I have a humorous idea. All of a sudden we just found our machines painted. Painted black to the back of the metal work (engine cowling to cockpit). And the wheel covers were black, [but] the struts were not black, nor were the wings black. Additionally, the four members of the Flight had their tactical names painted in small letters near the cockpit: Black Maria (Collishaw), Black Roger (Reid), Black Death (Sharnan), and Black Sheep (Nash).[16]

Collishaw later added: "The name *Black Maria* was painted in white on both sides of the cockpit just forward of the pilot's seat. I fancy that the letters were about three inches high. The idea of the Black Flight was in affinity with the need for distinguishing features. The main reason why squadron markings for [our] triplanes became necessary emerged when the German triplanes appeared on the scene."[17] And Mel Alexander continued: "Perhaps Collie called his machine *Black Maria* because he knew something about Black Marias [police cars]. Probably in some of his mischievous days, he'd been in one!"[18]

The honours for being one of the highest scoring small units on the Western Front during the bloody summer of 1917 must surely go the Black Flight of Naval 10. Flying many war sorties during the Messines offensive, their opposite numbers were the cream of the German Air Force, including von Richthofen's Flying Circus, *Jagdgeschwader 1*, and they soon locked in a form of ferocious, unrelenting combat. In two months, from 1 June until 27 July, Collie alone claimed 30 enemy aircraft destroyed, all but six of them Albatros scouts. Double and even triple victory days became regular events for him. On 15 June he accounted for four enemy aircraft, and three weeks later, on 6 July, he was credited with six victories in one engagement near Menin. Yet his accomplishments were only part of a larger whole, since collectively, Black Flight was credited with a remarkable 68 enemy aircraft during the period against a loss of only two of its own.

Great War aerial combat had become very dynamic by 1917, stressful and demanding, particularly during periods of intense activity. Collishaw later reflected upon some of the tactical fundamentals of the day, as he subsequently remembered them:

> It was commonplace for contending antagonists to meet "head-on." This introduced the most hair-raising experience for fighter pilots. At a distance apart of about 1200 feet, both opponents would open fire. Each pilot could see his own and his opponent's tracer bullets intermingling, and he could feel his aircraft shudder from the impact of bullets, while the near misses reacted harshly upon his ears. In about 3 1/2 seconds of fire, the intervening 1200 foot interval was covered and the contending pilots tried to dodge collision, over or under. There was no rule of the air. Escaping collision, each pilot had the same idea, how quickest to turn about and get on the other fellow's tail. Almost invariably, this resulted in another head-on encounter. A so-called "air dogfight" was the most exciting experience possible to the contestants. Dozens of waltzing couples could be seen in all directions. If one contender became disengaged and saw a likely opponent, it was highly likely that still another intervener would assault him

from the rear. No individual could do more than dodge his attackers and attack in turn. As the contending adversaries approached one another, each was possessed of the same idea, how to get on the other fellow's defenseless tail and at the same time, prevent the other fellow from doing it. Thus, when opposing air fighters met, it almost invariably resulted in a waltzing match. Tightly gripping his opponent in a spinning waltz and sharply banked, each pilot could watch one another's face closely.[19]

Black Flight's fabled luck could not hold out forever. On 26 June, after attaining six official victories, Nash was the first of the original group to fall when he became *Leutnant* Karl Allmenröder's 30th victory. Allmenröder was a high scoring ace with *Jasta 11* at the time, but Nash cheated death and became a prisoner of war. Sharnan was also lost on 22 July, shot down and killed by ground fire. He had scored seven out of his wartime total of eight victories while flying with Black Flight, and had been awarded a Bar to his Distinguished Service Cross (DSC), won during a previous tour. Ellis Reid scored 19 times during the period, and was awarded the Distinguished Service Cross and Mentioned in Dispatches (MiD) for his remarkable string of victories. Mel Alexander claimed eight times as a member of Black Flight, and four times later in the year. Before the war ended, he had amassed 23 confirmed victories and had also been awarded the Distinguished Service Cross. He had also accumulated 557 hours of flying time, many of them involving combat.

Mel Alexander's praise for Collishaw's leadership was unqualified, and he strongly believed that one of the keys to their collective success was Collishaw's inherent ability to keep a positive attitude, even when the going got rough: "This fellow Collishaw: I never saw him down, never once. No matter how bad things were — and they were pretty bad sometimes — he could keep built up. That was his long suit. Talk? He could talk his head off. Laugh? He was a wonderful fellow."[20]

By mid-summer Raymond Collishaw was a man in need of a respite from combat, so, festooned with decorations, including the French Croix de Guerre, the first of his two wartime MiDs, a DSC and, in August, the Distinguished Service Order (DSO), he was ordered back to Canada on leave. He would be back.

In late autumn, he returned to the front taking command of a succession of Sopwith Camel units, but he was initially ordered not to fly in combat. However, he was a charismatic leader and an inspiration to others. He made it a point of flying with new pilots, letting them spray bullets at relatively innocuous enemy two-seaters, and then, with little effort on his behalf, slipping in to firing position and downing the enemy aircraft. He would then selflessly slap the newcomer on the back and congratulate them on their first aerial victory.[21]

Finally being permitted to settle in at the helm of 203 Squadron RAF [after the amalgamation of the Royal Flying Corps (RFC) and the Royal Naval Air Service (RNAS) in April 1918], this second combat tour was also very successful for Collishaw. He racked up a at least 19 more confirmed victories during 1918, bringing him into a second place tie with the great Irish ace, Edward "Mick" Mannock on the overall empire scoring list with 61 aerial victories, though two of Collishaw's victories came in Russia in 1919]. He would add more honours, including the new Distinguished Flying Cross (DFC), another MiD, and a Bar to his DSO. The citation for the latter is a splendid testimonial to his skill and daring as a fighter pilot, and to his superb leadership skills:

> A brilliant squadron leader of exceptional daring who has destroyed 51 [at the time of award recommendation] enemy machines. Early one morning, he, with another pilot, attacked an enemy aerodrome. Seeing three machines brought out of a burning hangar, he dived three times, firing bursts at these from a very low altitude, and dropping bombs on the living quarters. He then saw an enemy aeroplane descending over the aerodrome; he attacked it and drove it down in flames. Later, when returning from a reconnaissance of the damaged hangars, he was attacked by three Albatros scouts, who pursued him to our lines, when he turned and attacked one, which fell out of control and crashed.[22]

On 1 October 1918, Collishaw was promoted to lieutenant-colonel, returned to the United Kingdom, and helped form the embryonic Canadian Air Force. However, he elected to remain in the RAF after the war, and in 1919, he led 47 Squadron to south Russia, assisting the White Russians against the Bolshevik revolution. There he shot down a further two Albatros scouts of the Red Air Force, bombed Bolshevik troops, and facilities, was awarded three tsarist Russian decorations, and appointed an Officer of the Order of the British Empire by Britain. Still, the Allied intervention in Russia was ultimately unsuccessful, and after many harrowing experiences, Collishaw escaped to the Crimea in January 1920.

He was then posted to Mesopotamia [Iraq] in command of 30 Squadron, operating against the Bolsheviks over Kurdistan, and for distinguished service in this theatre, he was awarded a third Mention in Dispatches. Many more adventures followed between the wars, as he steadily climbed the RAF ladder of rank and responsibility.

By 1939, Ray Collishaw was an air commodore and the AOC Egypt Group (No. 202 Group) in charge of RAF units in North Africa. From the war's outbreak in September, Collishaw and his command would concentrate on a strategy and the concomitant tactics designed to neutralize the Italian air force (*Regia Aeronautica*), and to gain air superiority in North Africa. This was a tall order, since all Collishaw's force had at its disposal was antiquated Gloster Gladiator biplane fighters and Vickers Wellesley bombers. However, from day one of the war, Collishaw's men were quick off the mark, attacking an enemy airfield and destroying 18 of their aircraft, for a loss of just three of their own. Further innovative attacks soon followed, designed to hold up Axis reinforcement of North Africa. They bombed enemy harbours, troop concentrations, and ships, which resulted, among other things, in the destruction of the Italian cruiser *San Giorgio* and a significant ammunition dump. Although Collishaw's forces were badly outgunned and outnumbered by the Italians, he offset these shortcomings through his expert advice to his staff and aircrews on aerial tactics, including aggressive offensive posturing and the use of wily deception tactics. For example, he had but one modern Hawker Hurricane fighter at his disposal. However, "he made the best of it by constantly moving it from base to base and letting the Italians see it. He came up with the idea of making many single-plane attacks on Italian formations to fool the Italians into thinking he had many Hurricanes. The result was that the Italians spread their superior fighters thinly across North Africa, and that seriously diluted their strength."[23] These innovative and aggressive tactics by Collishaw would later cause him to be referred to by Marshal of the Royal Air Force Lord (Arthur W.) Tedder as "the very epitome of the offensive spirit."[24]

However, by September 1940, the Italians had become somewhat more organized, and under the command of General Graziani, they commenced a ponderous offensive from Libya into western Egypt. British forces reacted with a strategic withdrawal. Collishaw's forces all the while harassed the Italians, forcing them to maintain wasteful, standing patrols over their fortifications. These attacks lowered Italian morale significantly.

Eventually, more modern reinforcements arrived for Collishaw's group in the form of Vickers Wellington bombers and two full squadrons of Hawker Hurricane fighters. Again, through the use of innovative harassment attacks, his crews took the Italians completely by surprise during Operation Compass, what was to be a reconnaissance in force around Sidi Barrani. However, the resounding success of these attacks, coupled with the significant ground gains of Major-General R.N. O'Connor, spurred the ground forces of the 7th Armoured Division even deeper into western Egypt and Libya. In the words of noted British historian John Terraine, "the cooperation between these two ardent spirits was never less than admirable."[25]

Due in no small measure to 202 Group's successful strafing of the enemy's rear areas and lines of communication, the British were eventually able to capture Benghazi and its rich cluster of airfields. Collishaw was in total charge of the air campaign, and the air attacks established complete moral ascendancy over the enemy, so much so that the *Regia Aeronautica* made no effective contribution to the fighting. When the final sums were done for Operation Compass, 10 Italian divisions had been destroyed, 20 generals, and 130,000 enemy soldiers were captured, and over 1,200 enemy aircraft were either destroyed or captured.

Nonetheless, the Germans belatedly acknowledged the strategic importance of North Africa, and sent a young "up and coming" general named Erwin Rommel to re-take and secure the region for the Axis powers. Thus began a protracted series of enemy offensives, which Collishaw and his limited air assets tried to stymie and delay. During this dismal period for the Allies, Collishaw handled his under-resourced command with great skill, enthusiasm, and courage, but suffered disappointments and, ultimately, criticisms. Although Arthur Tedder as commander-in-chief of the Desert Air Force was a great admirer of Collishaw, he felt Collishaw was "'a bull in a china shop': too eager to attempt every task required in daily operations himself (a practice which left his staff officers 'frustrated and miserable') and too often foolishly optimistic about what could be done with available resources in men and aircraft."[26]

While Collishaw's optimism and "hands-on" approach to leadership may not always have been appreciated at the time, he was acutely attuned to the capabilities of his force under the circumstances. In the post-Operation Compass North African theatre, Collishaw demonstrated the courage of his convictions in standing up to army demands to have the

RAF in-theatre concentrate upon enemy armour assets, and acting as free-ranging artillery. He astutely pointed out that during the 7th Armoured Division's advance associated with Compass, the *Regia Aeronautica* had dropped "thousands of bombs in intensified attacks upon the Division," attacks that were later deemed almost completely ineffective. He concluded that small, well-protected tanks were not appropriate targets, whereas thin-skinned vehicles in movement yielded much more profitable results. Attacks on enemy lines of communication, he argued, were the high value targets and the most effective use of air assets, and the army eventually came around to his way of thinking.[27]

In July 1942, Ray Collishaw was recalled to Britain, promoted to air vice-marshal, and given command of 14 Group, Fighter Command, responsible for the defence of Scotland and Scapa Flow. However, as it materialized, by mid-1942, the Germans had other significant problems in Europe and raiding Scapa Flow was not one of their priorities. Within a year, he was officially retired from the RAF, and although he had been appointed a Companion of the Most Excellent Order of the Bath (CB) "in recognition of the successful combined operations in the Middle East"[28] back in 1941, it is unlikely this gallant gentleman would have voluntarily retired during the middle of a shooting war. Rather, it appears to have been an embarrassing oversight on the part of the Royal Air Force.

Once back in Canada, Collishaw continued to serve as a regional air liaison officer with the civil defence organization for the rest of the war. After the cessation of hostilities, he returned to British Columbia, became a successful partner in a mining company and a historical writer. His memoirs, entitled *Air Command, a Fighting Pilot's Story*, were published in 1973, and before he passed away on 28 September 1976, he had been inducted into both the British Columbia and the Canadian Aviation Halls of Fame. In his later years, he had this to say about his Great War service:

> I felt that my days of command in North Africa, when we had to depend upon superior strategy, deception and fighting spirit, faced with a numerically — superior enemy, represented by far my best effort. Yet if I am known at all to my fellow Canadians, it is through more carefree days, when, as a fighter pilot, with the limited responsibilities of a flight commander of a squadron in France, I had the good fortune to shoot down a number of the enemy without in turn being killed.[29]

Given his own laconic assessment of his Great War aerial combat contributions, no one will ever accuse Raymond Collishaw of being a master of the overstatement.

LEONARD JOSEPH BIRCHALL

Leonard Joseph Birchall was born on 6 July 1915 in St. Catharines, Ontario. After initial service in the Royal Canadian Corps of Signals, he joined the RCAF in 1937 to train as a pilot. He was eventually assigned to coastal reconnaissance duties, flying Supermarine Stranraer flying boats with No. 5 Squadron out of Dartmouth, Nova Scotia. However, he was actually flying the antediluvian, although sound and dependable, "Strannies" on defensive patrols several months before the commencement of hostilities. Once war was declared, he regularly flew the biplanes on convoy and anti-submarine patrols around the coastal waters of Nova Scotia:

> In May 1940, the intelligence word was that Italy would soon declare war on Canada. Since a number of Italian merchant ships were still in Canadian waters, certain precautions were taken. On 1 June 1940, Birchall took off from Gaspé with orders to intercept and shadow the Capo Lena, which was churning down the St. Lawrence near Anticosti Island. Interception was made and the vessel kept under surveillance until nightfall, when Birchall and his crew returned to Gaspé. The next day, the ship had reached the Gulf of St. Lawrence, much closer to the sanctuary of the high seas, when Birchall made contact once more. No word was received about a declaration of war, so at nightfall, Birchall flew back to his base. Responsibility for the Capo Lena was turned over to the Royal Canadian Navy.
>
> In the early hours of 10 June 1940, Birchall and his crew were alerted for takeoff. They were airborne when they received the expected message: Italy had declared war on Canada. This turn of events increased the fliers' interest in Italian shipping generally, and specifically, in another Italian freighter, the Capo Nola. The Capo Nola had left Québec City and was making a run for the

Atlantic. Birchall and his crew were assigned to stop it. Near Big Bic Island, the freighter was spotted. The captain of the Capo Nola also spotted the Stranraer bearing down on his ship, and so, without further ado, he ran it aground and set fire to it. Birchall landed nearby as a small RCN vessel arrived on the scene. The Canadian sailors put a landing party on the Italian vessel to put out the fire. Birchall took off and radioed back to base what had occurred. This air force to navy cooperation had netted the first Italian prisoners of war for Canada.[30]

Shortly thereafter, the squadron converted to the relatively modern Consolidated Catalina twin-engine flying boats. Then, in December 1941, Birchall joined 413 Squadron, again operating Consolidated Catalinas out of Sullom Voe in the Shetland Islands, conducting monotonous, frigid patrols out over the North Sea. However, in the wake of the Japanese attack on Pearl Harbor and their successes in South-East Asia, such as in Hong Kong, Singapore, Malaya, and Borneo, 413 Squadron was sent to Ceylon, present-day Sri Lanka, with Squadron Leader Leonard Birchall appointed as the acting commanding officer of the squadron, to provide a reconnaissance force for the strategically vital island and the Royal Navy's Eastern Fleet under Admiral Sir James Somerville.

His new crew, now consisting of fellow Canadian navigator Warrant Officer "Bart" Onyette and seven British members of the Royal Air Force, had actually assembled for duty at Pembroke Dock in South Wales in March, where their Catalina was being fitted for the tropics. At least they would now be warmer while conducting operations! There was nothing unusual about that type of a crew mix at the time, even on a designated RCAF squadron of the line, and this situation also worked the other way, with nearly 60 percent of all wartime members of the RCAF being posted to RAF squadrons. However, when they departed Pembroke Dock, they had not yet flown together operationally as a crew and they were virtual strangers to each other. The outward flight to Ceylon would take 14 days, routed as it was through Gibraltar, Cairo, and Karachi.

They eventually arrived at Koggala in Ceylon on the afternoon of 2 April 1942. The next day was spent settling into their new surroundings. On 4 April, Birchall and his crew were scheduled for a day familiarization trip that would take them to Addu Atoll, a Royal Navy base some 680 miles southwest of Ceylon. The plan was to remain there overnight, then return to Ceylon the next day. However, a Dutch crew that had been scheduled originally with a war patrol mission out of Koggala on the 4th unexpectedly cancelled, and Birchall was asked to mount the patrol in their place. He agreed to do so:

> There was nothing special about the briefing the crew of Catalina QL — A received for their mission on 4 April 1942 — a flight to patrol a patch of the Indian Ocean, starting about 250 miles southeast of Ceylon. [It was] the kind of op 413 Squadron had flown many times in the North Atlantic and the Norwegian Sea from the squadron's former base at Sullom Voe in the Shetland Islands. On his first sortie out of the squadron's new home at Koggala, the skipper, S/L Leonard Birchall, expected to be back at base in less than 24 hours.
>
> It didn't turn out that way.
>
> By early evening, three of the crew would be dead. All of the others would be on a Japanese destroyer, beginning an odyssey described in a book by the late Canadian journalist Dave McIntosh as "three-and-a-half years of hell on earth."[31]

Unbeknownst to Birchall and his crew, the Japanese First Air Fleet, under the command of Vice-Admiral Chuichi Nagumo, was steaming towards Ceylon. This powerful force, which had previously attacked Pearl Harbor, consisted of more than 300 first-line combat aircraft embarked aboard five carriers, accompanied by four battleships, two heavy cruisers, a light cruiser, and eight destroyers. At the time, the primary purpose of this flotilla, in a war tasking known as Operation "C," was to help secure the Japanese western flank, including the sea route from Singapore to Rangoon, Burma, by striking at British naval assets and bases in the Indian Ocean, including the port of Colombo on Ceylon. It was, however, an attack or a raid, and not a planned invasion at this particular time.

After takeoff before daylight, the flight to their designated patrol area was uneventful, as was the cross-over patrol pattern itself. While thus engaged, the crew received word from Colombo to extend their patrol further south. At around 1600 hours, with dusk approaching, they were just about to turn towards home when navigator Onyette, asked "Birch" to fly an additional cross-over pattern so he could obtain a two-position navigational line fix and calculate an accurate return heading to "home plate." This was accomplished, and Onyette determined that they were then 350 miles south of Ceylon. Just as they were altering course to head home, Sergeant L.A. Colarossi, manning the aircraft's port observation blister, spotted a speck on the distant southern horizon:

> Believing that it could be a ship, Birchall turned to investigate, descending to 2000 feet. But as they came closer, it became clear that the "speck" was only the lead ship of a huge armada of cruisers, battleships, destroyers and supply ships, which now came into view.[32]

However, since there had been no indication at their pre-flight briefing that a large Japanese flotilla might be anticipated in the area, the crew initially assumed the warships were part of the British Eastern Fleet, and operating out of Addu Atoll. Birchall later recalled:

> "As we got close enough to identify the lead ships, we knew at once what we were into, but the closer we got the more ships appeared, and so it was necessary to keep going until we could count and identify them all. By the time we did this there was little chance left … All we could do was put the nose down and go full out — about 150 knots." Without cloud cover, the Catalina was easy prey for the carrier-borne Japanese fighters: "We immediately coded a message and started transmission when a shell destroyed our wireless equipment … We were now under constant attack. Shells set fire to our internal tanks. We managed to get the fire out, and then another started, and the aircraft began to break up. Due to our low altitude, it was impossible to bail out, but I got the aircraft down on the water before the tail fell off."[33]

Fred Phillips, the British wireless operator, who had been pounding out a message of the sighting to Colombo, managed to repeat the warning twice before a Japanese Zero fighter aircraft knocked the wireless key out of his hand and destroyed his radio. He later recalled what happened once they had crash-landed into the ocean:

> "It wasn't long," says Phillips, "before we were hip deep in water, searching in the semi-darkness for a way out.

The acrid smell of cordite and burning gasoline filled the cabin. At the finish, with the aircraft breaking up and sinking, Onyette comes up and grabs me, puts me into a Mae West, drags me to the hatch and gives me a helluvva push. I went out of there like a cork out of a champagne bottle. Bart saved my life …

"Everything happened quickly after that. There were now eight of us in the water, swimming as fast as we could to get away from the burning gasoline spreading over the water, and the suction of the sinking 'Cat, knowing too that under the wings hung four depth charges, set to go off at a depth of 20 metres. When she finally went under the surface, we realized that Colarossi, nowhere in sight, had gone down with her.

"As we bobbed around, I believed that the worst was over and that we would all survive, even though it would have to be as prisoners of war. I was wrong.

"The Zeros came back, their guns wide open, strafing us on every pass. Some of us were able to time our dives just as they passed over, and so avoided being hit. Davidson and Henzell, wearing fully inflated life jackets, were not so lucky. Both were shot to pieces.

"Suddenly, the Zeros broke off and left, no doubt, we thought, because they were out of ammunition. Shortly after, a small boat appeared, picked us up and took us aboard the destroyer Isokaze."[34]

They then quickly learned that this had not been an act of compassion. Len Birchall continues:

The Japanese had picked us up to find out whether we had been able to send a warning, and to obtain information on the defences of Ceylon.

We denied having gotten a message away and said we had only arrived in Colombo the day before and had no knowledge of the defences. Despite severe beatings, we stuck to our story and it appeared to be accepted. We were then placed in the forward paint locker where three could lie down, two could sit, and one had to stand. We remained like this for three days following the attack on Ceylon. We were given no medical treatment and only a cup of soup each day.

Following the attack, we were transferred to the aircraft carrier Akagi. We arrived at Yokohama the day after the famous Jimmy Doolittle air raid on Tokyo. We were paraded before the populace, who vented their anger on us. It was not until the end of the war that I found out our message had gotten through and had been of value …[35]

Indeed, the Japanese had decided to carry on with their attack on Ceylon, which took place on 5 April 1942. However, Birchall's message had given the island time to get ready, and the British merchant ships located there all left the harbour and sailed to safety. Additionally, " … the Japanese found the sky thick with British fighters and bursting shells. They lost 18 aircraft to the Hurricanes of the RAF and the Fulmars of the Royal Navy (RN) Fleet Air Arm. An additional five Japanese were shot down by anti-aircraft fire. The next day, the Japanese made two small raids on India, and again, they suffered defeat at the hands of the RAF and the RN."[36]

The downstream ramifications of these attacks would cost the Japanese dearly. Ceylon was not badly damaged by the raiding, and the

Canadian Forces Joint Imagery Centre PL-7405

Squadron Leader L.J. Birchall in the cockpit of his airplane, March 1942.

Japanese had lost enough aircraft in the attacks that only two of the five carriers were able to participate in the Battle of the Coral Sea the next month, a shortfall that greatly assisted the Americans. Additionally, the three carriers that returned to Japan were replenished with rookie crews to replace those lost over Ceylon. The replacements performed poorly when placed in action at the Battle of Midway, which took place exactly a month after Birchall's warning. It is of course hyperbole to suggest that Birchall actually saved Ceylon from invasion, and Winston Churchill, in spite of persistent references to the contrary, never dubbed Birchall the "Savior of Ceylon."[37] However, Len Birchall was subsequently awarded a Distinguished Flying Cross (DFC) while in captivity:

> his timely warning enabled preparations to be made which resulted in considerable losses to the enemy. Squadron Leader Birchall had recently arrived from England where he has had many operational successes … He did not return from this mission …[38]

However, the most arduous and courageous part of Leonard Birchall's war was just beginning. Promoted to wing commander while in captivity, he would become the senior Allied officer, initially of Prisoner of War (POW) work camp Yokohama. In that role, while exhibiting exemplary conduct as the senior prisoner, he endured brutal treatment by virtue of his repeated interventions when the Japanese beat prisoners or denied them medical treatment. His shining example served as a source of comfort and inspiration for prisoners incarcerated in other camps as well. After the war, when his remarkable courage under extreme duress was reported to the Allied authorities, he was given an extremely rare and prestigious "Gallantry" appointment to the Order of the British Empire in the grade of Officer. The citation is well worth quoting in its entirety:

> In April 1942, this officer was shot down and captured after sending out the warning from his patrolling sea-plane that a large force of Japanese warships was approaching Ceylon. Throughout his three and a half years as a prisoner of war, Wing Commander Birchall, as Senior Allied Officer in the prisoner of war camps in which he was located, continually displayed the utmost of concern for the welfare of his fellow prisoners. On

many occasions, with complete disregard for his own safety, he prevented, as far as possible, Japanese officials of various camps from sadistically beating his men and denying prisoners the medical attention which they so urgently needed.

Typical of his splendid gallantry was when in the Niigata Camp, he called a sit-down strike in protest against ill-treatment of his men. On another occasion when the Japanese wanted to send some sick prisoners of war to work, Wing Commander Birchall found it necessary, at great personal risk, to forcibly prevent the Japanese non-commissioned officer in charge from making these prisoners work. As a result, Wing Commander Birchall spent several days in solitary confinement. Nevertheless, the sick prisoners of war did not have to work. Knowing that each time he forcibly intervened on behalf of his men he would receive brutal punishment, Wing Commander Birchall continually endeavoured to improve the lot of his fellow prisoners. He also maintained detailed records of personnel in his camps, along with death certificates of deceased personnel. The consistent gallantry and glowing devotion to his fellow prisoners of war that this officer displayed throughout his lengthy period of imprisonment are in keeping with the finest traditions of the Royal Canadian Air Force.[39]

Following the war, Len Birchall enjoyed a rich and full career in the RCAF. He was a member of the U.S. Prosecuting Team at the War Crimes Trials held in Japan during 1947. His appointment by the Americans as an Officer in their Legion of Merit in 1950 cited that during his wartime incarceration "… Group Captain (then Wing Commander Birchall worked tirelessly and fearlessly to improve the physical and mental welfare of British, American and Canadian prisoners under his command. His exploits became legendary throughout Japan and brought renewed faith and strength to many hundreds of ill and disheartened prisoners. Subsequent to his liberation, he contributed information and material of inestimable value in connection with war crimes investigations."[40]

Later, as a group captain, he commanded RCAF Stations Goose Bay and North Bay, became assistant attaché to the Canadian Joint Staff in

Washington, DC, served as a senior staff officer at Air Material Command Headquarters, and became a member of the Canadian NATO Delegation in Paris. Then promoted to air commodore (brigadier-general) in 1960, he was made chief of operations at Air Force headquarters. Finally, in 1963, he was appointed commandant of the Royal Military College of Canada, where, until active duty retirement in 1967, he served with exemplary inspiration as a leadership role model to the young cadets under his charge.

Leonard Joseph Birchall passed away in Kingston, Ontario, at the age of 89. But his Regular Force service did not constitute the end of the Leonard Birchall contribution to the betterment of Canada. Active in the Air Reserves for many years after retirement, he eventually became the honourary colonel of his old wartime unit, 413 Squadron. In fact, he has been the only member of the Canadian military to date to have earned five clasps to his Canadian Forces Decoration, representing 62 years of service with the air force. In spite of his many wartime ordeals and painful memories, this irrepressible soul exuded a marvellous sense of humour and zest for living, right up until the end. When he was informed that Elizabeth, the Queen Mother had qualified for the award of a fifth clasp to her own Canadian Forces Decoration, based upon her own service as an honourary colonel, the cheeky man quipped that he should go to Buckingham Palace to present it to her, based upon his own seniority with the decoration!

For many years, Leonard Birchall was a strident, articulate and unrepentant advocate for improving the pension benefits of the survivors of the Hong Kong debacle, and those of others who had been incarcerated under the most inhumane of conditions by the Japanese during the Second World War. This was a very politically unpopular and uncomfortable stand to take, since a very different relationship existed between Canada and Japan during the 1990s than that of the 1940s. His many friends had lobbied for years to have him inducted into the Order of Canada, based upon his many contributions to the nation, and his nomination had been summarily rejected many times. Finally, in 1999, the efforts of his many friends bore fruit, and the government, being no longer able to resist, inducted him into the Order. However, Leonard Birchall was inducted at the level of Member, the lowest possible grade, while others not fit to carry his parachute pack in relative terms, or who consciously avoided risking their lives through military service during wartime, have been inducted as Companions of the Order, the highest possible level.

Suffice it to say, from time to time, Canadians need to do a little soul searching to determine just exactly what constitutes heroism, dedication, accomplishment, and stellar citizenship in our nation of free souls; a state of affairs paid for in blood and in suffering by the likes of Leonard Joseph Birchall.

ROBERT WENDELL MCNAIR

Born on 15 May 1919 in the small town of Springfield in Nova Scotia's Annapolis Valley just six months after the end of the Great War, Robert Wendell "Buck" McNair was the middle of three sons. A product of Scottish upbringing and early association with his mother's Germanic family, Robert would grow up to be both stubborn and determined. That growing up would take place in a variety of venues, ranging from rural Nova Scotia, to Prince Albert, Saskatchewan, and Edmonton, and Rocky Mountain House, Alberta. School proved to be generally distasteful to young Robert, and he eventually signed on with Canadian Airways in the late 1930s as a radio operator. It did not take him long to catch the flying bug. Early hops in a Noorduyn Norseman really whetted his appetite, and it was while he was working in Prince Albert as a relief operator for the Airways in early September 1939 that he heard Neville Chamberlain solemnly declare to the world that a state of war now existed with Germany.

> Robert was now 20 years, three and a half months old. There was no hesitation about what he had to do. He immediately typed out an application to the Royal Canadian Air Force in Ottawa, and within a few weeks, no doubt due to his knowledge of radio and his experience with aeroplanes, came an offer from the RCAF of a provisional commission in the service. However, the company could not replace him at a moment's notice. Robert also felt he could not embarrass his friends in Canadian Airways — amongst whom were Wilfred "Wop" May DFC and Con Farrell, both distinguished airmen from World War 1 — so he lost out on his initial chance. Wop May had been involved in the action which resulted in the death of Baron von Richthofen, the German air ace, in 1918.

When finally he was able to be released, he contacted the RCAF again, only this time he was informed he had lost his chance of a provisional commission, and if he joined now he would have to start at the bottom, as an Aircraftman Second Class (AC2), the lowest grade. Robert didn't care how he started, so long as he started, but the RCAF was slow. Everyone was clamouring to join and with the initial influx of volunteers, it took time to clear everyone and get them on the training road. In desperation, Robert even applied to the French Air Force at their office in Ottawa, but they were sorry, they were not taking recruits. He would just have to wait his turn.[41]

At any rate, the war soon accommodated Buck McNair. Just a week after the capitulation of France, on 28 June 1940, he reported to the RCAF manning depot in Toronto. The great adventure had begun. From the outset, in what was perhaps an early manifestation of his independent and headstrong personality, Buck was determined to fight the war as a fighter pilot flying Spitfires into combat. After normal pilot training in Windsor and Kingston Ontario, McNair was progressing through the mill nicely, apart from a couple of youthful transgressions, which his superiors tended to view as demonstrative of a fighting spirit. By the end of January 1941, his flying progress had been officially assessed as being "Above Average" and his flying time had topped the 100 hour mark. Towards the end of March, Buck McNair received his pilot wings, a commission as a pilot officer, and a posting overseas as a fighter pilot. Destiny was beckoning:

> The pilots left Kingston on 25 March, Robert going home to North Battleford. During this leave he visited Mickey Sutherland [an old mentor] and his wife in Winnipeg, where Mickey was working as an engineer with Trans-Canadian Airways. Mickey was very proud of his protégé, although naturally a little envious. Once Robert was ordered to report to Debart [Nova Scotia], he visited some relatives in the Maritimes on the way.
> Finally a ship was available. They boarded the SS California, a ship converted into an armed merchant cruiser. Within a day they had sailed, heading out into the Atlantic for England — and the war.[42]

Once in England, the authorities wasted no time in sending Buck and some of his colleagues to a Spitfire Operational Training Unit (OTU) at Grangemouth on the Firth of Forth in Scotland. By 16 May, he had been sent off for his first flight, and it was love at first sight:

> The first half of June 1941 was an in intense learning period on the Spitfire. Robert was immensely impressed with the sleek, trim, manoeuvrable fighter, as all fighter pilots were. As his flying hours increased, he began leading others about in the sky. He would fly along Scottish valleys, round mountains, and zoom up over them as the valley came to an end. In fact, he got so advanced on Spitfire time he had to be told to slow down. He would then fly [Miles] Masters, so long as he could keep in the air …[43]

McNair's naturally aggressive fighting spirit was nurtured and mentored by the combat veterans on staff, particularly Squadron Leader "Hilly" Brown, DFC and Bar, the OTU's commanding officer, a fellow Canadian, and an 18-victory veteran who had fought in France and during the Battle of Britain. Brown was, in the words of those who served under him, "a hell of a fine guy,"[44] someone admired and emulated by all the young novices.

The next stop for Buck McNair was RAF Digby, where he joined 411 (RCAF) Squadron, his first operational unit. Shortly thereafter, on 27 September 1941, he participated in his first combat during a bomber escort sortie over northern France, and he was able to damage a Messerschmitt 109 [Bf 109] in the process:

> Several weeks later, while returning from a fighter sweep, McNair spotted seven Bf 109s circling low over a shot-down British pilot in the English Channel. Ignoring the odds, he plunged into the middle of them, one German fighter falling quickly to his guns as he calmly radioed for Air Sea Rescue Service help. Then the Bf 109s ganged up on him. Smoke filled his cockpit as his aircraft was hit from all sides. But he managed to shoot down another one before his aircraft caught fire. Down at 400 feet, he bailed out, his parachute opening just as he hit the water.[45]

A short time later, a very colourful character in the form of Squadron Leader Percival Stanley Turner arrived to take command of 411 Squadron. He was an aggressive fighter pilot and leader who had served in the French Campaign, and under the legendary legless British ace, Douglas Bader, with 242 (Canadian) Squadron during the Battle of Britain, Turner's combat record brought him instant respect. He also had an eye for leadership talent, which, as the winter of 1941–1942 dragged on, he focused on the young McNair. When Stan Turner received a posting to the beleaguered island of Malta in February 1942 as a squadron commander, he asked Buck McNair to join him at 249 (RAF) Squadron as a flight commander. By early March, both men were in place on the island to welcome the arrival of the first Spitfires.

Robert McNair would really win his spurs during the defence of Malta, becoming one of his squadron's most remarkable pilots. He flew his first combat sortie in the area on 19 March and, as was now his custom, damaged a Bf 109. Just a week later, he shot down a Junkers 88 twin-engine bomber and damaged two others. Later on, while leading a section of four Spitfires, he attacked a gaggle of Messerschmitts escorting a mixed formation of Junkers 87 Stuka dive bombers and Junkers 88 bombers. In the ensuing mêlée, he shot down one of the escorting fighters and damaged another of the bombers. Awarded a well-deserved DFC in May, the citation singled him out as "… a skilful and courageous pilot. He invariably presses home his attacks with the greatest determination irrespective of the odds. He has destroyed at least five and damaged seven enemy aircraft."[46]

He also developed a reputation for speaking his mind and for providing impromptu leadership, however blunt, when he thought the circumstances dictated. On 25 March 1942, a shambles developed over Luqa airfield when two Hurricane pilots, short on fuel, attempted to land but were stymied by Bf 109 aircraft menacing the airfield. It was then that the senior RAF controller, Group Captain "Woody" Woodhall, another Fighter Command legend, asked for assistance from McNair and his section. In spite of attempting to draw off the '109s, the Hurricane pilots hesitated and balked their approaches to land. By now, an irate McNair knew that he and his wingman, Paul Brennan, were also in danger and running dangerously low on fuel. Buck McNair, who was rarely short of succinct instructions, then yelled over the radio at the hesitant Hurricane pilots: "For Christ's sake, pull your f****ng hook out and land next time. If those '109s don't get you, I will!"[47] Later, Paul Brennan recounted the event in his own book:

Buck's language over the R/T was lurid, and he kept telling the Hurriboys [Hurricane pilots] that if they didn't get down, he'd shoot them down. We were running short of gravy [petrol] and were thoroughly annoyed. The Hurriboys hurled back some affable abuse, but eventually all got in and we beetled off back to Takali.

I still had no airspeed indicator, and Buck had to formate [guide] me in. I got into position in echelon starboard on Buck and we started a circuit. The upwind end of the landing path was a maze of bomb holes, and I realized I would have to land very short. As we approached, Buck called "You're doing 120 now," and a few seconds later, "Now you're down to 100, but I think you're too high. Go round again." I was too brassed off to worry whether I pranged or not, so I decided to go on in.

We were rather anxious about the new boys, but they landed shortly afterwards. Neither had got anything but Buck and I had each shot down two confirmed. We celebrated in front of dispersal with a war dance.[48]

"Laddie" Lucas was another Fighter Command legend who served on Malta. In his book, *Malta: The Thorn in Rommel's Side*, he wrote the following of Buck McNair:

Robert Wendell McNair was ... a Canadian of easily recognizable calibre. He was, by nature, a critic of anything or anyone he thought to be sub-standard. He spoke his mind and never hedged his bets. He did not suffer fools gladly.

[When being told reinforcements were coming ...] over his customary pink gin, [Group Captain Woodhall] confided the news: "'Jumbo' says it won't be long now before reinforcements are here." Buck McNair gave the group captain the collective reaction, "And about f*****g time too, sir!" Buck had a ready knack of picking up the mood and giving it graphic expression.

He was, of course, a first-rate fighter leader, aggressive to the extent of being ruthless, yet inside him was a very private worry which he confided in me — that his eyesight was deteriorating [from a later accident after

Malta] and might not last the war. He lived in fear that at some point the medics would discover his defect and take him off operations. For Robert McNair, in the middle of World War II, that would have been worse than the end.[49]

In late June, McNair was posted back to England, but not before he shot down another Bf 109. Back in Britain, he rejoined 411 Squadron, this time as a flight commander, shooting down a Focke Wulf 190 over Dieppe in August. In September, he was sent back to Canada on a War Bond drive, returning to England in 1943. In May, now a squadron leader, he took temporary command of 416 Squadron, then transferred to 421 Squadron as commanding officer a month later.

> On the afternoon of July 28, while escorting Flying Fortresses, McNair's engine began to vibrate uncontrollably. Ten miles off the French coast his Spitfire caught fire, forcing him to parachute into the Channel. Badly burnt about one eye and with his dingy in shreds, he could only bobble about in the sea and rely on his Mae West lifejacket to keep him afloat. Rescued by a Walrus flying boat, he knew from the pain he had suffered permanent damage. But despite severe migraine headaches and some loss of sight, McNair kept on shooting, bringing his list of kills up to sixteen and receiving two Bars to his DFC.[50]

Following McNair's fearless and inspirational leadership of 421 Squadron, was promoted to wing commander and given command of 126 Airfield at Biggin Hill, the new designation for a fighter wing being readied for the upcoming invasion. Totally focused and uncompromising, he was characteristically blunt with superiors and subordinates alike, as recalled on separate occasions by Hugh Godefroy, another talented Canadian fighter wing leader from the war. The Godefroy recollections occurred during McNair's tenure as a squadron commander, and later as a wing commander under the British Air Vice-Marshal Harry Broadhurst, during the build-up phase to the Normandy invasion:

> Buck McNair, who had completed a very successful tour in Malta, was in command of 421 Squadron. He was a

handsome blond westerner renowned for his outspoken criticism of headquarters personnel. His fearless aggressiveness as a fighter pilot and his natural ability to lead forced the higher-ups to tolerate him. His squadron was the most important thing in his life. He insisted on implicit obedience to his flying orders, which included following his example of bulldog aggressiveness in battle. Anyone he found hesitating, he turfed. Those who stood behind him he would defend, even though he was threatened with court martial. He believed in the merit system, and he had no use for promotion based on seniority. On one occasion, when he was away on a 48 hour pass, a signal arrived promoting one of his pilots to flight commander. Buck had not authorized this change in leadership. With his face white with rage, he picked up the telephone and called Air Chief Marshal [Sir Trafford] Leigh-Mallory at Fighter Command Headquarters.

He was put straight through.

"Leigh-Mallory here."

"McNair here. If you want to run this squadron, you come down here and lead it. As long as I'm in command, I'm gonna decide who gets promoted. Do you understand?"

Without listening for an answer, he slammed down the receiver. The air marshal spent the next half hour trying to find out who had called him. Fortunately, he was unsuccessful. Buck made his own choice for the flight commander vacancy and the appointment was changed quietly at a local level.

When day gave way to night, he became a different person. He absolutely refused to talk shop. He mixed with everyone on an equal basis. If anything, alcohol seemed to increase his tolerance, and he drank just enough to enjoy such carefree moments to the full. He was generous with women, claiming that he was incapable of watching them suffer. For a while, a striking looking plotter in the ops room received most of his attention, but not with a serious intent. Unbeknownst to anyone, the continuous bombing in Malta had opened a chink in his armour.[51] A raw nerve had been bared. One evening in the bar, a pilot touched that nerve. This lad was a new replacement in Buck's outfit and was fascinated by his commanding officer. He hung on buck's every word. While standing beside him, during a lull in the conversation, he began to whistle, imitating the sound of a falling bomb. Buck's smile evaporated. With a lightning right to the jaw, he knocked the lad to the floor. Then slowly and emphatically he said: "I don't find that a bit funny. Never do that again."

As soon as his field headquarters was established, Broadhurst started weekly conferences for all the wing leaders under his command. Broady, as he was referred to, had led a wing in the Battle of Britain and subsequently made a name for himself as an efficient staff officer and a hard-nosed field commander. He openly admitted at first that he had little use for Canadians and Buck McNair in particular. Buck had flown under him at Hornchurch before he left for Malta. As far as Buck was concerned, the feeling was mutual. I distinctly remember the first wing commander's conference that Broady called in his headquarters. In desert tradition, the meeting was held in a long rectangular field tent furnished with a mobile conference table, field maps and collapsible chairs. Broady chaired the meeting from one end of the table, and by chance, Buck McNair occupied the chair at the other end. Through the meeting, Buck sat with his chair pushed back, his arms folded, with a disgruntled frown on his face. The meeting had no particular purpose, except to give the air vice-marshal an opportunity to tell us exactly what he expected of us. His remarks required no comment, and instead of asking if there were any questions, Broadhurst hunched forward in his chair and, glaring at Buck, said: "McNair, I'm disappointed in you. This is the first time I have seen you sit there without opening your big mouth. Are you ill?"

There was a long silence as Buck measured his gaze without blinking an eye. Finally, he said with a smile: "These meetings of yours are interfering with my social life, sir."

For a second, Broady's jaw stiffened, and he glowered down the table at Buck. Just when the tension was getting unbearable, Broady suddenly threw his head back and laughed uncontrollably. Nervously, the company followed his example.[52]

But McNair's premonition about his deteriorating eyesight was bearing fruit, even though his brave heart was driving him on through near-constant pain. In April 1944, after extensive examinations, Air Commodore Livingstone, a Canadian and the chief eye specialist in the RAF, gently informed Buck that his operational flying days were over. They had found about three dozen tiny blood clots, known as a thrombosis, behind the left eye. He was immediately taken off operations and made 17 Wing headquarters operations officer, working on Overlord, the code word for the upcoming invasion in Normandy. His only solace at the time was official recognition of his stellar leadership of 126 Wing, in the form of a well-deserved Distinguished Service Order:

> Since being awarded a second Bar to the Distinguished Flying Cross, Wing Commander McNair has completed many further operational sorties and destroyed another enemy aircraft, bringing his total victories to at least sixteen enemy aircraft destroyed and many others damaged. As officer commanding his wing he has been responsible for supervising intensive training in tactics. The results achieved have been most satisfactory. The wing, under his leadership, destroyed at least thirteen enemy aircraft. Throughout, Wing Commander McNair has set a magnificent example by his fine fighting spirit, courage and devotion to duty, both in the air and on the ground. He has inspired his pilots through his confidence and enthusiasm.[53]

Buck McNair would finish the war as the deputy commander of a Tactical Air Force wing with responsibility for five airfields on the European continent and oversight of fifteen operational fighter squadrons. Postwar, the French honoured him with the Croix de Guerre avec Palme and made him a Chevalier de la Legion d'Honneur.

Throughout his wartime service, McNair had fought and led with great tenacity and courage, never asking of others what he would not willingly do himself. Many of his young charges owed their lives to his uncompromising behaviour, and Flight-Lieutenant Karl Linton, DFC, from Plaster Rock, New Brunswick, an eventual five-victory ace, was no exception. McNair was rarely neutral on any subject, and since he had personally experienced unpleasant forced excursions into the Channel, he was bound and determined to prevent it from happening unnecessarily to his pilots. Karl Linton recalls:

> One time during 1943, we were in a dogfight 5–10 miles inside France, buzzing around like bees with 60+ '109s and '190s. Suddenly I noticed a plane on my tail, guns and cannons blazing, but I knew it was a Spitfire. However, I also thought that the pilot did not have enough deflection and that he must have been on the tail of a Jerry behind me. Anyway, the Spit hit my aircraft, Buck McNair and others saw it, and Buck radioed for us to head towards England, and for the rest to "cover me." We figured later that I was about six miles inside France. My engine was sputtering but I managed to climb to 36,000 feet and put the old Spit in its best gliding attitude. Buck took off after the other Spit that had hit me, but lost him in the haze around London and could not get his serial number. Buck then came back and took command of the squadron. I then radioed twice that I was going to bail out into the Channel. Buck came back on both occasions over the radio with an adamant "No!," stressing that I could glide back to British soil. So I did, and after I had picked out a fairly nice field for a belly landing and positioned myself into the wind, I did not see the concrete columns [camouflaged to keep enemy gliders from landing en masse] until I was 100'—150' above ground and heading straight into the mess! But I was lucky ... I swept between several, tearing up a bit of the wing tips and tail, and finally ground to a halt, fuselage and myself intact ...[54]

McNair's concern for his charges was legendary, as was his characteristic bluntness, though it was frequently laced with sarcastic humour. Arthur Bishop, a Second World War fighter pilot and the son of the legendary Great War ace "Billy" Bishop, recalls one such experience:

One day, while flying over the Channel, Buck ordered us to empty our guns. I didn't hear him. My radio was not working. At the debriefing, in front of the rest of the wing, he asked me why I hadn't fired. I told him. He then asked whether I had reported it to the ground crew when I landed. My reply was negative. I'd forgotten to do so. "Bishop," Buck bellowed, "Some day there'll be a Hun up your tail and I'll yell 'Break!' But you won't hear me and you'll be shot down. Then what's old man Bishop going to say?"[55]

Postwar, Buck McNair elected to remain in the RCAF, and he further distinguished himself by holding a number of senior leadership positions, including command of 4 (Fighter) Wing in Baden Söllingen, West Germany, as a group captain.

He also served with distinction at a western sector NORAD headquarters in Duluth, Minnesota. Before these postings, however, during the Korean War, he had been air attaché at the Canadian Embassy in Tokyo. Posted back to Canada in September 1953, his wife Barbara had returned earlier with the intention of getting their son Bruce established in a proper school in Vancouver. Robert, posted to Lac St. Denis

Canadian Forces Joint Imagery Centre PL-4988

in Quebec, missed the family Christmas that year, but got to see them in Vancouver between Christmas and New Years.

On 30 December, he was aboard a North Star (DC-4M) transport aircraft that crashed on landing at Vancouver Airport. Always at his best during an emergency, when courage, quick-wittedness, and fortitude were required, McNair was

Pilot Officer R.W. McNair, 411 Squadron RCAF, on his motorbike at a fighter airstrip in England, November 1941.

quick off the mark to aid his fellow passengers. Although his clothes were soaked in aviation gasoline, he returned time and again to the battered fuselage to help more passengers escape, in spite of an actively burning engine, the imminent danger of a fuselage fire erupting, and an injury to his own back.

For his heroism that cold December morning, he was later awarded the Queen's commendation for Brave Conduct. The back injuries eventually developed into Mariestrumpell Disease, a calcifying of the spinal column. This, in turn, led to some painful radiation and cobalt treatment in 1956. Sadly, the treatment in time produced a blood disorder, which developed into leukemia by November 1965. Not one to mope, Buck McNair did not even seek to retire. In August 1968, the McNairs were posted to the Canadian High Commission in London as the Senior Air Liaison Officer to Britain. His terminal illness at last forced him into hospital in January 1971, and he passed away on the 15th, with his wife and son close by.

> Robert "Buck" McNair had lost his last fight, but one
> which he had fought and lost with dignity and with the
> same bravery and fortitude he had shown in wartime.
> Valhalla is full of such men.[56]

He was buried at Brookwood Cemetery with full military honours. On 8 June 1990, Robert Wendell McNair was admitted into Canada's Aviation Hall of Fame in Edmonton, Alberta. The citation of entry reads, "His leadership, courage, dedication and his indomitable will to survive were manifestations of his contribution to Canadian aviation."[57]

SOME CLOSING THOUGHTS

What did these four gallant Canadian airmen all have in common? First, they were all proven and distinguished warriors in their own right, and as such, all were adorned with the mantle of operational credibility. They had all shared the dangers of their subordinates and peers, and they all demonstrated tremendous empathy for them. Furthermore, their courage was of the sustained variety, demonstrated time and time again under many different circumstances. All of them also fearlessly demonstrated, in one form or another, the courage of their convictions by either railing against conventional and unreasonable authority, or by challenging antediluvian or misguided thinking, no matter how arduous or unpopular a cause might be. All were prepared to stand up to those higher authorities on behalf of their subordinates, while demonstrating tremendous faith in their own judgment and abilities. These shared character attributes truly qualify Clifford Mackay McEwen, Raymond Collishaw, Leonard Joseph Birchall, and Robert Wendell McNair as exceptional Canadian air force personalities and leaders, men worthy of the highest emulation.

NOTES

1. "Leadership," in *Airmail* section of *Airforce*, Vol. 30, No. 2, Summer 2006, 57.
2. Directorate of History and Heritage (DHH), Barker Biographical Files, Creagen Collection, Canadian Aviation Museum, gleaned from the *Toronto Telegram*, April 1920.
3. Wayne D. Ralph, *Barker, VC* (London: Grub Street, 1997), 139.
4. Arthur Bishop, *Courage in the Air — Canada's Military Heritage*, Volume 1, (Toronto and Montreal: McGraw-Hill Ryerson, 1992), 62–63.
5. DHH, McEwen Biographical File, Creagen Collection, Canadian Aviation Museum.
6. *Ibid.*
7. *Ibid.*
8. *London Gazette*, 8 June 1944 and AFRO 1729/44, dated 11 August 1944, accessed at *www.airforce.ca/wwii/ALPHA-MC.D.html*, 20.
9. A.R. Byers, ed., *The Canadians at War 1939–1945* (Westmount, QC: Reader's Digest Association of Canada, 1986), 285.
10. Howard Ripstein, letter to author, 21 November 2000.
11. Quoted from Larry Milberry, *Canada's Air Force, at War and Peace*, Vol. 2, (Toronto: CANAV Books, 2000), 225. Readers should note that the *Immediate* category awards were submitted for particularly striking or *singular* acts of heroism, and the *Non-Immediate* awards were granted for *conspicuous gallantry*, which was interpreted to mean longer-term, sustained courage or particularly evident devotion to duty in an operational sense.
12. *London Gazette*, 1 January 1945 and AFRO 132/45, dated 26 January 1945, accessed at *www.airforce.ca/wwii/ALPHA-MC.D.html*, 20.
13. Christopher Shores, Norman Franks, and Russell Guest, *Above the Trenches — A Complete Record of the Fighter Aces and Units of the British Empire Air Forces 1915–1920* (London: Grub Street, 1990), 114.
14. DHH, Creagen Collection, Canadian Aviation Museum, Raymond Collishaw, letter to RV Dodds, RCAF Air Historical Branch, June 1962.
15. DHH, Collishaw Biographical File 53.71, Raymond Collishaw, letter to Mr. Alexander, 9 December 1962, from Canada, Department of National Defence.

16. DHH, Biographical File, Creagen Collection, Canadian Aviation Museum, H.E. Creagen, February 1965, from Alexander.
17. Raymond Collishaw, letter to Mr. Alexander, 9 December 1962.
18. DHH, Alexander Biographical File, H.E. Creagen, February 1965.
19. DHH, Collishaw Biographical File 53.71, Raymond Collishaw, unidentified personal recollections.
20. DHH, Alexander Biographical File, H.E. Creagen, February 1965.
21. *Raymond Collishaw World War I Fighter Ace*, accessed at *www.accessweb. com.users/mconstab/collishaw.htm*, 30 August 2006, 6.
22. *London Gazette*, 21 September 1918, accessed at *www.airforce.ca/wwii/ GONG-2.C-D.htm*, 29.
23. *Raymond Collishaw World War I Fighter Ace*, accessed at *www.accessweb. com.users/mconstab/collishaw.htm*, 5 September 2006, 10.
24. John Terraine, *The Right of the Line — The Royal Air Force in the European War 1939–1945* (London: Hodder and Stoughton, 1985), 311.
25. *Ibid.*, 314.
26. Vincent Orange, *Coningham — A Biography of Air Marshal Sir Arthur Coningham* (London: Methuen, 1980), 78.
27. Terraine, 344–345.
28. *London Gazette*, 4 March 1941, accessed at *www.airforce.ca/canraf/CAN-RAF.A-D.htm*, 21.
29. DHH, Collishaw Biographical File, Creagen Collection, Raymond Collishaw.
30. Tom Coughlin, *The Dangerous Sky — Canadian Airmen in World War II* (Toronto: Ryerson Press, 1968), 116–117.
31. Paul Nyznik, "The Saviors of Ceylon," *Airforce*, Vol. 22, No. 2, Summer 1998, 4.
32. *Ibid.*, 5.
33. From *Reader's Digest*, A.R. Byers, ed., *The Canadians at War 1939/45* (Montreal: The Reader's Digest Association [Canada], 1986), 102, in Brereton Greenhous, Stephen J. Harris, William C. Johnston, and William G.P. Rawling, *The Crucible of War, 1939–1945 — The Official History of the Royal Canadian Air Force*, Volume 3 (Toronto: University of Toronto Press, 1994), 386.
34. Fred Phillips, quoted in Nyznik, 7.
35. Leonard Birchall, quoted in *Reader's Digest, The Canadians at War*, 102.
36. Coughlin, 121.
37. In fact, that sobriquet or moniker was given to Birchall by the Canadian press. The Japanese were only concerned with destroying Somerville's Eastern Fleet, and they had never intended to actually invade Ceylon, at least, not at that time. However, Churchill *would* obliquely bestow a great tribute upon Birchall when he was later asked what he considered the most dangerous moment of the war. He replied that his greatest concern was when he learned that the Japanese fleet was heading for Ceylon at the time that the Germans were threatening to seize Egypt. Occupation of Ceylon

would have given the Japanese control of the Indian Ocean. This, on top of Axis control of Egypt, would have "closed the ring" and made the future very bleak for the Allies. "Disaster was prevented, said Churchill, by the man who spotted the Japanese fleet. His was 'one of the most important single contributions to victory.'" *Reader's Digest, The Canadians at War 1939/45*, 102.

38. As per *London Gazette*, dated 18 May 1943, and AFRO 1078/43, dated 11 June 1943, accessed at *www.airforce.ca/wwii/ALPHA-BI.html*, 10.
39. As per *London Gazette*, dated 5 February 1946, and AFRO 280/46, dated 15 March 1946, accessed at *www.airforce.ca/wwii/ALPHA-BI.html*, 11.
40. As per AFRO 443/50, dated 8 September 1950, accessed at *www.airforce.ca/wwii/ALPHA-BI.html*, 11–12.
41. Norman Franks, *Buck McNair Spitfire Ace* (London: Grub Street, 2001), 7.
42. *Ibid.*, 14.
43. *Ibid.*, 18.
44. *Ibid.*, 19.
45. Bishop, 221.
46. As per *London Gazette*, dated 22 May 1942 and AFRO 880–881/42, dated 12 June 1942, accessed at *www.airforce.ca wwii/ALPHA-MC.L.html*, 36.
47. Franks, 64.
48. Paul Brennan, quoted in Franks, 64.
49. Laddie Lucas, quoted in *Ibid.*, 65.
50. Bishop, 222.
51. By way of example, on 21 March 1942, the Luftwaffe scored a direct hit on the Officer's Mess at Rabat at the Pointe de View Hotel. Five local pilots were killed, as well as an intelligence officer. Another pilot lost his sight and a leg, and later died of his wounds. McNair had reached the hotel entrance just as the bomb hit. When he came to, stunned and dazed, he was appalled by the carnage taken in measure upon his close friends. He was a tough man, but this was an exceptionally traumatizing experience. Franks, 51–52.
52. Quoted in David L. Bashow, *All the Fine Young Eagles — Canadian Fighter Pilots and the Second World War* (Toronto: Stoddart, 1996), 185–186.
53. As per *London Gazette*, dated 14 April 1944 and AFRO 1020/44, dated 12 May 1944, accessed at *www.airforce.ca/ wwii/ALPHA-MC.L.html*, 37.
54. Karl Linton, letter to author, April 1993.
55. Bishop.
56. Franks, 160.
57. *Ibid.*, 161.

CHAPTER 7

Leading from the Front: Lieutenant-Colonel Cameron "Cammie" Ware, DSO

by Tod Strickland

> They had first class leadership. Cammy Ware, I think,
> was their Commanding Officer.[1]
> — General B.M. Hoffmeister

When one examines the picture of Lieutenant-Colonel Cameron "Cammie" Ware, the commanding officer (CO) of the Princess Patricia's Canadian Light Infantry (PPCLI) receiving his Distinguished Service Order (DSO) from Sir Oliver Leese, he does not appear to have been a very big man.[2] Ramrod-straight in khaki battle dress, wearing his new beret, which had just replaced the field service cap in the Canadian Army, he looked straight to his front, eyes boring into his superior as his decoration was presented to him. It was 1944 and the "Patricias" had been under Ware's careful hand for just over four months. They would serve in Italy together for another five, culminating in the cracking of the Hitler Line west of Monte Cassino. Afterwards Cammie would leave his beloved Regiment[3] until after the close of the war, but as the medal, with its maroon and blue coloured ribbon, was being pinned on his chest he was literally at the top of his craft, leading his troops in battle up the Italian countryside. Respected by his peers, loved by his men and now formally acknowledged by his superiors — he was a notable combat leader who years later was remembered, in Canada's *National Post*, as "an officer who led his soldiers from the front."[4]

Cammie Ware led his Regiment through three distinct battles, namely, the fight for Villa Rogatti[5], the cauldron of Vino Ridge, and the breaking of the Hitler Line. Throughout, he motivated his soldiers in a style that engendered their loyalty and respect, while accomplishing the missions he had been given. This raises two particularly pertinent questions. First, how did he lead and what kind of leader was he? Second, did his leadership style affect his ability to command? To answer these questions, it is important to examine the context that Ware operated in, specifically the battles in which he led his Regiment. However, before that matter is addressed, it is important that the terms *command* and *leadership* be appropriately defined and understood.

Leadership and command are not the same and must be treated as separate, if related, entities. Well-known scholar Joseph Rost defines leadership as "an influence relationship among leaders and followers who intend real changes that reflect their mutual purposes."[6] The first point to note in this definition is the fact that Rost believes leadership to be based firmly on "influence," and not upon either a stated authority or the practice of coercion. Additionally, because relationships are multi-directional, it must be recognized that both leader and follower can influence and have effects upon the other. Lastly it is worth acknowledging the focus Rost places on the importance of "mutual purposes." These purposes are not the product of one's authority over another; rather they are the result of persuasion and communication.[7]

By contrast, command is defined as the "exercise or tenure of authority."[8] Many, including the Canadian Forces and the former head of the Department of Military Psychology and Leadership at the Royal Military College in Kingston, Ontario, Lieutenant-Colonel (Retired) Dr. Peter Bradley, tend to view command as the blending of leadership and management behaviours.[9] A more recent view, from defence scientist Ross Pigeau and Carol McCann, is that command is based on a structure derived of three dimensions, namely, competency, authority, and responsibility (CAR).[10] This structure is a noteworthy development in the study of both leadership and command because of the importance it places on responsibility — both that assigned by a legal authority placing a commander in charge, and the moral responsibility that is assumed by a leader undertaking the dominant position in the leader-follower relationship.

From these definitions, there are some important inferences to be made. First, not all leaders are commanders. Leadership can be, and frequently is, exercised by those who lack any formal authority. Second, commanders are not always leaders who build relationships or establish mutual purposes with their subordinates. If a commander relies more upon managerial rather than leadership techniques he may not be viewed by his subordinates as someone who is sufficiently involved in the relationship to ever have goals similar to the people under his command. This may or may not be entirely appropriate for the situation at hand. Lastly and perhaps most important, the traits and abilities that make for good commanders may not universally make for good leaders; conversely the competencies that exist in an excellent leader may not be suited to some-one in a position of high command. Succinctly put, the skill-sets used by a commander and a leader are often different. Indeed, the demands imposed by subordinates and superiors will have different effects as well, with ever-changing constraints being imposed on leaders as they move higher in a given chain-of-command. These subtle distinctions are com-monly lost with both terms being used as if they were interchangeable; to do so is wrong. Leaders and leadership are different from commanders and the practice of command. That now being established let us return to Cammie Ware and his appointment to command of the PPCLI.

After being a member of the Regiment for just over five years, Ware was appointed to command the Patricias after a perceived poor showing by the unit during an attack on Mount Seggio at the close of the Sicilian

Photographer Jack H. Smith, Library and Archives Canada PA-166755

PPCLI troops in action near Valguarnera, July 1943.

Campaign. The outgoing CO, Lieutenant-Colonel Bob Lindsay, was "unjustly blamed and fired" by the then commander of 2 Canadian Infantry Brigade (CIB), Brigadier Chris Vokes.[11] No matter the circumstances, Ware immediately began imprinting his personality on the Regiment and rebuilding the unit's reputation. His first days of command were filled with briefings to his officers and men, during which he passed along a farewell from the outgoing CO, detailed the "future policy for the Battalion," and issued a demand for the cooperation of all ranks.[12] Additionally, he undertook several organizational changes, moving Major Rowan Coleman into the position of unit second-in-command (2IC) and organizing a "Scouts and Snipers" Platoon.[13] The changes were positively received in part because, as one of his officers later related, Ware knew the Regiment "intimately and exemplified its great spirit." As well, the way he took charge served to "put an end to the rumours and uncertainties that Lieutenant-Colonel Lindsay's removal had caused."[14] Ware, writing to the founder of the PPCLI, Brigadier Hamilton Gault[15] was immensely happy stating, "I am now commanding the Regiment. I do not need to tell you all that the Regiment means to me … it is a proud day for anyone who gets command. The greatest privilege and honour that anyone could ever have …"[16] Following this brief operational pause, on 4 September 1943, Cameron Ware led his soldiers ashore on the shores of Italy near Reggio.[17]

The amphibious landing went incredibly well, with units of 3 CIB[18] disembarking unopposed following a massive bombardment and seizing not only their own objectives but those of 2 CIB as well.[19] Immediately following the landings, Ware and the PPCLI rapidly moved up the southeastern coast of the Italian mainland. Moving at first on foot and later by whatever vehicles were available, the unit covered distances as great as 145 miles in a single day against minimal opposition.[20] Initially the Patricias and 2 CIB were held in reserve; however, after being committed to the advance they quickly discovered that their main enemies were the mines and demolitions left behind by the withdrawing Germans.[21] Aggressively patrolling forward, by mid-October the Regiment was just south of the town of Campobasso. The advance had been quick, and without large-scale battles or their associated casualties. Ware had spent much of his time dispatching patrols, or accompanying them, moving his battalion forward and demonstrating his propensity to lead from the front. This was recorded in the unit's War Diary, which during the advance to Vinchiatura, noted that "as each coy [company] arrived, the coy comd [commander] was given his orders by the CO."[22] This would not have been possible if Ware had not been at the head of his unit.

On 21 October 1943, Ware received orders to attack the town of Spinette.[23] Following a detailed reconnaissance, the Patricias advanced, crossed the Biferno River and seized the town. The only enemy interference had been shell fire; the only casualties two mules.[24] To a degree Ware had been lucky and it is probable that the soldiers under his command believed that under his hand the Regiment was succeeding at its missions, with minimal costs. This was reinforced on 26 October when Ware dispatched a patrol to the Matese spurs, and retrieved 26 escaped prisoners of war who had been in hiding there.[25] For the month of November, the Patricias and Ware rested and trained in the area around Campobasso. Their next challenge came in early December, near the Moro River and the town of Villa Rogatti as the 1st Canadian Infantry Division prepared to advance and seize the port-town of Ortona.

Villa Rogatti was a small village situated between two ravines, and split by a third. Lying less than half a mile north of the Moro River and dominating the main crossings in the area, it had been occupied by members of the 90th Panzer Grenadier Division who knew their craft well.[26] German armour also figured heavily in Ware's planning, necessitating that Allied tanks cross the river as early as possible.[27] After Ware received the results of his reconnaissance patrols, he also knew that the Germans had organized themselves into a "hedgehog"[28] type defence and that he was facing at least five machine-gun posts. His map study also showed that the Germans could reinforce their positions from the twin villages of Villa Caldari and Villa Jubatti.[29] Lastly, and pivotal to Ware's plan, he knew that the reports of a bridge over the Moro, south of Villa Rogatti were false, and that only a ford existed with which he could bring over his supporting armour.[30]

Planning quickly, Ware decided that he would attack on the night of 5–6 December 1943 with the battalion in a column of companies, using the ford to get his men across the river.[31] "B" Company, under Captain Robertson, was the lead element of the battalion. He was charged with attacking the town from the northeast. They would be followed by Major "Bucko" Watson and "A" Company who would attack from the southwest. "C" Company would cross the river and push through the lead elements of the battalion to establish a defence oriented to the north, while "D" Company would cross on order and remain in reserve.[32] Tanks from the 44th Royal Tank Regiment (44 RTR) would wait until dawn, then ford the river and enter the town.[33]

Artillery support for the attack was somewhat confused. Support had been planned, however, at some point either the division commander

Library and Archives Canada PA-183275

"Patricias" advancing towards Adrano, Italy, August 1943.

(Vokes) or the brigade commander (Hoffmeister) changed the plan, deciding the attack was to be carried out silently.[34] Unfortunately this was not passed on to Ware, who scant minutes before midnight had to determine whether he should commit his Regiment without the artillery fire he had expected. "[W]orried, not knowing whether the Arty [*sic*] was called off or merely delayed"[35] Cammie ordered "B" Company to "kick off."

The Patricias commenced crossing the Moro River without alerting the Germans in Villa Rogatti. The ford that was critical to getting the armour over the river had been left unprotected by the Germans, and shortly after midnight the lead companies poured across. Further downstream the Seaforth Highlanders of Canada fought to gain access over the Moro and seize the town of San Leonardo.[36] "B" Company's advance started extremely well, with the men moving silently towards the town, in marked contrast to the sounds of fire and combat emanating from the area of the Seaforths.[37] As the Patricias advanced, the mules carrying reserve ammunition and radios apparently felt that a night silent attack was not in their best interest and started to make noise. Ware then made the decision to leave the animals behind until battle was joined;[38] he did not have long to wait. As "B" Company continued to advance, the Germans opened fire.

Initially, the fire came from machine guns located on the flanks, apparently firing on fixed lines, high and largely ineffective. Captain Robertson quickly dispatched two platoons to remove these using their own Bren guns, 2-inch mortars, and grenades. "A" Company immediately closed up on "B" Company and then attacked into the town.[39] In approximately four hours of fighting the Patricias secured Villa Rogatti, taking prisoners and occasionally finding the enemy's breakfast still on the table.[40] By 0700 hours, the mopping up was essentially complete and Ware set about consolidating his hold on the town while he awaited the arrival of the tanks from the 44th RTR.[41] At this point, with the Sherman tanks being held up "by mud and mines," the Germans commenced shelling with artillery and mortars that were "more accurate than at any previous time."[42] They twice struck a location just vacated by Ware's battalion headquarters (BHQ). Then the counterattack began, falling on Bucko Watson and the soldiers of "A" Company.

Following their artillery with infantry, the Germans came through the early-morning mist with every intention of retaking the ground that they had just lost, bringing "food and blankets" and an anti-tank gun along with them.[43] This attack came close to succeeding, overrunning the forward platoon of "A" Company and taking its platoon commander prisoner. With the Patricias running low on ammunition,[44] the tanks of the 44th RTR now arrived. Together, the tanks and infantry beat the Germans back using "superb" cooperation.[45] By this point it was approximately 1130 hours, and as Ware continued to strengthen his hold on the town, the mules carrying the ammunition arrived. After examining the situation, Ware decided that "D" Company would remain down by the river, while "C" Company would occupy the centre of the town and "A" and "B" Companies would hold the northern perimeter.[46] As for the tanks, he opted to site them to protect the main armoured approach into the town, positioning them in the "B" Company sector.[47] After dispatching standing patrols to cover the approaches and with his work done for the moment, Ware relaxed in his relocated BHQ and fell asleep.

His mortar platoon commander, Lieutenant Jerry Richards, later recalled the scene when he reported to BHQ and saw Ware asleep in the corner. In Richard's estimation "he seemed to have aged overnight. I thought he looked terribly tired and worn out and I even began to wonder whether he wasn't too old for the job."[48] Ware was barely thirty years old at the time. Shortly thereafter, at approximately 1330 hours, with artillery again beginning to fall on the Patricias, a standing patrol reported that they had German infantry and armoured vehicles approaching.

This time the attack fell on "B" Company, with nine German Mark IV tanks and accompanying infantry attacking with the benefit of artillery and mortars. Under the strong hands of their officers and non-commissioned officers (NCOs), the men of "B" Company held fast, giving ground only when the tanks got in among the houses.[49] At a range of 50 yards, the men of the 44th RTR engaged the Germans, destroying the momentum that the Germans had built, and two hours later this attack was over leaving the Patricias still holding their gains.[50] The Germans counterattacked five times in total, but at the end of the day, the Patricias had won their first major battle on the Italian mainland.

Ware and his men could be justifiably proud. Theirs was the only portion of the divisional plan that had been executed according to design, the Seaforths having been unable to seize their crossing over the Moro River or the town of San Leonardo. Indeed, during their stand at Villa Rogatti, the Patricias had been the only British or Canadian unit north of the Moro River.[51] They had captured over 40 prisoners, six mortars, a motorcycle, numerous small arms and machine guns, and the anti-tank gun that the Germans had brought with them on the first counterattack.[52]

Ware's actions during this engagement were noteworthy and earned him the DSO. By many accounts, he was everywhere. During the initial counterattack on "A" Company, Ware showed up in Bucko Watson's company HQ to ask "what can I do for you?"[53] This support of a subordinate commander and the manner by which it was offered, "injected confidence" into the men under Ware's command.[54] Ware also led somewhat of a charmed life, escaping injury even though he traversed the battlefield. On at least two occasions he vacated a location with his BHQ, only to have shells strike its former position. The citation for his DSO detailed that he crossed and re-crossed ground swept by machine gun fire without being wounded. This "soldier's luck" probably added to the feeling the troops had for their commander: Ware was lucky and as long as they were under his command, they would be too. Ware's actions were set out in his nomination for the DSO, which specifically listed his "determination and absolute disregard for his personal safety" and the fact that he "assisted" first one company commander then another in beating the enemy back.[55]

Courtesy PPCLI Museum and Archives

Brigadier Cameron "Cammie" Ware receiving his Distinguished Service Order from Lieutenant-General Sir Oliver Leese.

In Ware's own modest words it had been "a very fine battalion attack that had been sort of made to order." He later remarked, "that DSO, all it was, was running from one side to another and there isn't [*sic*] much to run to, because it wasn't very big."[56] The war diarist was somewhat more positive, stating "the CO … in everybodies [*sic*] estimation did a marvellous job."[57] After the attack, the plan for the seizing of Ortona changed and on the night of 7–8 December the Patricias conducted a relief-in-place with the Royal West Kents of the 8th Indian Division.[58] The battles were far from over, and Ware now turned his attention to his next task. The Patricias would be in for a bitter fight as part of 2 CIB, attacking a vital crossroads, and the southern lip of the infamous "Gully," in what would come to be known as the battle of Vino Ridge.

After pulling back across the Moro, the Patricias began preparations to take part in a brigade level attack along the road running from San Leonardo to the cross-roads known as "Cider," with a view to gaining access to the road into Ortona. The plan was relatively straightforward. The Seaforths would be the led battalion, advancing to objective "Punch," following which the Loyal Edmonton Regiment (the "Eddies") would seize the crossroads at "Cider" and the Patricias would swing right and clear Vino Ridge, thus giving the brigade possession of the high ground that dominates Ortona to the southwest as well as the vital crossroads that controlled movement through the area.[59] Slated for 10 December 1943, the plan did not survive contact with the enemy.

First, while coordination was going on with the supporting armour, two of Ware's company commanders became casualties. Ware, Major Brain (commanding "C" Company) and "Bucko" Watson were in the area of San Leonardo when it began to be heavily shelled by the Germans. Ware and Watson were in a tank, with Brain on the outside when a round struck the tank, wounding Watson and killing Brain. Ware escaped "without a scratch," perhaps reinforcing the notion that he possessed exceptional luck.[60] Later, as the battalion began moving forward, the Germans again began shelling, this time wounding the commander of the leading company.[61] The Patricias had not even reached the start line and Ware had lost three of his four rifle company commanders.

Ware by this time had moved forward to the BHQ of the Loyal Edmonton Regiment, and was there when the code word "Cider" came over the radio, indicating that the lead elements of the Eddies had seized the crossroads. In fact this was in error, and although Ware was sorely aware of it,[62] the orders were that the Patricias would advance along the ridge; this they commenced to do with their left flank wide open. Ware was livid and felt that the attack "made no sense at all," knowing that "if he sent his troops onto the ridge, they could be cut to ribbons by any enemy forces still at the crossroads and the high ground around it."[63] The flexibility he had in orchestrating a battalion attack did not evidently exist when operating in the context of a brigade or divisional operation.

The Patricias advanced and, after struggling through the late afternoon, it was dusk when the order was given to dig-in for the night. In the confusion of artillery fire, olive groves, mines, mud, and the enemy it was difficult to know where they were in any definitive fashion. On 11 December, they again continued to advance, however the Germans remained tenacious in their defence, using mines, booby-traps, and artillery to slow the advance as much as possible.[64] On their left flank, the Eddies were still trying to seize Cider, while their right flank was wide open as the Patricias had yet to link-up with the Hastings and Prince Edward Regiment of 1 CIB. The Germans naturally worked to exploit this gap.[65]

With his attack progressing at a miserable rate, the divisional commander decided that a change was in order and opted to push three brigades along a frontage normally assigned to a battalion, with the advance preceded by a massive artillery barrage. The necessity to keep the forward troops safe from their own artillery in turn forced the Patricias to pull back on the night of 12–13 December.[66]

The attack on 13 December failed. As soon as the artillery lifted, the German defenders reoccupied their fighting positions. When "B" Company advanced they found the "Germans sitting in their weapon pits waiting for them."[67] Additionally, the Germans had artillery of their own, which they used to extremely good effect, knocking out Ware's radios and depriving him of the ability to talk to his lead elements.[68]

Once again however, Ware escaped without a mark. The decision was then made to pull the lead companies back to the start line.

The 14th of December continued in the same vein as the previous three days, with Ware pushing his two lead companies up Vino Ridge, taking casualties from the artillery, mortars, snipers, and machine guns that poured into them from the Gully. However at this point, the Royal 22nd Regiment seized Casa Barardi and outflanked the Gully, making its defence untenable, even if the German defenders continued to fight.[69] By 15 December, with casualties mounting, Ware amalgamated "C" and "B" Companies. That same day it appeared that the battle was stabilizing and the commander of 2 CIB offered Ware wire and mines to protect his front. Ware's response was recorded in the war diary — "the CO decided not to wire, and replied that the enemy had already mined our area for us."[70] His sense of humour, if now slightly sardonic, was clearly still present.

The Patricias would remain in place on Vino Ridge for five more days while other elements of the 1st Canadian Division fought and clawed their way into Ortona. On the 19th the Regiment advanced again, finally halting approximately 600 yards from Ortona,[71] while the Eddies and the Seaforths moved into "Canada's Stalingrad." Christmas brought reinforcements and the reforming of "C" Company, as well as the gift of a German pistol for Ware from his Scouts and Sniper Platoon.[72] Obviously, they felt both respect and affection for their commander.

The costs of the December battles had been heavy; the Regiment has lost 32 killed and 154 wounded.[73] Just before Christmas, Ware again wrote Hamilton Gault:

> I have not been out of my clothes for three weeks ... The fighting has been bitter and a different proposition from the early days of Italy and Sicily. The Hun's stubborn and has lots of guts and skill. Have lost many fine men and officers but its been a grand show ... The troops are absolutely superb and the spirit is wonderful ... They are so proud of being Patricias and I am so proud of them and I hate losing any of them.[74]

For the next six weeks, the Patricias would remain in the Ortona area, patrolling against a "vigorous and bad tempered adversary."[75] In early March they were pulled out of the forward area, and by April they had been pulled out of the battle altogether. The focus for the Canadians had shifted during the pause afforded by the winter, and the Patricias, along with much of the Canadian Corps, were moved away from the eastern coast of Italy in preparation for their next task — the breaching of the Hitler Line in the Liri Valley.

The Liri Valley lies on the western coast of Italy, near the infamous site of Monte Casino. Here, in a space barely five miles wide and 10 miles long, the Germans had blocked the route to Rome with two well-constructed defensive positions named the Gustav and Hitler lines. After examining the problem, Allied planners decided that the 1st Canadian Infantry and 5th Canadian Armoured Divisions would breach these positions and allow the Allied Armies to advance and liberate Rome.[76] For the PPCLI, this plan would come in the form of orders for the execution of Operation Chesterfield and on 12 May 1944, the Patricias commenced their move forward from rear assembly areas, using the Apian Way to move up towards the Hitler Line.[77]

On the 19th, the initial orders detailing the breaking of the Hitler Line were issued. They called for an attack on 22 May. By that evening they had been cancelled. This would set the tone for the next 48 hours, with orders and plans being issued, changed, and then rescinded,[78] causing anger and frustration among the three battalion commanders of 2 CIB.[79] Initially, Ware was directed to plan for an attack as the rightmost unit of 2 CIB. Next he was told that the plan had changed and he now had to focus on the left. Over the course of 21 and 22 May, Ware conducted his planning in an atmosphere of confusion and uncertainty, even coordinating supporting fires and armoured support only to be told that, owing to the fluctuating nature of the battlefield, the plan had changed again.[80]

When the final plan was decided upon, the Patricias[81] were on the right flank of 2 CIB and the 1st Canadian Division, with the British 78th Division to their right. The brigade plan called for the Seaforths and the Patricias to advance to the Pontecorvo road, and breach the line, with the Eddies following behind the Patricias.[82] Tank support for 2 CIB would be provided by 51st Royal Tank Regiment (RTR). This, like many details of the battle, was then changed after coordination had been conducted between the PPCLI and the 51st RTR, and the Patricias were then assigned a squadron of the North Irish Horse.[83] The area assigned to Ware was formidable, being a triangle formed by the Aquino-Pontecorvo road, the inter-unit boundary with the Seaforths on the left and a stream known as the Forme D'Aquino on the right. The length of the advance was approximately 1,500 yards, broken down into five report lines each 300 yards apart (known as January, February, March,

April, and Aboukir, which was the last report line that also designated the battalion's actual objective on the Aquino-Pontecorvo road).[84] This areawas liberally strewn with wire and mines, covered by interlocking anti-tank guns and machine guns in concrete pillboxes.[85] The enemy was initially under-rated, as shown in the post-operation report written by 2 CIB that stated: "The appreciation of the strength of the Hitler Line varied, but generally, a very optimistic view was taken and the tendency was to underestimate it's [*sic*] strength."[86] This optimism was to prove disastrous during the battle.

Ware decided to advance with "two companies up" — "A" Company under the indefatigable Bucko Watson on the left and "C" Company under Major Hobson on the right. "B" Company would follow in depth approximately an hour later.[87] The attack would start with a rolling barrage that the infantry would be expected to follow. However, even with "about 500 guns"[88] in support of the attack, Ware and Coleman (now in command of the Eddies) were not satisfied and attempted to petition their brigade commander on the night of 22 May. Upon arrival at the HQ of 2 CIB however, they were rebuffed by the brigadier, who sleepily announced from his tent, "no further changes could be made."[89] The next morning, the barrage commenced at 0558, and the Patricias advanced.

Things started to go badly almost from the beginning. When the Allied barrage commenced, the Germans fired artillery and Nebelwerfers[90] into the area where the Canadian infantry were starting their advance.[91] By 0620 hours, the forward companies radioed in that they were at phase line January, a little less than an hour later, they reported that February had been attained.[92] Room for the tanks had ceased to exist, narrowing down to 150 yards for the affiliated squadron, and this was now discovered to be covered by anti-tank guns that were extremely well sited. The infantry companies pushed forward leaving the tanks behind. There was one more signal from "A" Company stating that they "were through the wire." At this point the radios ceased functioning and Ware was left blind to what was going on ahead of him, as the battle began to deteriorate further.[93]

Runners were sent forward to get situation reports, but they either did not make it back or were wounded in the process. Artillery and machine gun fire raked the Patricias from the open right flank. The attack by the 78th Division had either been only a diversion or had not gone off well. In either case, the Patricia right flank was left unguarded. Ware decided to move his tactical HQ forward, to February,[94] as the only information that Ware was receiving was from "casualties streaming back with tales of platoons decimated and all officers dead or wounded."[95]

Ware then decided to move up to March to get a better picture of the situation. In the process of the move his accompanying forward observation officer (FOO) was killed by shellfire, and his battery commander (BC) was wounded.[96] The decision to move to March was a poor one, as Ware acknowledged, stating "I made the fatal error, for a commanding officer, I was too far forward … I was caught up virtually with the forward companies … all wireless sets were out … I could talk to nobody."[97] With command and control deteriorating, Ware moved back to February to re-establish his tactical HQ.

Here, he and his HQ took cover behind a destroyed tank, which promptly came under enemy fire, "knocking pieces off it" and destroying one of Ware's radios. Ware then moved the HQ off, away from the tank, into a ditch. Once again, Ware's luck saved him when the HQ was brought under machine gun fire as it moved to the ditch. The men on either side of Ware were hit, while he escaped injury.[98] The remainder of the afternoon was spent commanding his battalion and leading his men, answering queries on his radios, sorting out calls for fire, and getting re-enforcements moved up. Ware was yet again everywhere, motivating his men, striving to preserve cohesion, and building and maintaining the limited momentum that they had.[99] By this point the situation on the right flank was incredibly confused, with men of all three rifle companies and the Loyal Edmonton Regiment intermixed. At approximately 1500 hours, Ware managed to get in contact with the commander of 2 CIB and report on the state of his battalion. He was promptly informed that the line had been breached outside of the brigade sector and that the battalion simply had to hold on as German transport was now "streaming" northwards.[100]

The attack had been successful from a divisional perspective, but for the PPCLI it was the Regiment's worst day of the Second World War.[101] Speaking of it years later Ware said, "the right flank was not a success, a glorious failure if you want to call it that, because there wasn't anybody left."[102] Ware was sadly correct in his assessment, with only 77 out of the 287 Patricias who had begun the battle being able to answer the roll call at the end of the day.[103]

Through the late afternoon, the Regiment continued to hold on and consolidate its limited gains in the area of March. The North Irish Horse had lost 10 of the 18 tanks that had been supporting the Patricias.[104] Early in the evening, Ware was ordered out of the battle by the commander of 2 CIB "for a rest."[105] His second-in-command, Major D.H. Rosser, came forward to replace him, and Cammie returned to the HQ of 2 CIB in accordance with his orders.[106] Although reasons for the brigadier's decision were not recorded, there is no doubt that the battle and its associated casualties had had an affect on Ware, which the Brigadier seems to have sensed or anticipated.

Accounts of Ware's appearance and demeanour after being called back to the HQ vary in their descriptions of the intensity of Ware's emotions. An officer attached to the HQ recalled:

> After the show Lt. Col. Camy [*sic*] Ware ... came to Brigade Headquarters. Brig Gibson was very enthusiastic and praised Ware for the splendid job that had been done. The Canadians had done what others failed to do. But Camy was heartbroken. "Those were fine boys. They are gone. I haven't anybody left. They are all gone.[107]

War correspondent Doug How, as author Daniel Dancocks recorded, remembered meeting Ware "whose eyes were glazed and understandably so" in the immediate aftermath of the battle.[108] Additionally, one of Ware's own soldiers Sydney Mckay remembers, "I recall Colonel Ware that day, standing there with a handful of tags ... the bottom half of the ID tags. That was kinda [*sic*] sad."[109]

The effect that the Regiment's losses had on Ware, and his ability to command, was significant. Historian Mark Zuehlke asserts that Ware was "broken" during this battle.[110] Zuehlke's choice of words is important, and should not be taken to imply that Ware had suffered a mental or nervous breakdown, but that he had lost his spirit for the fight; that he had seen too many men of his Regiment destroyed in battle to be willing to commit any more than he had to. At the least, his brigade commander felt the necessity to remove him temporarily from command. Regardless of the effect however, Ware resumed command the next day. By the 25 May, the battle for the Hitler Line was essentially over and operations evolved into a pursuit to the town of Frosinone. Ware handled the Regiment in a cautious fashion, lending at least a small degree of credence to Zuehlke's assertion.[111] Following this Ware immediately set to record the efforts of his soldiers, writing Gault on 27 May:

> The Regiment cracked the Hitler Line allright [*sic*] as you will probably know. It was a glorious victory — though as you realize tempered with the inevitable losses which must accompany a victory. I have never seen

troops so thoroughly courageous and wonderful in every way. They were too magnificent … it almost seems the impossible was accomplished.[112]

Ware, had again been everywhere, and had seen the effects of the fight first-hand on the soldiers under his command. Leading yet again from the front, he had seen his men cut down beside him while he worked to mitigate the chaos of combat and inspire them to accomplish their tasks. Following the conclusion of the battle, the month of June was spent rebuilding, with Ware visiting his wounded in the hospitals and hearing their "terrific" stories.[113] Sadly, however, Ware was due for a respite from the rigours of battlefield command and on 29 June 1944, he handed over the responsibilities of CO to newly promoted Lieutenant-Colonel David Rosser.

G.R. Stevens, the Regiment's historian, recorded that Cammie was "sped upon his way with roaring cheers but there was a catch in many throats, for Lieut.-Colonel [sic] Ware had been the very body of the Regiment throughout his period of command and his loss was equivalent to that of an essential member."[114] Writing later to Gault, Ware explained, "I hate to have to tell you though that I am not commanding the Regiment any longer. David Rosser has taken over and I'm sure that the Regiment is in good hands, but I hated to have to leave after all this year although commanding a year in action is quite enough I guess."[115] His time as a combat leader was over. He would later go on to command Canadian brigades in peacetime and head the National Defence College, but his opportunities to lead soldiers in action, using his distinctive up-front style, were finished.

Ware's manner of leading men in combat bears further examination to draw out its hallmarks. What is readily apparent is that Cammie was not a leader in the authoritative style; rather he opted to be more paternalistic, using the "velvet glove" approach to motivate his men. William Sutherland, who served under Cammie following the war, noted that he:

> got the job done by inspiring troops, by quietly keeping the impetus up, by his own presence. When things got nasty, Cammie was right there … Cammie was a follow-me leader. He was an infantryman by intuition, by instinct by training.[116]

Sutherland also noted the physical characteristics of the man, writing that "he was a strong, burly man of medium height — but he always

Brigadier C.B. Ware after the war, Ottawa, October 1955.

seemed just slightly at ease in a chair and a bit rumpled."[117] This was echoed by Jock Mackie, who had served as a soldier in Italy under Ware, stating that "old Cammie Ware, he was … loveable, but he was brains … you could pour him into a uniform and it would still hang on him … But he was a wonderful soldier."[118]

Sydney Frost remembered the "casual manner … boisterous laugh" and "quiet determination"[119] that Cammie had shown while leading his soldiers. That Ware's manner of leading was effective there can be little doubt, as Frost later remembered when thinking of Ware's departure from the Regiment, writing that he "would have done anything for him."[120]

Ware's quiet confidence and luck also played a role in the way he led his Regiment. Noted historian and author David Bercuson related that Ware "bore himself with a confidence that inspired confidence in his men." Going further, he saw Ware as having a "rare combination of charisma and quiet self-assurance that reassured his soldiers … would keep them alive and get them through, or at least ensure that their sacrifices would not be in vain."[121] That Ware was also personally exceptionally lucky in battle probably enhanced this aspect of his ability to lead. Many times men around him were killed or wounded, while Cammie escaped the war intact. Felix Carriere described Ware as "fearless" and "magnificent" recounting a story from Sicily where Carriere had been blown over by a shell, only to be grabbed by Ware who recrossed a road under enemy observation and fire, to know if Carriere was all right and able to carry on.[122]

One enduring aspect of his leadership was his emotional proximity to his soldiers, which in turn may have been a double-edged sword. His onetime signaller, Felix Carriere described him as "a humanist in uniform" stating that:

We loved that guy. He knew the name of every guy in the Battalion and he cared ... He knew my wife and he knew my kids ... After a battle the first thing he'd do ... walk among his troops and comfort them, encourage them, listen to their tales.[123]

Sydney Frost asserted, "The officers and men loved him and he repaid their devotion by his constant concern for their welfare"[124] Carriere went further noting that "he would place himself in our place" and that "he was completely understanding of small failings." However, this familiarity and devotion may have had an affect on his ability to command. Carriere perhaps states it best:

He would do things with the men. As a matter of fact it was one of his failings. A commander is supposed to be in a specific place ... a lot of the time when he was Battalion Commander they couldn't find this guy, because he's sitting with the troops in the front trenches, talking to them, wanting to know how they're feeling and ... how life is and what can happen to make it nicer for them ... He was a person concerned with individuals ... too much concerned ...[125]

However, as big a factor as emotional proximity may be in leading soldiers, for Ware, the element which stands out the most is his sense of personal responsibility for the men that he felt privileged to lead. On that theme, Cammie stated:

When you are a commanding officer, you are responsible for everything that happens in that Battalion and every man and so on ... they are never out of your mind ... You never get a night's sleep ... command entails everything ... You're responsible for every man in the Regiment ... You're responsible for every operation.[126]

However, Ware also commented that this is not a responsibility that can be borne unceasingly.

Following the war and a lifetime of service, he remarked, "You can command for so long ... when you start wondering whether you should put Bucko Watson in because you didn't want Bucko to get killed or

Colin Macdougal who you didn't want to get killed either, or you didn't want all the nice guys in A Company dead…."[127] Not stated, but clearly obvious, is the fact that Ware realized that there is a time to leave, and turn the responsibilities over to someone else.

Cammie Ware's time as CO of the PPCLI highlights some of the best and worst experiences an officer can have. Aside from the history of the campaign, his period as CO points to an aspect of command beyond leadership or management, specifically a requirement for emotional distance. The existence of this element may mean that command behaviours have to be considered as a separate component within a commander that is really neither leadership nor management. The commander that can maintain the leader's touch with his men, while being pragmatic and realizing that their sacrifice may be the only way to accomplish his given tasks is not frequently encountered. It takes a strong willed individual to truly be effective without sacrificing any more of his humanity than is actually demanded by the missions he is forced to execute.

Examined in light of the definitions introduced earlier, Cameron Ware was an effective commander and an exceptional leader of men. However his leadership style, specifically his emotional proximity to his soldiers, may have had an adverse effect on his suitability for higher command during Second World War. This is supported by the fact that he never led a combat formation larger than battalion size during the war. Emotional distance is not built between an officer and his men for its own sake; rather it should be viewed as a means of self-protection undertaken by commanders who know that they may be ordering their soldiers "into harms way." It could be viewed as an essential element in those who are employed in positions of high command. Leading from the front, a sense of personal responsibility for his soldiers, and an enduring emotional proximity to them made Ware an excellent combat leader. That one of these traits might have adversely affected his suitability for higher command is unfortunate. I doubt however that his soldiers would have wanted it any other way.

NOTES

1.   General B.M. Hoffmeister on the Princess Patricia's Canadian Light Infantry (PPCLI) when he commanded 2 Canadian Infantry Brigade (CIB) during the advance up Italy. Department of National Defence, Directorate of History and Heritage, Bert M. Hoffmeister, interview by B. Greenhous and W. McAndrew, 1982, transcript, 67.

2. *National Post*, 28 January 1999.

3. At this time, the Regiment known as the PPCLI was a single battalion. As such, the terms *regiment, battalion,* and *unit* all equate to the same thing. In this case an organization comprised of three to four rifle companies each normally commanded by a major, and a headquarters company also commanded by a major.

4. *National Post*, 28 January 1999.

5. This battle, owing to a typographical error on the original maps, is also known as Villa Roatti.

6. Joseph Rost, *Leadership for the Twenty-First Century* (New York: Praeger, 1991), 94.

7. Rost takes over 20 pages (102–123) in his book to fully explain his definition. Interested readers are strongly encouraged to read the entire section Rost devotes to the topic.

8. J.B. Sykes, ed., *The Concise Oxford Dictionary of Current English: Seventh Edition* (Oxford: Oxford University Press, 1982), 187.

9. Lieutenant-Colonel Peter Bradley, "Distinguishing the Concepts of Command, Leadership and Management," in Bernd Horn and Stephen Harris, eds., *Generalship and the Art of the Admiral: Perspectives on Senior Canadian Military Leadership* (St. Catharines, ON: Vanwell Publishing, 2001), 80.

10. Ross Pigeau and Carol McCann, "What Is a Commander," in *Ibid.*, 79–93.

11. Sydney C. Frost, *Once a Patricia: (Memoirs of a Junior Infantry Officer in World War II)* (St. Catharines ON: Vanwell, 1988), 534–536.

12. PPCLI War Diary, August 1943, Sheets 10–11.

13. Frost, 128–129.

14. *Ibid.*, 125.

15. For an excellent account of the founding of the PPCLI and the life of its founder, see Jeffery Williams's *First in the Field*.

16. PPCLI Archives, Calgary, Alberta, Lieutenant-Colonel Cameron Bethel Ware to Brigadier Hamilton Gault, 20 August 1943.

17. G.R Stevens, *Princess Patricia's Canadian Light Infantry 1919–1957, Volume III* [henceforth Stevens, *PPCLI*] (Montreal: Southam, 1958), 98–99.

18. The PPCLI were part of 2 CIB, of the 1st Canadian Infantry Division. The formations of the Division included 1, 2, and 3 CIBs.

19. Stevens, *PPCLI*, 98–99.

20. *Ibid.*, 104.

21. *Ibid.*, 107–108. The Patricias had lost approximately half of their wheeled vehicles when the ship carrying them was torpedoed while on route to Sicily. Ware was on board when this occurred and had to join the Regiment after fighting had commenced in Sicily.

22. PPCLI War Diary, October 1943, Sheet 17.

23. Stevens, *PPCLI*, 114.

24. *Ibid.*, 115.

25. *Ibid.*, 116.
26. Lieutenant-Colonel G.W.L. Nicholson, *Official History of the Canadian Army in the Second World War, Volume II, the Canadians in Italy 1943–1945* (Ottawa: Queen's Printer, 1966), 292; and Stevens, *PPCLI*, 127.
27. *Ibid.*
28. A hedgehog defence is established to protect a given area from an attack from any direction. In modern Canadian military parlance it is similar to an "all-round" defence.
29. PPCLI War Diary, December 1943, Sheet 3; and Stevens, *PPCLI*, 123
30. *Ibid.*, Sheet 3.
31. *Ibid.*, Sheets 3–4; and David J. Bercuson, *The Patricias: The Proud History of a Fighting Regiment* (Toronto: Stoddart, 2001), 202.
32. PPCLI War Diary, December 1943, Sheets 3–4; and Stevens, *PPCLI*, 123–124.
33. Stevens, *PPCLI*, 123.
34. PPCLI War Diary, December 1943, Sheet 3; Stevens, *PPCLI*, 124; and Mark Zuehlke, *Ortona: Canada's Epic World War II Battle* (Toronto: Stoddart, 1999), 78.
35. PPCLI War Diary, December 1943, Sheet 3.
36. Bercuson, 203.
37. PPCLI War Diary, December 1943, Sheet 3.
38. Stevens, *PPCLI*, 124.
39. *Ibid.*, 124–125.
40. Bercuson, 205.
41. Operation Reports — PPCLI — Moro River, 4–7 December 1943 "Crossing of the Moro and Capture of V. Roatti, PPCLI, Italy, 1944," [henceforth Op Report — Moro River], Paragraph 11.
42. PPCLI War Diary, December 1943, Sheet 4.
43. *Ibid.*
44. "C" and "D" Companies were now redistributing their ammo forward to the troops in contact. Op Report — Moro River, Paragraph 16.
45. PPCLI War Diary, December 1943, Sheet 5.
46. Op Report — Moro River, Paragraph 18.
47. Nicholson, 295.
48. PPCLI Archives, Calgary, Alberta, Jerry Richards, interview by Brian Munro, recorded 28 January 2000.
49. PPCLI War Diary, December 1943, Sheet 5; and Stevens, *PPCLI*, 128.
50. *Ibid.*, Sheet 5
51. *Ibid.*, Sheet 7; and Stevens, *PPCLI*, 129.
52. *Ibid.*, Sheet 5.
53. Colonel (Retired) W.B.S. CD. Sutherland, "Some Remembrances of Cammie Ware," Edited by Lieutenant-Colonel J.W. Hammond, 6 February 2002, 8.
54. *Ibid.*
55. Ware Papers, PPCLI Archives, Calgary, Alberta.
56. Ware interview.

57. PPCLI War Diary, December 1943, Sheet 7.
58. *Ibid.*, Sheet 6.
59. Stevens, *PPCLI*, 130.
60. PPCLI War Diary, December 1943, Sheet 8.
61. *Ibid.*
62. Stevens, *PPCLI*, 131,
63. Daniel G. Dancocks, *The D-Day Dodgers: The Canadians in Italy, 1943–1945* (Toronto: McClelland & Stewart, 1991), 164.
64. PPCLI War Diary, December 1943, Sheet 9; and Stevens, 132.
65. *Ibid.*, Sheet 10.
66. Stevens, *PPCLI*, 132.
67. PPCLI War Diary, December 1943, Sheet 10.
68. *Ibid.*
69. Bercuson, 213.
70. PPCLI War Diary, December 1943, Sheet 15.
71. Stevens, *PPCLI*, 135.
72. *Ibid.*, 136–137.
73. Stevens, *PPCLI*, 140.
74. PPCLI Archives, Calgary, Alberta, Lieutenant-Colonel Cameron Bethel Ware to Brigadier Hamilton Gault, 21 December 1943.
75. Stevens, *PPCLI*, 141.
76. For an excellent account of the battles and their complete background, see Mark Zuehlke, *The Liri Valley: Canada's World War II Breakthrough to Rome* (Toronto: Stoddart, 2001).
77. *Ibid.*, 262; and Stevens, *PPCLI*, 151.
78. Stevens, *PPCLI*, 154–157.
79. Mark Zuehlke, *The Liri Valley*, 262.
80. PPCLI War Diary, May 1944, Sheets 15–17.
81. It should be noted that owing to casualties and a lack of replacements, the rifle companies of the Regiment at this time were operating at approximately half of their normal strength.
82. Mark Zuehlke, *The Liri Valley*, 265–266.
83. *Ibid.*, 266.
84. PPCLI War Diary, May 1944, Sheet 18; and Bercuson, 218.
85. Bercuson, 218–219; and PPCLI War Diary, May 1944, Sheet 23.
86. Operation Reports — 2 CIB- Liri Valley, 8 May — 2 June 1944 "2 Cdn Inf Bde in the Liri Valley Battle by Comd 2 Cdn Inf Bde," [henceforth Op Report — Liri Valley], Paragraph 22.
87. PPCLI War Diary, May 1944, Sheet 18.
88. *Ibid.*
89. G.R. Stevens, *A City Goes to War* (Brampton, ON: Charters Publishing, 1964), 263.
90. This is a six-barrelled rocket launcher, also known as "Moaning Minnie," which fired either 15- or 21-centimetre-diameter rockets up to eight kilometres.

91. PPCLI War Diary, May 1944, Sheet 18.
92. *Ibid.*, Sheet 19.
93. *Ibid.*
94. Op Report — Liri Valley, Annex A, Paragraph 20.
95. Nicholson, 419.
96. PPCLI War Diary, May 1944, Sheet 19.
97. Ware Interview.
98. PPCLI War Diary, May 1944, Sheet 20.
99. Stevens, *PPCLI*, 160.
100. PPCLI War Diary, May 1944, Sheet 21.
101. Bercuson, 224.
102. Ware interview.
103. Zuehlke, *The Liri Valley*, 293.
104. Op Report — Liri Valley, Annex A, Paragraph 26.
105. PPCLI War Diary, May 1944, Sheet 21.
106. *Ibid.*
107. Howard Mitchell, *"My War": With the Saskatoon Light Infantry (M.G.), 1939–1945* (Rosetown Publishing, n.d.), 97.
108. Dancocks, 261.
109. PPCLI Archives, Calgary, Alberta, Sydney McKay, interview by D'Arcy Best, recorded 13 December 1999.
110. Zuehlke, *The Liri Valley*, 293. Clarification regarding the meaning of the word *broken* was obtained in an email exchange between Mark Zuehlke and the author 21 March 2005.
111. From discussions between Mark Zuehlke and the author, 22 March 2005.
112. PPCLI Archives, Calgary, Alberta, Lieutenant-Colonel Cameron Bethel Ware to Brigadier Hamilton Gault, 27 May 1944.
113. *Ibid.*, 11 June 1944.
114. Stevens, *PPCLI*, 171.
115. PPCLI Archives, Calgary, Alberta, Lieutenant-Colonel Cameron Bethel Ware to Brigadier Hamilton Gault, 20 July 1944.
116. Sutherland, 5 and 12.
117. *Ibid.*, 3.
118. PPCLI Archives, Calgary, Alberta, Jock Mackie, interview by Ken Villiger, recorded 22 October 1999.
119. Frost, 271.
120. *Ibid.*
121. Bercuson, 194.
122. Felix Carriere, interview by Tom Torrie, recorded 1987, University of Victoria Library Archives, Roy Collection.
123. Sutherland, 2.
124. Frost, 271.
125. Carriere interview.
126. Ware interview.
127. *Ibid.*

CHAPTER 8

Bradbrooke, Nicklin, and Eadie: A Tale of Command

by Bernd Horn

Command, which is commonly accepted to be "the authority vested in an individual of the armed forces for the direction, co-ordination, and control of military forces," is arguably a very personal endeavour.[1] After all, each person approaches it in different ways depending on their experience, circumstances and personality. It is this dynamic that individualizes the command experience.

However, there is another complicating factor that adds to this individualistic/personality-centric mix. Command is not a uni-dimensional concept. It comprises of three components—— authority, management (e.g., allocating resources, budgeting, coordinating, controlling, organizing, planning, prioritizing, problem solving, supervising, and ensuring adherence to policy and timelines) and leadership (i.e., "directing, motivating and enabling others to accomplish the mission professionally and ethically, while developing or improving capabilities that contribute to mission success").[2]

As such, commanders invariably place a different emphasis on the different components. Some rely on authority, others have a bureaucratic managerial bent, while still others personify leadership and emphasize that component.[3] The best commanders are able to use a balanced approach, specifically tailoring the degree of emphasis on each component based on circumstance, their subordinates and their own personality. As a result, some commanders reach greatness while others disappear into history in ignominy.

The 1st Canadian Parachute Battalion (1 Cdn Para Bn) provides an excellent example of how commanders can vary, even within one small unit. During its brief three year history, from 1942 to 1945, the airborne unit had three commanding officers (COs) each of whom emphasized a different component of command.[4] As such, as will be seen, some commanders have more talent than others in leading troops in battle, while others excel in organizational skills. In other words, each practiced the art and science of command differently — some relying more on leadership while others placed more focus on the authority and managerial components.

The unit, 1 Cdn Para Bn, was itself a dark horse. During the early years of the war Canadian commanders and politicians dismissed the idea of airborne forces as a luxury that the Canadian Army could not afford and frankly could not use. However, the continuing American and British development of these forces and their subsequent belief that paratroopers were a defining element of a modern army led the Canadians, in July 1942, to form a similar capability, but on a much smaller scale.

Despite the Army's initial reluctance to the idea of airborne soldiers, it now undertook an all out effort. In fact, the parachute battalion was given elite status and was widely advertised as such.[5] It was granted "the highest priority."[6] The Army also attempted to provide the Battalion with the best available personnel. "Only the best men," directed the Army commander, "will do."[7] Although only limited experience was available on which to base selection, it was clear that paratroopers needed characteristics such as resourcefulness, courage, endurance, and discipline.[8] The Canadian Army Training Memorandum explained that "parachute training is tough ... It needs young men, alert and clever young men, who can exploit a chance and who have the guts necessary to fight against overwhelming odds and win."[9] But, it was also evident to the leadership that the airborne soldier required a level of intelligence above the normal infantry requirement. "Only physically perfect men of high intelligence and good education were admitted," explained Captain F.O. Miksche, a renowned military writer of the time.[10]

Senior commanders acknowledged the higher standards required of paratroopers. They knew that the paratroopers would require "greater stamina and powers of endurance than is generally asked of an infantry soldier." The director of military training succinctly asserted, "'guts' all along the line" were a necessity.[11] Brigadier F.G. Weeks, the deputy chief of the general staff (DCGS), elaborated, "the Dominion's aim was to develop such a hard striking unit that it would have an efficiency excelled by no other such group in the world."[12]

The Army leadership also decided that all serving members should be of the rank of private and they made it mandatory for all volunteers to revert prior acting or substantive rank to that of private before proceeding for training.[13] As a result, many senior non-commissioned officers rejoined the ranks. The conceptual model was such that one journalist quipped, "You've practically got to be Superman's 2IC in order to get in."[14]

Significantly, the Army tried to make certain that theory was backed up with practice. A very complex and discerning screening process was undertaken to ensure that only the finest candidates were selected for further training. Army psychiatrist, Dr. A.E. Moll, developed a rating system that was used to grade volunteers during selection boards. His system ranked an individual from a range of A (outstanding) to E (rejected).[15] Only those who achieved an "A" score were kept for airborne training.[16]

The requirements imposed on the volunteers demanded an exceptionally high standard of mental, physical, and psychological fitness. Criteria were quickly developed and promulgated.[17] Initially soldiers were required to be fully trained before they could qualify to apply for parachute training. However, within three months this restriction was lifted and volunteers needed only to be "basically trained." This ensured that there was a larger pool of talent to draw from.[18]

All volunteers were required to pass a discerning selection process. Once an individual volunteered for parachute training he was then put through a personality appraisal that comprised of a review of the individual's service record and qualification card data, the completion of a questionnaire, administration of a word association test and a self-description test. Finally, there was a psychiatric interview to overcome. The examiners deemed the psychiatric interview essential to determine not only if the volunteer would "take the jumps" but also on whether or not he would "become an efficient paratrooper in every sense of the word."[19]

Early on in the process military commanders and examiners agreed that "only those whose suitability is beyond reasonable doubt are to be recommended."[20] A rigorous application of the selection criterion was imposed despite the understanding that this would make it difficult to meet the quota requirement.[21] By December 1942, a report from the director of personnel selection said that approximately 50 percent of those volunteering were rejected.[22]

Clearly, the screening procedure was severe. But this was just the beginning. A further 35 percent of successful volunteers were lost because of the normal parachute training wastage rates.[23] However, the process ensured that 1 Cdn Para Bn had the cream of the Canadian Army. On the whole, they were some of Canada's fittest, most motivated, and capable soldiers. A great many were former non-commissioned officers (NCOs) with years of experience.

Not surprisingly, as a result of the strenuous selection and subsequent training the paratroops faced, the Army hierarchy decided that the "Parachute Corps must be considered an elite Corps in every sense."[24] The *Canadian Army Training Memorandums* aptly summarized that "Canada's paratroop units are attracting to their ranks the finest of the Dominion's fighting men ... these recruits are making the paratroops a 'corps elite.'"[25]

The media was even more pronounced in their description of the new airborne unit. "The army picked them out of thousands of fit young Canadian soldiers," wrote journalist Robert Taylor, "who sought berths in the Canadian army's newest and already its elite corps, the first parachute battalion."[26] Other reporters and newspapers were equally impressed. They described the paratroopers as "action-hungry and impatient to fill their role as the sharp, hardened tip of the Canadian army's 'dagger pointed at the heart of Berlin.'"[27] With unanimity, newspapers invariably described the parachute volunteers as "hard as nails" representing the toughest and smartest soldiers in the Canadian Army.[28] One journalist wrote: "They are good, possibly great soldiers, hard, keen, fast-thinking and eager for battle," while another asserted that they were "Canada's most daring and rugged soldiers ... daring because they'll be training as paratroops: rugged because paratroops do the toughest jobs in hornet nests behind enemy lines."[29] Others painted a picture of virtual super-men. "Picture men with muscles of iron," depicted one writer, "dropping in parachutes, hanging precariously from slender ropes, braced for any kind of action ... these toughest men who ever wore khaki."[30] Another simply explained, "[Y]our Canadian paratrooper is an utterly fearless, level thinking, calculating killer possessive of all the qualities of a delayed-action time bomb."[31]

Clearly, the unit had outstanding potential. However, with such a roster of talent, the requirement to select able leaders, specifically a capable CO, was critical. As such, the Army Commander chose Lieutenant-Colonel George Frederick Preston Bradbrooke as the unit's first CO. Bradbrooke was a Westerner and an accountant who worked for a farm implement company in Regina. When war broke out he joined the Saskatoon Light Infantry.[32] By 1942, he had already participated in the commando raid on Spitzbergen and had made a visit to Russia. He also volunteered for the paratroops and underwent his parachute training at the Parachute Training School, Royal Air Force Station, Ringway, in England.

To some, Bradbrooke may have seemed a strange choice. At 30 years of age, he was reportedly the youngest man in the Canadian Army to hold the rank of lieutenant-colonel.[33] But, the six foot one inch, blue-eyed officer was soft-spoken and of "normal stature and of rather slender proportions."[34] He appeared, as one writer described, "every inch a 1930s matinee idol and sometimes acted like one, in the memory of some of the men."[35] This did not seem in consonance with the aggressive, explosive image of paratroopers being portrayed in the press. Moreover, many of his soldiers found him aloof, if not socially elitist.[36]

Nonetheless, on 12 October 1942, Bradbrooke undertook his new duties with enthusiasm and conviction.[37] Initially, he seemed to prove to be the perfect selection. He was a talented administrator in the early days when the battalion had to be formed, training schedules created, the necessary equipment procured, aircraft allocated, and most of all, a role for the new neophyte parachute unit found.

Library and Archives Canada PA-213629

Early days: Major G.F.P. Bradbrooke (right), CO designate, and his soon-to-be DCO, Captain Jeff Nicklin, after their parachute course, England, August 1942.

These were no easy tasks. Unfortunately, once the Army had created 1 Cdn Para Bn and established the process of selecting drafts of volunteers to be sent to Fort Benning for parachute training, it largely forgot about the unit.[38] As a result, a number of serious issues began to appear. Problems in selection cropped up and the attrition rate blossomed, thus, creating difficulty with achieving the necessary personnel levels. In addition, needed equipment such as personal and section weapons, radios, and vehicles, to name a few, were not being allocated to the new unit. Therefore, keen, enthusiastic newly trained paratroopers found themselves sitting idle with nothing but physical fitness training and foot drill to occupy their time. In fact, the lack of follow-up training designed to challenge the neophyte paratroopers once they had finished their jump course, coupled with the on-going problem of obtaining parachutist pay, the unavailability of unit insignia, and distinct items of dress, compounded with numerous administrative problems and increasing questions raised as to the Battalion's operational role, thwarted the development of the unit's esprit de corps and lowered morale. Some disheartened paratroopers even requested to be posted back to their previous units.

Part of the problem stemmed from the fact that the senior command at national defence headquarters (NDHQ) still struggled with the issue of 1 Cdn Para Bn employment. Focused on building a Canadian Army capable of fighting on the modern mechanized battlefield, the problem of what to do with a small, unique specialty unit just did not seem to be a priority. This confusion and lethargy created great challenges for Bradbrooke.

The creation of the First Special Service Force, a joint U.S./Canadian commando unit in August 1942, was crippling. The Canadian component was initially called the 2nd Canadian Parachute Battalion as a security cover name. However, its existence threatened that of 1 Cdn Para Bn. On 1 December 1942, Captain R.W. Becket of 2 Cdn Para Bn arrived in Fort Benning with specific orders from NDHQ to recruit qualified paratroopers for this newly formed unit. During his address Becket guaranteed that "this unit [2 Cdn Para Bn] will see action before this one [1 Cdn Para Bn] does."[39] Consequently, Sergeant Herb Peppard, who had been with the Battalion since its beginning, and 96 other paratroopers, requested an immediate transfer. They saw this as a welcome opportunity to get out of Fort Benning and the dull regimen that was in place. "We had nothing to do so we spent hours marching singly, or in pairs, saluting fenceposts," said Peppard. "We felt," he added, "that we were making jackasses of ourselves in front of the Americans and that we had been put on indefinite hold."[40]

On all levels, Bradbrooke made every effort to solve the problems and he ably battled NDHQ to move the realization of the new parachute unit forward. First he tackled the issue of personnel. He demanded more volunteers and extra parachute training serials to bring up his unit to the necessary strength. In addition, he provided advice on how to improve the selection process based on his observations of the failed candidates at Fort Benning to date.[41] He also worked feverishly at developing a parachute training directive modeled on the existing Canadian Army Basic and Advanced Infantry Training Syllabuses so that advanced training could be undertaken. Bradbrooke also fought for equipment.

Disheartened by the loss of so many of his trained men to 2 Cdn Para Bn, Bradbrooke immediately expressed his concerns to the Directorate of Military Training requesting urgent clarification in regard to the Battalion's operational status.[42] The Battalion's War Diary captured the state of frustration and uncertainty that prevailed. "The personnel," it revealed, "began to feel as though they were lost souls of a lost Battalion."[43] By late December equipment and weapons finally began to arrive.

At the same time, in an attempt to stem any further loss of personnel, Bradbrooke took it upon himself to implement many initiatives from December 1942 to February 1943. These efforts proved crucial in developing and maintaining unit morale while providing new challenges to bored paratroopers. Personnel were organized into Battalion sub-units, specifically, headquarters (HQ), "A," "B," "C," and training companies. This established a much needed administrative and operational infrastructure. In addition, it instilled a competitive spirit and unit identity.[44] These small steps increased the morale and motivation of the paratroopers. "Operation of the Battalion is becoming more efficient every day," revealed the War Diary, "morale has improved tremendously."[45]

In March 1942, Chief of the General Staff Major-General Ken Stuart, informed the Overseas Commander, Lieutenant-General A.G.L. McNaughton that 1 Cdn Para Bn could be made available to the British.[46] On 7 April 1943, Canada agreed to contribute its parachute battalion to a second British airborne division that was being formed,[47] so, in late June 1943, the Battalion's 31 officers and 548 other ranks deployed to England for overseas duty. They were subsequently attached to the 3rd Parachute Brigade (3 Para Bde), as part of the 6th Airborne Division (6 AB Div).

Their new brigade commander was the incomparable Brigadier James S. Hill. He was an experienced airborne commander who saw action in Tunisia, North Africa during Operation Torch as the commanding officer of the British 1st Parachute Battalion. While in North Africa he was severely wounded and evacuated to England. Hill, based on his operational experience, believed that the unforgiving nature of airborne warfare was such that the survival of his paratroopers depended to a great extent on their physical fitness. Therefore, he set demanding standards. Hill expected a unit to cover 50 miles in 18 hours with each soldier carrying a 60 pound rucksack and weapon. Ten mile marches within a two-hour time period were also considered the norm.

Unfortunately for many reasons, many not its fault, the Battalion had not yet reached proficiency in many of the individual and collective battle skills that Hill demanded. Parachute skills, marksmanship, and fieldcraft were some of the areas still lacking. Although a skilled administrator and bureaucrat, what Bradbrooke was not, was a dynamic up front leader or trainer. Lieutenant William Jenkins felt he "relied on his rank."[48] Private Doug Morrison assessed Bradbrooke as "a good administrator, but he wasn't a field soldier."[49] Neither was he a strict disciplinarian. This was significant. The Canadian inspector-general noted that although overall discipline was good, he felt, "Due to the youth of the men they are sometimes hard to control." He added, "The men came in with a little Paratroop complex in their soul, which will be ironed out when they get along side other paratroop battalions."[50]

In the end, despite Bradbrooke's administrative expertise and ability to stand the unit up, it seemed he was beginning to show some weakness in the ability to lead and control his battalion. Corporal John Ross felt he "was over his head."[51] This was not always readily obvious because luckily for Bradbrooke, his deputy commanding officer (DCO) was Major Jevon Albert "Jeff" Nicklin, an officer from the Royal Winnipeg Rifles, who was more than willing to swing the "big stick" and enforce rules, regulations, and the unit standards.

Already back in Canada, 28 year old Major Nicklin, a former Canadian Football League (CFL) star who played with the Winnipeg Blue Bombers, continually worked at instilling a sense of urgency and professionalism. He constantly tested and pushed everyone in the Battalion, including officers, even the company commanders. One officer remembered that Nicklin "punished officers who tried to sneak out of the two-mile morning runs by turning them over to the regimental sergeant-major (RSM) for punishment drill on the parade square.[52]

Nicklin demanded attention to detail and he was intolerant of mistakes. Jenkins noted that Nicklin was "tough, very tough, but he would not ask anything of anybody that he would not do himself."[53] As training progressed, Nicklin ceaselessly criticized the level of intensity and effort being put forth by members of the Battalion. Each week, he drafted and posted the upcoming training schedule. Anyone not directly tasked on garrison duty was expected to participate in the training activities. Even sports days designed to provide a bit of a diversion and relaxation failed to meet with Nicklin's favour. "This is not a holiday for certain personnel to be sitting around, lolling in the sun," declared Nicklin. "This time was to be used," he asserted, "with the view and in mind at all times of developing personnel of companies into able physical condition, which is one of the two prime requisites of our training."[54]

Nicklin's approach was inflexible. He was relentless. Colin Brebner, the unit medical officer who was constantly at odds with Nicklin, described him as "tough as hell. He expected everyone to be as strong and as fit as he was." Brebner lamented, "He'd [Nicklin] drive them to the limit."[55] Each week new faults were uncovered. Nothing seemed to escape his eye. "The condition of the feet of personnel of this unit," he complained, "seems to be in a very soft state."[56]

By the beginning of May, Nicklin observed, once again, that individuals were not putting forth the required level of effort. "Training," he seethed, "has been carried on in a very desultory manner and this must cease, especially under the present situation." He now focused his renewed effort at the leadership levels. "Training will be really intensified at once," he ordered, "emphasis being laid on junior officers and NCOs."[57]

Nicklin worked at improving the Battalion's state of readiness and fitness, even if it was not appreciated by everyone. Private Morrison repeated a common sentiment when he stated Nicklin "wasn't really popular."[58] But the DCO's efforts were important. He ensured method of instruction in the classroom was adequate to achieve the necessary levels of learning. He increased the complexity of training, as well as the self-reliance of the paratroopers. They were now required to cook their own meals in their mess tins while in the field and route marches now included ambushes and immediate action drills.

Despite his efforts, the Battalion was not progressing as fast as it should. Following an inspection carried out during the last week of June, Nicklin, reported, "that not one coy. is ready to proceed to higher training such as collective platoon training."[59] But Nicklin's constant protestations and exhortations were justified. A Directorate of Military Training report revealed that the Battalion was still only at the individual or "trained soldier" level. As a result, they recommended that training be accelerated, "as it was felt [that this unit] to be below Parachute Battalion standard."[60]

Before leaving Canada, during the first week of July 1943, the Battalion was inspected one last time by Major-General J.P. Mackenzie, inspector-general Western Canada. Mackenzie assessed Bradbrooke as "a very efficient officer — energetic with plenty of imagination." He rated Nicklin as "a good leader and as a Training Officer, thoroughly satisfactory."[61] In essence, the character, as well as command and leadership styles of both officers were evident but each supported or covered for the weakness and possible problems of the other.

Nonetheless, Brigadier Hill welcomed the Canadians. He saw in them the making of great soldiers. "As the days passed," wrote Hill, "General Gale

Before the storm: Lieutenant-Colonel Bradbrooke and Major Nicklin in England preparing the Battalion for the return to the continent, January 1944.

[6 AB Div Commander] and I realized what a unique and interesting Battalion had joined us as brothers."[62] However, he was not blinded by their strengths. Hill consistently "kept a tight rein" on his Canadians. Although he admired their spirit he also felt that they were neither well-disciplined, nor adequately trained when they first joined the Brigade.[63]

Their shortcomings were quickly addressed by Hill's rigorous training regimen and demanding standards. By spring 1944, it was merely a matter of time before the Canadians would be tested in battle. The planning and preparation for the invasion of Europe was now in the final stages. Missions had already been assigned. The 6th Airborne Division was responsible for protecting the left flank of the 3rd British Infantry Division that was to land on a beach west of Ouistreham. In turn, 3 Para

Bde was given the daunting tasks of destroying the coastal defence battery at Merville, demolishing a number of bridges over the River Dives, as well as controlling the high ridge centred on the small village of Le Mesnil, which dominated the landing beaches.

Brigadier Hill assigned 1 Cdn Para Bn the responsibility of covering the left flank of the Brigade's drop zone (DZ) and protecting its movements within the DZ. The Battalion was also given three primary missions — the defence and protection of 9 Parachute Battalion's left flank during its approach march and attack on the Merville battery; the destruction of two bridges spanning the River Dives; and the of destruction of German positions and a headquarters, as well as a bridge at Varaville.

The Battalion crossed the channel and jumped into France between 0030 hours and 0130 hours, 6 June 1944. The drops were badly scattered over a wide area as a result of the lack of navigational aids and the heavy dust and smoke that drifted over the drop zones from the heavy bombing of nearby targets. Heavy enemy anti-aircraft fire also panicked many of the pilots who immediately took evasive action that only magnified the difficulty of delivering the paratroopers accurately onto their objectives. On the first drop alone, only 30 of a possible 110 paratroopers of "C" Company landed on the DZ. The subsequent drops were no better. The second group, made up of the main body of the Battalion, was scattered over an area 40 times greater than planned. To add to the problems, many leg kit bags ripped open, scattering the unit's vital heavy machine guns, mortars, and anti-tank weapons across the Normandy countryside. This significantly reduced the firepower available to the airborne soldiers in the critical days that followed.

In the midst of the growing chaos, the physical and psychological toughness honed by careful training, showed its importance and value. The paratroopers, as individuals and a collective unit, not only persevered, but flourished despite the unexpected situations and set-backs. By the end of the day, the resiliency of the Canadian paratroopers enabled them to attain all their assigned objectives with less than 30 percent of the troops and equipment originally allocated to the tasks. Having completed their allotted missions, the surviving paratroopers grimly dug in to hold the ground they had fought for so ferociously. Despite heavy losses, the Battalion held off all German counterattacks until the eventual Allied breakout.

By mid-August, the tide had finally turned and 1 Cdn Para Bn, as part of 3 Para Bde, for the first time since the Normandy drop, was back on the offensive. Commencing on 16 August, and continuing for the next 10 days, the unit participated in an advance and series of attacks against the German rearguard until finally being pulled from the line. On 4 September, the Battalion began its departure from France and returned to its adopted home in Bulford three days later.

Unquestionably, 1 Cdn Para Bn distinguished itself in its first combat action. However, this came at great cost. During the three month period between 6 June and 6 September 1944, the battalion sustained heavy losses. Of the original 544 paratroops dropped, 83 were killed, 187 were wounded, and 87 became prisoners of war. In regard to 1 Cdn Para Bn's performance on D-day, Brigadier James Hill wrote, "they really put up a most tremendous performance on D Day and as a result of their tremendous dash and enthusiasm they overcame their objectives, which were very sticky ones, with considerable ease ..."[64] Hill was justifiably proud of his Canadians. "The battle," he wrote, "carried on for three months till the Germans were driven across the Seine. In this period, the 6th Airborne lost some 4,457 men killed, wounded, and missing. Throughout that time, the Canadian Parachute Battalion had never been out of the line. They won their spurs and glory ... and paid the price. Nearly half the battalion were either killed, wounded or missing ... It had been a bloody battle with high stakes. No quarter asked or given."[65]

Despite the unit's fine showing in its first combat experience not everything was acceptable. The CO was found wanting. Sergeant John Feduck observed "he was no active commander — he should have been assigned to a desk."[66] It was not lost on anyone that the CO was seldom seen among the forward trenches.

This was in stark contrast to Nicklin who continued his larger than life presence. He regularly visited the soldiers in their forward positions. Furthermore, he enjoyed the action and even took part in reconnaissance patrols. "He was very strict," conceded Sergeant Feduck, "but he was a real paratrooper."[67] In short, he shared the risks of his men. In fact, Nicklin was seriously wounded on 23 July 1944, while participating on a patrol. He tripped a wire that set off an improvised mine made of two mess tins packed with ammunition and metal scraps. Shrapnel hit him in the arms, legs and buttocks, and he was evacuated to England. His closest friend, a fellow native of Winnipeg and former officer of the Royal Winnipeg Rifles, Major Fraser Eadie, took over as DCO.

The obvious absence of the CO among the forward trenches did not elude Brigadier Hill. In fact, upon taking over as DCO, Hill counselled Eadie not to leave the CO alone as "he's a bit nervous."[68] Eadie recalled sitting by a slit trench as an 88 mm shell came whistling by slamming into the paratroop position nearby. "He [Hill] didn't move, so I didn't either," recalled Eadie, "Hill was testing me."[69]

Brigadier Hill rated Bradbrooke as "a good administrator, a very good CO in peacetime and an intrepid parachutist."[70] However, Bradbrooke's leadership during the defence of the Le Mesnil crossroads and the subsequent pursuit of the retreating German forces was not up to Hill's, or the unit's, expectations. Hill noted that Bradbrooke lacked the aggressive leadership required to lead his men during combat.

Major Richard "Dick" Hillborn acknowledged that the problem was evident to everyone. As a result, according to Hillborn, Brigadier Hill, who was seriously wounded on 6 June, but refused evacuation, spent a disproportionate amount of time in the 1 Cdn Para Bn lines and personally led the famous Bréville counterattack on 12 June, because of his concerns for the lack of leadership shown by the CO.[71] Hillborn further reveals that in later discussions Hill confessed he did not know what to do about the problem because of the "political aspect."[72]

This problem was later solved for him by Hillborn. On 23 August, during a lull in the fighting Lieutenant-General Ken Stuart, the chief of the general staff (CGS), visited the unit. Hillborn, was known by Stuart because he had visited the CGS at his home in Barriesfield during the pre-war days when Hillborn was a student at the Royal Military College of Canada with Stuart's son. Hillborn asked for a few minutes of the CGS's time and in a private discussion in a Normandy orchard laid out the problem to Stuart.[73] As a result, or coincidently, that same day, Bradbrooke was assigned to a position on the general staff at Canadian military headquarters in London. Major Eadie became the acting CO for the remainder of the unit's time in Normandy.

The Battalion's return to England provided the opportunity to reconstitute itself and prepare for its next mission. The unit's first priority was bringing itself back up to strength through the integration of reinforcements from the 1 Cdn Para Training Company. The general feeling that prevailed recalled Sergeant R.F. Anderson was one of "tremendous relief and of great success and of having survived a most harrowing experience."[74] During the next four days, activities were mostly administrative in nature consisting of clothing, pay, and medical parades. While discipline remained high, the officers and the senior NCOs ensured that the tempo of activity was relaxed and that the men were not rushed. Everyone knew that these first few days would prove difficult. Many familiar faces had vanished. "Out of my company's 120 men," recalled John Kemp, "there were 22 of us that returned to Carter Barracks."[75]

The survivors were well treated. The base staff went out of their way to welcome the paratroopers back home and great care was taken to prepare excellent meals. Furthermore, many day passes were issued enabling the paratroopers to go out on the town, dance and have a few pints. For those who preferred to stay in camp, they had the option of taking in a movie or show. On 11 September, the paratroopers were given a well-deserved 13 day furlough. Before heading off to their various destinations, they were warned that the day following their return, training would start once again in earnest.[76]

As promised, on 26 September 1944, Acting Lieutenant-Colonel Jeff Nicklin, the battalion's new CO had the unit formed up for a special parade.[77] His address was short and to the point. He wanted to command the best battalion in the Division. As a result, he insisted that training would be very demanding.[78] His previous "in your face," harsh disciplinary style as the unit's DCO had been tolerated by the untested troops in the training leading up to Normandy. However, it now annoyed the hardened combat veterans. Nonetheless, Nicklin's command approach was fully endorsed by Brigadier Hill who believed that strong leadership was necessary to ensure that the paratroopers put forth full commitment and effort during training. In fact, Hill's Evaluation Report of Nicklin stated:

> An officer of the highest integrity who possesses unusual drive and determination. He sets a very high standard in the Battalion and is prepared to accept no compromise. He is a stern disciplinarian, but takes infinite trouble to safeguard the welfare of the men. He is a good trainer of troops and is tactically sound in his ideas. He requires further experience in the tactical handling of his Battalion.[79]

Part of the problem, however, also lay in the difference between the old and the new CO. Lieutenant-Colonel Bradbrooke, was a behind the scenes individual and he not a stickler for strict discipline. This was in complete contrast with the new CO. Nicklin was up front and tolerated no deviance from the rules.

"Jeff Nicklin," observed one senior NCO, "was one who almost seemed indestructible, 6'3" tall, football hero back home, a stern disciplinarian, physical fitness his specialty."[80] Those who played football with Nicklin back home "rated him almost immortal."[81] Sergeant Feduck remembered

Nicklin as "a strong commander with very severe discipline — what he did or said you obeyed."[82] Unquestionably, Nicklin was a rugged physical individual, who was feared and could sense fear, recalled Brigadier Hill.[83] In this officer, Hill discerned the leadership qualities that could prove useful to supervise the battalion's post campaign training.

Although Hill respected the accomplishments and sacrifices of his Canadian paratroopers, he had nevertheless learned a valuable leadership lesson while commanding soldiers during the Battle of France, in 1940 and paratroopers later in North Africa, in 1942. The brigadier had observed that "blooded" veterans who returned from combat duty to resume daily training routine showed an unwillingness to "snap to it" and put up with various aspects of garrison duties and discipline. Therefore, he believed that a strong hand was required to once again motivate, closely supervise, and control battle hardened troops. Hill was right. Having faced death and survived, many veterans now thought that they were better than their new untested comrades. Hill identified this type of combatant as, "heroes and crooked berets that had to be knocked on the head and have discipline reimposed."[84]

This post operational mind-set was seemingly now developing within 1 Cdn Para Bn. "Here we have very tough chaps, heroes," explained Hill, "They had to be disciplined. So, I popped in Jeff Nicklin."[85] In the end, regardless of what the paratroopers had accomplished, Hill would not shy away from his two airborne tenets — discipline and physical fitness. There was still much to accomplish and the war was from over.

Nicklin now focused on correcting the deficiencies and shortcomings experienced during the Normandy Campaign. He specifically targeted those skills required for offensive operations. The Battalion had its work cut out for itself. It was a long way from its pre–D-Day level of operational readiness. Lieutenant-Colonel Jeff Nicklin accepted this challenge without hesitation. The men immediately noted the change in the tempo. "The training got more severe," recalled Sergeant John Feduck, "and nothing was let go. Nothing was overlooked." He added that "Nicklin was the type of guy who did everything strictly by the book, and he had his own way of training, making sure you went for your runs. There was no slacking off." Nicklin's training schedule was very simple. "You trained all the time," stated Feduck. "You had no time for yourself," he added, "Leaves were a little shorter and you worked harder."[86]

Physical training under Nicklin "was a hell of a lot tougher," recalled Sergeant Harry Reid, "He wanted us to become linebackers."[87] Doug Morrison lamented, "[H]e was so determined that we would all be as fit as him that he lost a lot of people."[88] The new CO's objective was clear. "He wanted to have the best battalion in the Brigade," explained Sergeant Andy Anderson. "Nicklin had us out on the parade square at six o'clock in the morning," he recalled, "and worked us till dark." The senior NCO noted, "Brigadier Hill was thrilled and he did not object to that." Nicklin really enjoyed the physical part of the training. He personally led the bimonthly 10-mile forced march. As the paratroopers arrived at the finish line, "he [Nicklin] and the RSM [regimental sergeant-major] would stand at the gate with a clipboard," recounted Anderson, "and took down the names of the stragglers." No quarter was given. "If they could not keep up," stated Anderson, "they were gone."[89] Nicklin wanted each platoon to arrive at the finish line as a group.

Nicklin's Normandy experience had confirmed in his mind that a well-trained group that worked skilfully together could inflict greater damage than a few isolated paratroopers. Since the Battalion's return from France, Nicklin inculcated the importance of teamwork in all training to both the veterans and to the reinforcements. He had personally experienced the benefits and results of this concept as well as the close-knit camaraderie that it fostered during his tenure with the CFL's Winnipeg Blue Bombers. He realized that teamwork was vital in winning football games. Nicklin knew that it would also enhance the effectiveness of his paratroopers.

Furthermore, Nicklin insisted that all his officers become team players. They were now ordered to take part with their men in all training activities. Under Nicklin there were no exceptions. "He started pushing them hard," recalled Sergeant Roland Larose, "He ordered all the officers to take part in these runs and physical training exercises."[90] This was one of the rare Nicklin training directives that the troops appreciated.

The hard training and demanding exercises assisted in integrating the reinforcements that the unit received. Nonetheless, the first few weeks proved difficult for the new men. "That's when the BS [bull shit] started, the attitude of some of veterans was, 'We were there [Normandy] and you weren't,'" explained Major Hilborn.[91] The new men had to prove to the veterans that they could indeed fit in and, more important, keep up.

Nicklin had anticipated this situation and told his officers he would not put up with such behaviour. "There was no lording over others," recalled Lieutenant Alf Tucker. Nicklin insisted that all veterans use "their experience to show the replacements how to react and protect themselves or how to act in a manner that was in their best interest. I remember," explained Tucker, "that the officers took that to heart."[92]

"The problem," conceded Hilborn, "now became one of reintegrating the old with the new. They all had to be taught to think alike."[93] A redeeming factor was that the reinforcements were all qualified paratroopers. They had also undergone advanced weapons and fieldcraft training similar to those of 1 Cdn Para Bn. The men had a good handle on their basic skills. Now, they just had to be accepted by the veterans.

The integration of the new members eventually worked itself out. By mid-October 1944, the Battalion's training program was progressing well and the undesirables had been weeded out. Corporal Richard Creelman commented, "There were quite a few that did not come up to what they were expected to and they were replaced. They [battalion headquarters] found out quickly who were the leaders and who weren't." Those who chose to remain knew that they would have to work hard. "We had some experience by now," said Creelman, "and we knew what was expected of us. We knew what it was like getting shot at."[94]

It was also easier to keep the men in line. "All you had to do," explained Sergeant Larose, "was to tell them to smarten up, or they'd be back to the Canadian Army. That was it."[95] Even though the training was difficult, the pride of wearing the distinctive maroon beret and the unique Canadian Parachute Qualification Badge, as well as the fact that they were the first to take the fight to the enemy were reasons enough for the paratroopers to dig deeper and find the energy to keep up with the unrelenting tempo.

Those who remained were extremely professional. They were self-motivated and possessed good leadership skills and initiative. "In the Nicklin regime, we had to be prepared and were expected to take on a lot of initiative," revealed Andy Anderson. "Certain phases during the exercises were especially prepared to evaluate candidates [all ranks] and their use of initiative," he explained, "You would be briefed and once you landed [during an exercise], referees would black arm band [identification system used during an exercise to simulate casualties and wounded personnel] a certain percentage of your stick." A paratrooper would then be designated by the referees to carry on with the unit's task. "You had to know where you were," stated Anderson, "who was missing, what you had to do and what resources were at your disposal. This was a new part of the training that had been derived from our Normandy experience." He concluded, "This training really paid off." Quick thinking and adapting to any situation resulted in the mission's success. It also kept casualties to a minimum.

Despite the challenging training the paratroopers were becoming increasingly disgruntled with certain aspects of the CO's uncompromising level of discipline. Fraser Eadie, the new DCO, frankly stated, "Nicklin's attitude was to simply charge to the hilt [those who did not comply with his regulations or orders."[96] Private Morrison believed he "was too strict and over did it with discipline." He added, "[H]e would toss people out or charge them for very slight problems."[97] Roland Larose recalled one particular case. "Sometimes NCOs, had to give drill exercise to defaulters [paratroopers who had committed infractions or had not performed up to expectation]. He [Nicklin] got them to wear a smock

Lieutenant-Colonel Fraser Eadie, the CO who seemed to achieve the right amount of balance in his command role, Grelingen, Germany, April 1945.

with a big yellow stripe down their back. That really cheesed us off," said Larose. "You can only push a guy so far … They weren't yellow, that's the part we didn't like."[98]

Even the smallest detail did not escape Nicklin's watchful eye. "We used to have to blanco [color] our stripes [rank insignia] white," stated Corporal Ernie Jeans. He went on, "I didn't do that because I wasn't on parade much. However, one day, Nicklin noted my stripes and hollered at me from across the parade square. I had to race over and I had a lot of explaining to do."[99] By all accounts the CO was unrelenting. "[Lieutenant] Colonel Nicklin," wrote Anderson, "was a by the book commander, absolutely no quarter given and he had no compassion for defences that were mounted." He added, "the number of soldiers punished severely for what might be minor infractions gave the colonel the un-kind title of the 'Tyrant.'"[100] Corporal John Ross felt that Nicklin was "isolated from the private soldier."[101] By late October, a group of paratroopers decided that they would no longer put up with this excessive discipline and organized a hunger strike.

The Battalion war diary entry for Friday, 20 October 1944, simply reads "One evening supper parade great confusion was caused when the men refused to eat." It explained, "The complaint lay not in the food but in the treatment of the men by the commanding officer."[102] What in fact transpired was a refusal of some 70–80 men to eat their meal. The following day, the war diary simply noted "Personnel still not eating." However, what it failed to highlight was the fact that the hunger strike had now spread through the whole battalion, including the training company.[103] On Sunday, 22 October, the war diary reported, "Personnel in camp refused to eat again today." Clearly, the hunger strike was meant to pass a serious message. The troops, however, "were observing all orders meticulously and were actually attending meal parades but were not eating."[104]

The protest, argued some of the senior leadership, was organized by a group of malcontents to complain about what Captain John Madden described as "a parade square type discipline."[105] Madden explained that "The men saw it as chickenshit … They knew that so many of the manifestations of this parade square discipline were unessential to getting the job done in war."[106] Private Jan de Vries added, "Many paratroopers were uncomfortable with this course of action." However, he conceded, "we were put in a position that we had to show solidarity and go with the flow."[107]

Whereas discipline was an integral element of a military life, Nicklin enforced it with an iron hand on absolutely every facet of the daily lives of his men. "He [Nicklin] imposed such requirements," complained Madden, "that when they went to the canteen at night, they couldn't go casually dressed. They had to go with their battledress jacket buttoned up. They couldn't wear their fatigue shoes; they had to wear proper ammunition boots, and that sort of thing."[108]

The hunger strike came at an inopportune moment. With the influx of a large number of new paratroopers, NCOs, and officers, the incident threatened to cause irreparable damage to the unit's cohesiveness and morale. Many officers were very concerned by this turn of events. While some backed the CO's actions wholeheartedly, others thought that Nicklin was unnecessarily hard on the men. "It was disconcerting," lamented Madden, "in that you were expected to go back to battle with these guys and here they had, you know, dug in their heels and shown that they weren't prepared to obey orders or do what was required."[109]

Lieutenant Jenkins, agreed. "It was an unpleasant experience around camp," stated Jenkins, "because morale was usually very very high. But, now whose part do you take." Jenkins added, "You could not condemn them [the men] for what they did. The position that most of us [officers] took, was that it was your business and do whatever you like … It was a tense period for a while."[110] The strike went on for three days and further strained the relations between the men, the NCOs, and the officers.[111]

By Saturday afternoon (22 October 1944), Brigadier Hill decided to take a closer look.[112] He monitored the situation and finally the next day decided to intervene. Hill was revered by the men. "Brigadier Hill was a tremendous officer," remembered Sergeant Flynn, "He was out every morning and did all the things he expected us to do. He had a smile all the time. I was certainly impressed with him."[113] Sergeant Anderson agreed. "I can hardly think of any general officer that the men could feel any affection for, except Hill," he stated, "He is always up front, he has been wounded at least six times, he is totally without fear, and what I always imagine as a great leader, however you measure it."[114]

Hill ordered the entire Battalion to be assembled in the base auditorium. Upon Hill's arrival all officers and Warrant Officers were asked to leave. The men were then given a few minutes to present their concerns. The brigade commander then interjected, "Look, you are letting the whole party down." He then appealed to their sense of pride. "More important-ly," he chided, "you are letting Canada down."[115] The meeting was short and to the point. Deep down, the paratroopers knew that the brigadier was right. He was a professional soldier and would not tolerate such nonsense. Hill ended the meeting abruptly. "Now," he emphatically asserted, "I am making it absolutely clear I am giving you an order, and you are going back to eat your lunch."[116] A few hours later, Brigadier Hill was informed that the Canadian paratroopers had done as they were told.

The following day, six paratroopers requested to meet with the brigadier. They identified themselves as the ring leaders and apologized for their behaviour. Hill was impressed by this show of character:

> I accepted their apologies and thanked them very much for coming in. I always loved those Canadians and that made me love them more and more. That couldn't have happened to any other battalion except a Canadian bat-talion. It was wonderful. Of course, really, that I had the grip on them to some extent was that I loved them, lit-erally. If you love people you are commanding and, lead, they will always reciprocate.[117]

A Canadian Army investigation into the hunger strike concluded that a number of factors caused the protest. These were reported as:

a) The battalion was being reconstituted and that roughly two-thirds of the men were new since the operation in Normandy.
b) Most of the junior officers were new.
c) The former CO had not been a strict disciplinarian and the men had been getting away with a lot, though discipline as a whole was not bad.
d) The new CO was an exceptionally strict disciplinarian and in his enthusiasm had been punishing minor offences on a much too severe basis and in some respects had produced regulations, particularly concerning dress within the camp area, which were not entirely reasonable ones.
e) Many of the new junior officers have not grown to know their men as they should.
f) It appears that a number of the new men in the Battalion were among those at Camp Shilo, Canada, who staged a similar hunger strike successfully there some time earlier this year.
g) Paratroops, as a whole, appear to be somewhat over-pampered and temperamental primadonnas, and they dislike going through the training process again after their operations in Normandy.[118]

No action was taken against the soldiers or instigators. Hill believed that the incident "had pretty well burnt itself out" and he felt it would be "unwise to exaggerate the importance of the whole matter by digging them out at this stage and making examples of them."[119] Part of the problem was also the rationale behind the protest. Although both Hill and the divisional commander, Major-General Richard Gale, expressed complete confidence in Nicklin, both were "satisfied that the main cause was the slightly excessive enthusiasm for perfection in disciplinary matters by the CO."[120]

Even though Hill and Gale believed that "the CO's appreciation of the disciplinary situation is cured," in the end, only the men had given in, Nicklin refused to change his rules.[121] "Major Eadie, the Battalion's Second in Command," remarked Sergeant Anderson, "told me after the war that on many occasions he asked Nicklin to back off on certain issues regarding discipline. But he refused to do so."[122]

Despite the embarrassing episode, neither the hunger strike, nor Nicklin's zealous attitude to discipline, adversely affected the Battalion's

Brigadier S.J. Hill, the beloved commander of the 3rd British Parachute Brigade. Although a disciplinarian and unrelenting taskmaster, his fairness, exceptional courage, and lead-from-the-front style won him the admiration and respect of all his subordinates.

performance. Their record of action and accomplishments to the end of the war was commendable. They distinguished themselves when they were rushed to Belgium to assist Allied efforts to stop the Germans during their Christmas offensive in the Ardennes in December 1944, commonly called the "Battle of the Bulge." They also performed admirably in Holland in the aftermath of the German attack during one of the coldest winters on record. In addition, they demonstrated their professionalism and effectiveness during Operation Varsity, the airborne assault across the Rhine in March 1945 and the subsequent pursuit of the German forces across North-West Europe. The Battalion ended the war in Wismar on the Baltic Sea, the only Canadian troops to link-up with the Russians.

Lieutenant-Colonel Nicklin, however, was killed in battle, on 24 March 1945, in the parachute assault during Operation Varsity. He was found hanging in a tree, still in his canopy, riddled with bullets. As a result of rumours and supposition as to the fate of Nicklin who had been reported missing, the Canadian Army sent an investigative team to determine what in fact had happened to the CO. In the end, his death was attributed to enemy action. He had landed in a tree directly above an enemy machine-gun nest — he never had a chance. Ironically, normally Nicklin jumped in the middle of the stick so that he could have half of his headquarters on either side of him upon landing. However, for this operation he wanted to be the number one jumper so that he could lead his troops into battle.[123] That decision cost him his life, but he stayed true to principles up to the end.

Command of the Battalion now fell to Major Fraser Eadie. The new CO was much like his predecessor in some ways; he was a former athlete who turned down an opportunity to play professional hockey with the Chicago Black Hawks in the NHL to serve his country. He was also direct and frank, with a fiery temper. Eadie was lucky in that he had evolved and grown with the unit virtually from the beginning. He knew the men, had experienced combat, had watched two other COs, and was familiar with the problems, strengths, and weaknesses of the Battalion. He was well-positioned to lead it to the end of the war which was mere months away.

From all accounts Eadie had learned well. He was an excellent CO who knew how to balance the three components of command. One soldier observed that he was a CO who knew "when to be on parade and when to be off parade."[124] Sergeant Feduck recounted, "[Eadie was] very strict but extremely smart." He added, "He had a way of talking to the men at their level — never mocked or down graded you."[125] Similarly, Private Morrison recalled, "Eadie was tough when he had to be but fair."[126] By his own accounts Eadie had a simple leadership philosophy. "I always believed," he affirmed, "that I must lead them [his soldiers] or I couldn't live with myself." He added, "The only way to be promoted was if I was held in good esteem by my men. I never asked them to do anything I wouldn't do myself."[127] It is no wonder then, that Fraser Eadie was highly respected and treated like "the CO" by his men until his death in 2005.

On 30 September 1945, the 1 Canadian Parachute Battalion was officially disbanded. The nation's first airborne soldiers had earned a proud and remarkable reputation. Their legacy would become the standard of excellence that would challenge Canada's future paratroopers and imbue them with a special pride. The Battalion never failed to complete an assigned mission, nor did it ever lose or surrender an objective once taken. The Canadian paratroopers were among the first Allied soldiers to have landed in occupied Europe, the only Canadians to have participated in the "Battle of the Bulge" in the Ardennes, and by the end of the war had advanced deeper into Germany than any other Canadian unit. "The Battalion," wrote Chief of the Imperial General Staff Field Marshal Sir Alan Brooke, "played a vital part in the heavy fighting which followed their descent onto French soil in 6 June 1944, during the subsequent critical days and in the pursuit to the Seine. Finally, it played a great part in the lightning pursuit of the German Army right up the shores of the Baltic. It can indeed be proud of its record."

In the end, this achievement is owed in large part to the unit leadership, particularly its commanding officers. Although each was in contrast to the others, all brought special skills, talents, and capabilities to the unit. In so doing, they all shaped and prepared the Battalion for its role and success during the war. G.F.P. Bradbrooke, the aloof administrator and intrepid parachutist, was instrumental in establishing and organizing the unit when it was in its infancy. He seemingly relied on his rank, and focused on the management and authority components of command. Although he failed to be the dynamic and courageous battle field commander, his instrumental role in establishing 1 Cdn Para Bn cannot be dismissed.

In contrast, the larger than life ex-star of the CFL, Jeff Nicklin, proved to be a dynamic, imposing commander who was feared by most, respected by many, and unpopular with the majority. Nonetheless, his superiors adored him as a paratroop commander. He instilled energy and drive, and a relentless pursuit for toughness and effectiveness. Nicklin always led by example and made certain he managed the unit properly — always, ensuring the necessary supervision of activities, proper priorities, and allocation of resources. He was never afraid to use his authority, and it seems was probably to ready to use it to the maximum to discipline even minor indiscretions. Nicklin, in his desire to shape and mould a tough battalion, one whose men were superbly fit and expert at their craft, sometimes went too far. He was too inflexible in his philosophical approach, too distant from the men on a human level, and arguably lacking a degree of compassion and humanity. As a result, many considered him a "tyrant." However, what cannot be lost is the fact that Nicklin's unrelenting pressure created a unit that was second to none and was able to operate effectively in the complex and unforgiving airborne battle ground. Although not all may have appreciated his methods — many owe their lives to his zeal and conviction in training them hard.

Finally, Fraser Eadie seemed to be the balance between his predecessors. Possessing a fiery temper, he could nonetheless easily let minor indiscretions go and never held a grudge. Courageous, he led his men in battle from the front "with utter disregard for danger."[128] He relied on leadership and was conscious of when to be a strict disciplinarian and when to allow the troops to relax and vent. Although he relied on leadership he was an able manager and ensured the unit was efficient in every facet of the word. Equally, he never shied away from using authority when required. He knew himself, and he knew his men, and as a result, he was able to balance the three components of command and use the right component to the right effect.

In the end, all three COs played a vital role in shaping the unit into what it was. Although all had a different approach to command, it seemed that each was the right individual at the right time. A Bradbrooke was necessary to stand the unit up. A Nicklin was required to take the veterans of Normandy and bring them back to earth so that they could properly prepare for the next battle and integrate with the new reinforcements. An Eadie, with his balanced approach, was vital to bring the troops down in the final days of the war and lead them into demobilization. Together, they and their soldiers laid the foundation of a proud airborne legacy for Canada's future paratroopers to follow.

Notes

1.   Canada, *Command* (Ottawa: DND, 1997), 4. The essence of command is the expression of human wills — an idea that is captured in the concept of commander's intent as part of the philosophy of mission command. The commander's intent is the commander's personal expression of why an operation is being conducted and what he hopes to achieve. It is a clear and concise statement of the desired end-state and acceptable risk. Its strength is the fact that it allows subordinates to exercise initiative in the absence of orders, or when unexpected opportunities arise, or when the original concept of operations no longer applies. Mission Command is a command philosophy that promotes decentralized decision-making, freedom, and speed of action and initiative. It entails three enduring tenets: The importance of understanding a superior commander's intent, a clear responsibility to fulfil that intent, and timely decision-making. In summary, command is the purposeful exercise of authority over structures, resources, people, and activities.

2.   Canada, *Leadership in the Canadian Forces: Conceptual Foundations* (Kingston: DND, 2005). It is within this powerful realm of influence and

potential change that leadership best demonstrates the basic difference between it and the concept of command. Too often the terms *leadership* and *command* are interchanged or seen as synonymous. But they are not. Leadership can, and should, be a component of command. After all, to be an effective commander the formal authority that comes with rank and position must be reinforced and supplemented with personal qualities and skills — the human side. Nonetheless, as discussed earlier, command is based on vested authority and assigned position and/or rank. It may only be exercised downward in the chain of command through the structures and processes of control. Conversely, leadership is not constrained by the limits of formal authority. Individuals anywhere in the chain of command can, given the ability and motivation, influence peers, and even superiors. This clearly differentiates leadership from command.

3.   The main difference between the concept of command and that of leadership (the two often being used interchangeably, which is incorrect) is that command is vested authority that is given by the chain of command. Only those so appointed can exercise it. Conversely, anyone can exercise leadership. Arguably, leadership is given by followers who choose to follow out inspiration, confidence, motivation, and/or a belief that by following the leadership of another their personal goals and aspirations will be achieved.

4.   The unit actually had four. Ottawa native, 31-year-old Major Hilton D. Proctor, was the Battalion's first designated CO when the unit was being created. He was part of the first group to be trained in Fort Benning in the fall of 1942. Once trained, this initial group would become the training cadre to instruct the volunteers of the new Canadian airborne unit. As the group's senior ranking officer, Proctor insisted on being the lead jumper. When the signal was given to jump, he exited the airplane. As his parachute opened, his lines were sheared by a following aircraft, causing Proctor to plunge to his death.

5.   Library and Archives Canada (LAC), Records Group (RG) 24, Series C-1, Vol. 21, File HQS 8846–1, Parachute Troops. Organization, Training 1941–45, Memorandum, DND HQ MD No. 2, "Serial 1351 — 1st Parachute Battalion," 27 November 1942, Microfilm C-5278, Vol. 21.

6.   *Ibid.*, Vol. 12, File HQS 8846–1, Letter, Major-General H.F.G. Letson (Adjutant-General), "1st Parachute Battalion — Serial 1351," Microfilm C-5278. As early as 29 July 1942, the deputy chief of the general staff (DCGS) declared that "the formation and individual training of the 1st Canadian Parachute Bn is an urgent matter and [I must] stress the importance of eliminating any delays in this regard." Canadian Airborne Forces Museum (CAFM), AB 1, 1 Cdn Para Bn, Vol. 2, File 19, Letter, DCGS to District Officers Commanding, "Canadian Parachute Battalion," 29 July 1942.

7.   Draft letter, Air Chief Marshal C.F.A. Portal, Air Ministry to GHQ Home Forces, January 1942. Public Record Office (PRO), AIR 39/26. Air

Ministry: Army Cooperation Command: Registered Files, Airborne Forces Organization, February 1941–43.

8. CAFM, AB 1, 1 Cdn Para Bn, Vol. 6, File 21, Major-General R.N. Gale, Pamphlet — "To All Officers in the 6th Airborne Division," June 1943.

9. "Training Paratroops," *Canadian Army Training Memorandums*, No. 20, November 1942, 10.

10. Captain F.O. Miksche, *Paratroops — The History, Organization and Tactical Use of Airborne Formations* (Faber and Faber Ltd, 1942), 133.

11. DND Department of History and Heritage (DHH), File 112.3M300 (D99), Memorandum, DMT to DCGS, "1st Canadian Parachute Battalion," 22 October 1942.

12. LAC, RG 24, Series C-1, File HQS 8846–1, Letter, Secretary DND (Army), "1st Canadian Parachute Battalion — Accounting of Personnel," 17 December 1942, Microfilm C-5277, Vol. 17; *Ibid.*, Memorandum, A.P. 3, "1st Canadian Parachute Bn — Documentation, Relinquishment of N.C.O. Appointment, 11 February 1943, Microfilm C-5277, Vol. 1; and LAC, RG 24, Series C-1, File HQS 8846–8, Promotions 1 Cdn Para Bn, 1942–43, Letter, Military Attaché Canadian Legation to the Secretary, Department of National Defence (Army), "Organization — 1st Canadian Parachute Battalion," 20 February 1943, Microfilm C-8379, File HQS 8846–8, No. 3.

13. LAC, RG 24, Series C-1, Vol 17, File HQS 8846–1, Letter, Secretary DND (Army), "1st Canadian Parachute Battalion—Accounting of Personnel," 17 December 1942, Microfilm C-5277; *Ibid.*, Vol. 1, Memorandum, A.P. 3, "1st Canadian Parachute Bn — Documentation, Relinquishment of N.C.O. Appointment, 11 February 1943; and LAC, RG 24, Series C-1, File HQS 8846–8, Promotions 1 Cdn Para Bn, 1942–43, Letter, Military Attaché Canadian Legation to the Secretary, Department of National Defence (Army), "Organization—1st Canadian Parachute Battalion," 20 February 1943, Microfilm C-8379, File HQS 8846–8, No. 3.

14. "Canada's Jumping Jacks!" *Khaki: The Army Bulletin*, Vol. 1, No. 22, 29 September 1943, 1.

15. 1 Cdn Para Bn Assn Archives, Letter, A.E. Moll, "Selection of Airborne Personnel," 52/Psychiatry/4/3 S.P.5. — 24 November 1943.

16. Moll was certain that the "A" candidates were the best material. He was equally sure that the "E" personnel should not be considered. However, he conceded some uncertainty in regards to the 80 percent who fell into the grey area in-between. But Moll and his staff decided that as long as the supply of volunteers remained strong they would continue to accept only the best. Letter, 15 November 1985, from Dr. Bill McAndrews (DHH Historian) to Brigadier-General E. Beno. CAFM.

17. As of 10 July 1942, the initial physical requirements for paratroops were:

    A) Alert, active, supple, with firm muscles and sound limbs: capable of development into aggressive individual fighter with great endurance.

B) Age: Officers — not over 32 years of age for captains and lieutenants and not over 35 years for majors; Other ranks (ORs) 18–32 inclusive.

C) Physically qualified as follows:
1. Weight — maximum, not to exceed 185 pounds.
2. Height — maximum, not to exceed 72 inches.
3. Vision — Distant vision uncorrected must be 20/40 each eye.
4. Feet — Greater than a non symptomatic 2nd degree pes planus [progressive flatfoot deformity] to disqualify.
5. Genito-urinary system — recent venereal disease to disqualify.
6. Nervous system — evidence of highly labile nervous system [prone to anxiety, emotionally unstable] to disqualify.
7. Bones, joints, and muscles — Lack of normal mobility in every joint, poor or unequally developed musculature, poor coordination, asthenic habitus [thin-muscle type], or lack of at least average athletic ability to disqualify.
8. Medical History — History of painful arches, recurrent knees or ankle injuries, recent fracture, old fractures with deformity, pain or limitation of motion, recurrent dislocation, recent severe illness, operation or chronic disease to disqualify.
9. Other than listed above, the physical standards to be the same as Army Standard "A.1."

DHH, File 171.009/ D223, Letter, Adjutant-General to All District Officers Commanding, "Parachute Battalion, Serial No. 1351," 10 July 1942. The Army definition of "A.1." category was: "The man shall be able to see to shoot or drive, and can undergo severe strain without defects of locomotion and with only minor remediable disabilities. Age — between 22 and 32 years of age; Height — usual heights — minimum 5'2," max 6'; Weight — minimum 125 lbs, maximum 196 lbs; Visual Standards — 20/40 both eyes without glasses. Colour vision should be 'defective safe'; Hearing W.V. — 10 ft. both ears, i.e., a man standing with his back to the examiner and using both ears, must be able to hear a forced whisper 10 feet away. Must have patent Eustachian Tubes; Dental — Men must not drop with false teeth, consequently there must be eight sound or reparable teeth (including two molars) in the upper jaw in good functional opposition to corresponding teeth in lower jaw; Injuries of limbs — it was agreed that men with old fractures of the lower limbs or spine, however well recovered, were not suitable. Flat-feet not acceptable. Must have full movements in all joints of lower limbs; Mental and intelligence standard: It was agreed that men with alert minds are required for these duties and that men with doubtful intelligence should be eliminated by an intelligence test." LAC, RG 24, Series C-1, File HQS 8846–1, Vol. 15. Microfilm C-5277, Medical Standards for Paratroops.

18. LAC, RG 24, Series C-1, File HQS 8846–1, Vol. 12, Letter, Adjutant-General to Commanders, "1st Parachute Battalion — Serial 1351," 2 October 1942, Microfilm C-5277. There were those who were ineligible to volunteer for the paratroops. They were: Tradesmen who have completed trade training; Personnel under instruction in Army Trade Schools, Technical Schools, or Vocational Schools; and Personnel earmarked for trades such as surveyors, instrument mechanics, wireless mechanics, radio mechanics, electrician sigs, and fitters.

19. 1 Cdn Para Bn Assn Archives, Letter, Major A.E. Moll, "Selection of Airborne Personnel," 52/Psychiatry/4/S.P.5. 24 November 1943, 3.

20. DHH, File 163.009 (D16), Memorandum, Colonel W. Line, "Selection of Personnel — 1st Parachute Battalion," 23 December 1942; and LAC, RG 24, Series C-1, File HQS 8846–1, Vol. 16. Microfilm C-5277.

21. Examiners reported that the chief non-physical causes for rejection were lack of enthusiasm for parachute work, which often became evident once individuals learned in more detail what they had volunteered for and evidence of emotional instability, defined as:

- Sociability: unfriendly, reclusive, lacking in social skills.
- Adjustment to Army Life: Discontented, complaining.
- Occupational History: Frequent changes, little responsibility or pay in relation to ability.
- School History: Poor progress, truancy, bad conduct.
- Family History: Home broken by death or divorce, foster parents, alcoholism, juvenile delinquency or crime, nervous disorders in relatives.
- Personal Health and History: Tremors, sweating extremities, stammering, nightmares, pounding heart, cold sweats, dizzy or fainting spells, nail-biting, alcoholism, vague stomach or nervous ailments, fear of dark or high places, sex problems, drug addiction, juvenile delinquency or crime, frequent visits to Medical Inspection Room (MIR).

22. LAC, RG 24, Series C-1, File HQS 8846–1, Vol. 16, Memorandum, Colonel W. Line, "1st Parachute Bn. (Serial 1351), 26 December 1942, Microfilm C-5277. An independent assessment of 613 personnel appraisals provides additional detail. Of the cases examined, 322 of the 613, or 52.5 percent were accepted. The personnel assessments consulted were found primari-

ly in LAC, RG 24, Series C-1, File HQS 8846–1, Vol. 19, Microfilm C-5277. They spanned the period September 1942 to early 1943. It became evident that the cases in January–March 1943 were less rigidly assessed then those in 1942. The major categories for rejection were nervousness or "tremulous hands for 29 percent;" "instability" accounting for 13 percent; "family background" (broken home, parental, or spousal disagreement with joining paratroops, family health history) for 12 percent; and "lack of aggressiveness" for 11 percent. The remainder of the reasons were: health reasons — 10 percent; voluntary withdrawal — 9 percent; mentally slow — 7 percent; non-swimmer — 1 percent; poor military record — 2 percent; and other — approximately 6 percent.

23. In January 1943, the medical criteria for screening were amended in response to feedback provided by the initial intake of volunteers and their success rates (italics indicate amendments):

> Alert, active, supple, with firm muscles, and sound limbs: capable of development into aggressive individual fighter with *GREAT* endurance. Age: *18–32, both inclusive.* [In June 1943, the lower end was amended to 18?].
>
> A) Physically qualified as follows:
>
> 1. Weight — maximum, not to exceed *190* pounds.
> 2. Height — maximum, not to exceed 72 inches.
> 3. Vision — Distant vision uncorrected must be 20/40 each eye.
> 4. *Feet and Lower Limbs: Flat feet not acceptable. Better than average bone structure and muscular development of lower limbs.*
> 5. Genito-urinary system — recent venereal disease to disqualify.
> 6. Nervous system — evidence of highly labile nervous system to disqualify. *History of nervous complaints to disqualify.*
> 7. Bones, joints, and muscles — Lack of normal mobility in every joint, poor or unequally developed musculature, poor coordination, asthenic habitus, or lack of *better than average* athletic ability to disqualify.
> 8. *Hearing: W.V. — 10 ft. both ears, i.e., a man standing with his back to the examiner and using both ears must be able to hear a forced whisper 10 ft. away. Must have patent Eustachian Tubes.*
> 9. *Dental: Men must not drop with false teeth; consequently there must be eight sound or reparable teeth*

(including 2 molars) in the upper jaw, in good functional opposition to corresponding teeth in lower jaw.

10. Medical History — History of painful arches, recurrent knees or ankle injuries, recent fracture, old fractures with deformity, pain or limitation of motion, recurrent dislocation, recent severe illness, operation or chronic disease to disqualify (*unless recurring, properly healed fractures not to disqualify*).

11. *Mental and Intelligence Standard: It was agreed that men with alert minds are required for this type of training and that men with doubtful intelligence should be eliminated by intelligence test.*

12. Other than listed above, the physical standards to be the same as Army Standard "A.1."

It was also a reflection of the fact that as the war progressed the rigorous selection process became an impediment in reaching the necessary quotas. By May 1944, the criteria were severely relaxed. The new standards for "Parachutists (Operational)" were very forgiving:

A) Physical

1.   PULHEMS [see below]: 1112111.
2.   Age: 18 1/2 — 32 years inclusive.
     Max Height: 6'2" max wt. 220 lbs. A proper correlation of height and weight will be required.
3.   Teeth: Must have a sufficient number of second teeth to masticate food reasonably well if dentures should be broken or lost.
4.   Must be in good physical condition: A history of participation in rugged sports, or in a civilian occupation or hobby demanding sustained exertion is very desirable.

B) Other Qualifications

1.   Should be emotionally stable, well-motivated, self-reliant, and relatively aggressive.
2.   Must be General Service prior to despatch for paratroop training.
3.   Must have completed Basic Training.
4.   If non-English speaking, must be sufficiently bilingual to take all instruction in English.
5.   Must have at least the equivalent of Gr. VI Education.
6.   Must be genuinely interested in paratroop training

> after having been thoroughly informed concerning the strenuous physical requirements and the emphasis on Infantry training.

But the loosening of the criteria was not enough. The director of personnel selection stressed to his examiners that a psychiatric examination was no longer required at the time of initial nomination. Furthermore, he reminded them that any personnel who met the minimum PULHEMS requirement and was otherwise suitable would be eligible for paratroop service. In fact, Army examiners were prodded to ensure that whenever a suitable recruit was encountered they should be immediately briefed on paratroop service. PULHEMS stood for: P — physique; U — upper limbs; L — lower limbs; H — hearing; E — eyes; M — mental; S — stability. Soldiers were graded from 1 to 5 for each of these factors, 1 being fit for any military employment, 5 being fit for none. Major-General F.M. Richardson, *Fighting Spirit: A Study of Psychological Factors in War* (London: Leo Cooper, 1978), 165. See 1 Cdn Para Bn Assn Archives, "Physical Standards and Instructions for the Medical Examination of Serving Soldiers and Recruits for the Canadian Army — 1943;" LAC, RG 24, Series C-1, File HQS 8846–1, Vol. 19. Microfilm C-5277, "Medical Standards for Paratroops — All Ranks," 18 January 1943; 1 Cdn Para Bn Assn Archives, Letter, Adjutant-General to GOCs, "Selection of Paratroops — Specifications General Instructions," 17 May 1944; 1 Cdn Para Bn Assn Archives, Letter, Director of Personnel Selection to All District Army Examiners, " Selection of Paratroops — Specifications General Instructions," 22 May 1944; and DHH, File 163.009 (D16), Letter, Director of Personnel Selection to All District Army Examiners, " Selection of Paratroops," 2 March 1945. DHH, File 112.21009 (D197) folder 6, "A.35 Canadian Parachute T.C.," 19 November 1943. Sergeant R.F. Anderson stated that, based on his discussions with others, a minimum of 60 to 70 percent of volunteers failed the selection/training process. Interview with Bernd Horn, 11 June 1998. This is consistent with the recollection of other veterans.

24. *Ibid.*
25. "Training Paratroops," *CATM*, November 1942, No. 20, 10.
26. 1 Cdn Para Bn Assn Archives, Lockyer, Mark, File 10–3, Robert Taylor, "Paratroop Van Eager to Be Tip of Army 'Dagger,'" *Toronto Daily Star*, 12 August 1942.
27. *Ibid.*
28. 1. Cdn Para Bn Assn Archives, Firlotte, Robert, File 2–11, James C. Anderson, "Tough, Hard-as-Nails Paratroopers Arrive to Open Shilo School," 22 September 1942; *Ibid.*, "Toughest in Canada's Army Back for Paratroop Course," *The Star*, 21 September 1942; and Ronald K Keith, "Sky Troops," *Maclean's*, 1 August 1943, 18–20 and 28. This is simply a representative sample. Virtually every article in newspapers nation-wide used similar adjectives to describe Canada's "newest corps elite."

29. LAC, "Assembling Paratroopers at Calgary," *Globe and Mail*, Vol. 99, No. 28916, 18 August 1942, 13, Microfilm N-20035; and 1 Cdn Para Bn Assn Archives, Lockyer, Mark, File 10–3, Robert Taylor, "Paratroop Van Eager to Be Tip of Army 'Dagger,'" *Toronto Daily Star*, 12 August 1942.

30. LAC, "Assembling Paratroopers at Calgary," *Globe and Mail*, Vol. 99, No. 28916, 18 August 1942, 13, Microfilm N-20035.

31. LAC, James C. Anderson, "Canada's Paratroopers Don't Have Stage Fright," *Saturday Night*, No. 11, 12 December 1942, 11, Microfilm 56A.

32. His father G.H. Bradbrooke had a distinguished record in the First World War. He was lieutenant-colonel and he earned both the Military Cross and the Distinguished Service Order.

33. 1 Cdn Para Bn Association Archives, "Man of the Week: No. 1 Paratrooper," Unknown newspaper clipping, unknown date.

34. Description of Bradbrooke given by *Maclean's* journalist Ronald A. Keith, quoted in Brian Nolan, *Airborne* (Toronto: Lester Publishing, 1995), 33.

35. *Ibid.*, 16.

36. Former 1 Cdn Para Bn officer, Lieutenant William Jenkins, wrote "he [Bradbrooke] was pleasant, but I had little contact with him." Jenkins concluded Bradbrooke was elitist. Letter, Jenkins to Nolan, 26 February 1994. Brian Nolan who conducted many interviews noted that this was a common sentiment. I found the similar view point in my interviews.

37. Bradbrooke was promoted to the rank of lieutenant-colonel on 12 October 1942, the same day he was appointed officer commanding of 1 Cdn Para Bn. He was posted on course to the Parachute School in Fort Benning, Georgia on 28 October 1942. LAC, RG 24, Part II, Order, 1st Canadian Parachute Battalion, Order No. 26, 29 October 1942.

38. The unit strength was to be 616 all ranks. To achieve this number, drafts of 55 volunteers per week (i.e., a parachute course serial) were sent to Fort Benning for parachute training starting in October 1942. The proposed War Establishment (Cdn. III/1940/127/1) of the 1st Canadian Parachute Battalion was based on the British War Establishment (BWE X/127/2). The Battalion was to consist of a battalion headquarters; a headquarters company that included an intelligence section, a signal platoon, a mortar platoon of four detachments, a protective section, and an administration platoon. Three rifle companies consisting of a: company headquarters, two mortar detachments, a anti-tank section, three rifle platoons each having a platoon headquarters and three rifle sections. The Battalion's War Establishment was notified in LAC, RG 24, CMHQ, Vol. 12260, File 1/Policy/Parachute Troops/1, General Order 452/42. As the war progressed, the Battalion's War Establishment underwent several modifications.

39. Herb Peppard, *The Light-Hearted Soldier: A Canadian's Exploits with the Black Devils in WW II* (Halifax: Nimbus Publishing Ltd., 1994), 28.

40. *Ibid.*, 27.

41. For example, see LAC, RG 24, Series C-1, File HQS 8846–1, Vol. 15, Letter from the Office of the Directorate of Military Training to D.C.G.S. (B),

Ottawa, 25 November 1942, Microfilm C-5277; *Ibid.*, Vol. 17, Letter from Lieutenant-Colonel G.F.P. Bradbrooke to the Director of Military Training, Fort Benning, 6 November 1942, Microfilm C-5277; DHH, File 112.3M3009 (D99), Training 1st Cdn Para Bn, October 1942-July 1943, Memorandum from Colonel R.H. Keefler to DCGS (B), Ottawa, 22 October 1942; LAC, RG 24, Series C-1, File HQS 8846–1, Vol. 15, Letter from the Office of the Directorate of Military Training to D.C.G.S. (B), Ottawa, 25 November 1942, Microfilm C-5277; and *Ibid.*, Vol 17, Letter from Lieutenant-Colonel G.F.P. Bradbrooke to the Director of Military Training, Fort Benning, 6 November 1942, Microfilm C-5277.

42. LAC, RG 24, Series C-1, HQS 8846–1, Vol. 15, Letter from Lieutenant-Colonel G.F.P. Bradbrooke to the Director of Military Training, Fort Benning, 3 December 1942, Microfilm C-5277.

43. LAC, RG 24, Vol. 15298, December 1942, 1 Cdn Para Bn War Diary, 3 December 1942. Entry, 4 December 1942: "From all comments, a majority of these men decided to leave the 1st Battalion because they felt that the 2nd Battalion or Special Service group would be first to see overseas action. Furthermore, most of them being impatient, wanted to go to a fully organized and equipped unit, rather than submit to New Battalion Growth."

44. LAC, RG 24, Vol. 15298, January 1943, 1 Cdn Para Bn War Diary, 11 January 1943.

45. *Ibid.*

46. LAC, RG 24, CMHQ, Vol. 12260, File 1/Policy Parachute Troops/1, Message (CGS 142) from C.G.S. Stuart to G.O.C.-in-Chief, First Canadian Army. Ottawa, 6 March 1943.

47. LAC, RG 24, CMHQ, Vol. 12260, File 1/Policy Parachute Troops/1, Message from Stuart to McNaughton, (CGS 212), Ottawa, 7 April 1943; LAC, RG 24, Series C-1, File HQS 8846–1, Vol. 24, Letter from the Chief of the General Staff, Lieutenant-General Stuart to the Adjutant General, the Quarter Master General and the Master-General Ordnance, Ottawa, 9 April 1943, Microfilm C-5278. Originally this division was designated as the 2nd Airborne Division, however, the designation was quickly changed to 6th Airborne Division to confuse German Intelligence.

48. Letter, Jenkins to Nolan, 26 February 1994.

49. Interview with author, 31 January 2002.

50. DHH, File 169.009 (D212) Inspector-General's Reports of 1 Cdn Para Bn, July 1943, Report on the 1st Canadian Paratroop Battalion, by Major-General J.P. Mackenzie, Inspector-General Western Canada, Brandon, Manitoba, 4 July 1943.

51. Letter to author, 7 May 2001.

52. Nolan, 121.

53. Letter, Jenkins to Nolan, 26 February 1994.

54. LAC, RG 24, Vol. 15298, Training Syllabus, week of 26 April-1 May 1943. 1 Cdn Para Bn War Diary, June 1943.

55. Quoted in Nolan, 53.

---

56. LAC, RG 24, Vol. 15298, Training Syllabus, week of 26 April-1 May 1943. 1 Cdn Para Bn War Diary, June 1943. No one escaped his eye either. He advised the company commanders to improve their planning, "instead of waiting for the last mad bustle."

57. *Ibid.*, Training Syllabus, week of 10–15 May 1943. 1st Canadian Parachute Battalion.

58. Interview with author, 31 January 2002.

59. Training Syllabus, week of 28 June-3 July 1943. 1st Canadian Parachute Battalion.

60. LAC, RG 24, Series C-1, File HQS 8846–1, Vol. 23, Microfilm C-5278, Report of Trip to Camp Shilo, Manitoba, (Canadian Parachute Training School, 1st Canadian Parachute Battalion) by Major R.A. Keane, 17 May 1943 to 22 May 1943.

61. DHH, File 169.009 (D212) Inspector-General's Reports of 1 Cdn Para Bn, July 1943, Report on the 1st Canadian Paratroop Battalion, by Major-General J.P. Mackenzie, Inspector-General Western Canada, Brandon, Manitoba, 4 July 1943.

62. Jean E. Portugal, *We Were There — The Army: A Record for Canada*, Vol. 2 (Toronto: The Royal Canadian Institute, 1998), 944.

63. DHH, File 145.4011 (D2) 1 Cdn Para Bn, Letter Brigadier James Hill to the Honourable P.J. Montague, Cdn Military HQ., 9 April 1945.

64. *Ibid.*

65. Portugal, 943–944.

66. John Feduck reply to Nolan questionnaire 31 January 1994. Feduck added, "he was rated poorly as a commander."

67. *Ibid.*

68. Interview with author, 20 November 2000.

69. *Ibid.*

70. 1 Cdn Para Bn Assn Archives, Brian Nolan Fonds, Brigadier James Hill file, Brigadier James Hill, interview with Brian Nolan, 33–34.

71. During the German breakthrough at the village of Bréville on 12 June 1944, Brigadier Hill gathered up a reserve force and personally led the counterattack to re-establish the Allied line. Major Murray Macleod stated: "The counter-attack went in led by Brig Hill, and his personal bravery was said to do a lot for the stiffened stand of all the troops there. His apparent lack of concern for the hail of bullets and shellfire about him as he walked back and forth between the defensive positions gave heart and the position held." Portugal, 963. For details on the battle of Bréville see Horn and Wyczynski, *Paras versus the Reich*, 149–151.

72. Interview with author, 30 May 2001.

73. *Ibid.*

74. R.F. "Andy" Anderson, interview with Michel Wyczynski, 7 February 2002.

75. Harold Johnstone, *Johnny Kemp, DCM, His Story with the 1st Canadian Parachute Battalion, 1942–1945* (Nanaimo: Private Printing, 2000), 17.

76. Battalion personnel boarded three trains on 11 September for Scotland,

London, and the Midlands. All personnel were ordered to return by 24 September 1944. LAC, RG 24, Vol. 15299, September 1944, 1 Cdn Para Bn War Diary, 11–24 September 1944.

77. Bradbrooke was transferred to a staff position in the Canadian Military Headquarters in London. Nicklin was promoted to the rank of acting lieutenant-colonel on 8 September 1944. LAC, RG 24, Part II Orders, No. 37, 8 November 1944, 2) Appointments — Promotions.

78. *Ibid.*, 26 September 1944.

79. 1 Cdn Para Bn Archives, Evaluation Report, Nicklin, Major Jevon, Albert. Prepared by Brigadier S.J.L. Hill, 17 February 1945.

80. 1 Cdn Para Bn Assn Archives, File 11–2, Sergeant R.F. Anderson, "From the Rhine to the Baltic."

81. 1 Cdn Para Bn Assn Archives, Joe Ryan, "Old Manager Pays Tribute to Nicklin," newspaper clipping, unknown date or publication.

82. John Feduck reply to Nolan questionnaire 31 January 1994.

83. *Ibid.*, 41.

84. Brigadier James Hill's speaking notes, November 1993, 22. *Ibid.*

85. 1 Cdn Para Bn Archives, Brian Nolan Fonds, Brigadier James Hill file, Interview of Brigadier Hill by Brian Nolan, 37.

86. John Feduck, interview with Michel Wyczynski, August 2002.

87. Harry Reid, interview with Michel Wyczynski, 24 January 2002.

88. Interview with author, 31 January 2002.

89. Sergeant R.F. Anderson, interview with Michel Wyczynski, 7 February 2002.

90. Roland Larose, interview with Michel Wyczynski, 10 January 2002.

91. Richard Hilborn, interview with Michel Wyczynski, 14 December 2002.

92. Alf Tucker, interview with Michel Wyczynski, 12 December 2001.

93. Interview with author, 27 April 2001.

94. Richard Creelman, interview with Michel Wyczynski, 27 December 2001.

95. Roland Larose, interview with Michel Wyczynski, 10 January 2002.

96. Interview with author, 20 November 2000.

97. Interview with author, 31 January 2002.

98. Roland Larose, interview with Michel Wyczynski, 10 January 2002.

99. Ernie Jeans, interview with Michel Wyczynski, 22 January 2002.

100. Letter to author, 4 August 2005.

101. Letter to author, 7 May 2001.

102. LAC, RG 24, Vol. 15299, October, 1 Cdn Para Bn War Diary, 20 October 1944. Another version of this story that has been circulating throughout the years inferred that the men were protesting the quality of the food. Most paratroopers agreed that the food wasn't the best; however, it was not the cause of this hunger strike. This is borne out by the official report on the incident. See LAC, RG 24, War Diaries, Series C-3, Vol. 15, 299, 1 Cdn Para Bn, February 1944-January 1945, Appendix 18, Memo, Cdn Liaison Section, 3 Para Bde, "Refusal to Eat," 23 October 44.

103. LAC, RG 24, Vol. 12, 721, File 2011, Para Battalion, Memo, "1 Cdn Para Bn," AAG to MAG, 24 October 44.

104. *Ibid.*

105. Jan de Vries, telephone interview with Michel Wyczynski, 8 December 2002; and DHH, Madden Biographical File, John Madden, 1st Canadian Parachute Battalion, taped recollections, non-dated, 21.

106. *Ibid.*, John Madden.

107. Jan de Vries, telephone interview with Michel Wyczynski, 8 December 2002.

108. DHH, Madden Biographical File, John Madden, 21.

109. *Ibid.*

110. William E. Jenkins, interview with Michel Wyczynski, 19 December 2001.

111. Many of the veterans who were interviewed confirmed that they did not go hungry during this period. They were provided with rations from other units, or had built up their own personal food stashes or had light lunches or snacks at the NAFFI. The impact of the hunger strike threatened to reach even beyond the unit. The press was soon on the story. Colonel W.G. Abel at Canadian Military Headquarters impressed on Rear-Admiral G.P. Thomson, the chief press censor at the Ministry of Information to kill the story. But the story was not a threat to security, so editors could only be asked to suppress the story. However, Abel argued that the "hunger strike amounted to mutiny and it would be valuable for the enemy to know that a Canadian formation was not at present battle worthy because of incipient mutiny." The War Office was of the same mind and was intent that "every possible step will be taken on the highest level necessary to prevent it [publication]." After all, the senior leadership was concerned of the "possible serious effect if publicity were to encourage the spread of the hunger strike as an instrument of protest in the Army." See LAC, RG 24, Vol. 12, 721, File 2011, Para Battalion, "Hunger Strike Story," DDPR to MGA, 24 October 44; and LAC, RG 24, Vol. 12, 721, File 2011, Para Battalion, Memo, "1 Cdn Para Bn," AAG to MGA, 24 October 44.

112. This was prompted by a call from the news editor of the *London Daily Mail*, who called to ask if he could come and take a look at the "hunger strike." Hill responded, "Look there is a war on. The war has to be won. Give me until Monday and if that strike isn't settled on Monday you can come and see me and look into it." See Nolan, 123–124.

113. Interview with author, 18 April 2001.

114. 1 Cdn Para Bn Assn Archives, File 11–2, Sergeant R.F. Anderson, "From the Rhine to the Baltic." He also stated: "In line of march and in any attack, you could always find the Brigadier at your elbow. His courage and leadership inspired our men, and to this day, he holds 'his Canadians' as special in his heart and prayers." Hill passed away in 2006.

115. 1 Cdn Para Bn Assn Archives, Brian Nolan Fonds, Brigadier James Hill file, Brigadier James Hill, interview with Brian Nolan, April 25, 1994, 40. The War Diary notes, "General training in the morning and a lecture from Brigadier Hill who promised that there would be an investigation into all grievances."

116. *Ibid.*

117. *Ibid.*

118. LAC, RG 24, Vol. 12, 721, File 2011, Para Battalion, Memo, "1 Cdn Para Bn," AAG to MGA, 24 October 44; and LAC, RG 24, War Diaries, Series C-3, Vol. 15, 299, 1 Cdn Para Bn, February 1944-January 1945, Appendix 18, Memo, Cdn Liaison Section, 3 Para Bde, "Refusal to Eat," 23 October 44.

119. LAC, RG 24, Vol. 12, 721, File 2011, Para Battalion, Memo, "1 Cdn Para Bn," AAG to MGA, 24 October 44.

120. *Ibid.*

121. *Ibid.*

122. Fraser Eadie interview with author, 20 November 2000; and R.F. "Andy" Anderson, interview with Michel Wyczynski, 7 February 2001.

123. Alf Tucker, interview with Bernd Horn, 23 June 2001. Tucker, the signals officer, was normally the number one jumper. Interestingly, a newspaper article at the time stated, "… the men who loved him as seldom a leader has been loved" was completely off the mark. The hunger strike, or more accurately, the causes for it drove an irreparable wedge between the soldiers and Nicklin. Many veterans to this day still voice their criticism of their former CO. See 1 Cdn Para Bn Assn Archives, Joe Ryan, "Old Manager Pays Tribute to Nicklin," newspaper clipping, unknown date or publication.

124. Nolan, 162.

125. John Feduck, interview with Michel Wyczynski, August 2002.

126. Interview with author, 31 January 2002.

127. Interview with author, 20 November 2002.

128. Extract from Eadie's citation for his Distinguished Service Order (DSO) — Lieutenant-Colonel George Fraser, see 1 Cdn Para Bn Assn Archives, "Paratroop Leader Lt. Col Fraser Eadie, Awarded D.S.O." Unknown newspaper clipping, unknown date.

CONTRIBUTORS

Lieutenant-Colonel (Retired) David Bashow has written extensively in books and periodicals on a variety of defence, foreign policy, and military history topics. He retired from military service after a long career as a Canadian Air Force fighter pilot, a senior staff officer, and a military academic. His flying time includes nearly 2,400 hours in the F-104 Starfighter, and he is a graduate of the USAF/GAF Fighter Weapons School and the U.S. Navy's TOPGUN at the postgraduate level. Bashow is currently the editor of the *Canadian Military Journal* and is an adjunct associate professor of history at the Royal Military College of Canada in Kingston, Ontario.

Major Douglas E. Delaney is a serving infantry officer with operational experience in Somalia, Cyprus, and the Balkans. He holds a doctorate in war studies from the Royal Military College of Canada, is also the author of *The Soldiers' General: Bert Hoffmeister at War* (2005), and is currently the professor in charge of the Military and Strategic Studies Undergraduate Program at the Royal Military College.

Major Andrew Godefroy is an independent scholar working with the Canadian Army's Directorate of Land Concepts and Doctrine where he serves as head of the Research, Publications, and Outreach Programs. A Primary Reserve Army officer with 16 years service, he holds a Ph.D. in war studies from the Royal Military College and is the author of two books and several book chapters and scholarly articles on Canadian strategic studies and military history.

Colonel Bernd Horn is the deputy commander of Special Operations Forces Command and the former director of the Canadian Forces

Leadership Institute. He is a seasoned infantry officer with command experience at the unit and sub-unit level. He holds a master of arts and Ph.D. in war studies from the Royal Military College where he is an adjunct associate professor of history. He has authored, co-authored, edited, and co-edited 20 books and numerous articles on military affairs and military history.

Dr. P. Whitney Lackenbauer is an assistant professor of Canadian history at St. Jerome's University (University of Waterloo). His current research interests focus on arctic security, Aboriginal peoples and warfare, and the environmental impacts of military activities. He is the author of *Battle Grounds: The Canadian Military and Aboriginal Lands.* Lackenbauer has also edited three other books, authored a short monograph on military base closures, and has published widely in the *Canadian Military Journal*, *Journal of the Canadian Historical Association, Urban History Review*, and *Ontario History*, among others.

Craig Leslie Mantle graduated from Queen's University in 2002 with a master of arts in Canadian military history and has been employed by the Canadian Forces Leadership Institute as a historian and researcher ever since. He is a doctoral candidate at the University of Calgary and is the editor of two volumes relating to disobedience in the Canadian military.

Major Tod Strickland is a serving infantry officer in the Canadian Forces. He joined the Princess Patricia's Canadian Light Infantry (PPCLI) in 1989 and has served in various positions with the First and Third Battalions in Victoria, Edmonton, and the Balkans, and at the Infantry School and headquarters of the First Canadian Mechanized Brigade Group. He returned from Operation Archer, Roto 1, in Afghanistan in August 2006, where he was employed as the deputy commanding officer for the 1 PPCLI Battle Group. He has earned a bachelor of military arts and sciences degree and is now pursuing a master of arts in Middle Eastern history.

Dr. Michael Whitby is the senior naval historian at the Directorate of History and Heritage. He is co-author of the official history of the Royal Canadian Navy (RCN) in the Second World War and leads the team preparing the official post-war history of the RCN, 1945–68. He also edited *Commanding Canadians: The Second World War Diaries of AFC Layard* and *The Admirals: Canada's Senior Naval Leadership in the 20th Century*.

INDEX

Abel, Colonel W.G., 259
Adamson, Agar Stewart Allan
    Masterson, 15, 21–39, 41–47, 49,
    50, 52–55, 57–58
Addu Atoll, 175, 177
Aircraft, 75, 128, 159, 165–168,
    170–172, 176–180, 185–186,
    191–193, 227, 233, 248
    Consolidated Catalinas, 175
    Hawker Hurricane, 171–172
    Lancaster bomber, 160–161
    Messerschmitt 109 (Bf 109), 185
    Sopwith Camel, 158, 166, 169
    Sopwith Pup, 165
    Sopwith Triplane, 166–167
    Spitfire, 184–186, 188, 192
    Supermarine Stranraer, 174
    Wellington bomber, 172
Alberta, 109, 183, 194
Aleutian Islands, 99, 128
Alexander, Mel, 167, 169
Algiers, 81–84, 87, 92
Amersfoort, 42
Anderson, Sergeant R.F., 235,
    238–240, 242–243
Anzio, 102–104, 106
Ardelian, Sergeant Don, 117
Ardennes, 244, 246
Atlantic, 16, 75, 78–80, 85, 165,
    175–176, 184
Atlantic, Battle of, 16, 84, 86

Attu, 99

Badfontein Valley, 43
Barker, Major William George "Billy,"
    157–159
Bashow, David, 17
Battle of the Bulge (*see also*
    Ardennes), 244, 246
Becket, Captain R.W., 228
Bercuson, David, 115, 215
Bertram, Sergeant Instructor, 31
Birchall, Leonard Joseph, 17, 155,
    174–183, 195, 196
Bishop, William Avery "Billy," 192–193
"Black Flight," 167
Boers, 33–38, 40–41, 43, 47–48
Bomber Command, 155, 160–163
Borden, Camp, 112–113
Borden, Dr. Frederick William, 25, 52
Bradbrooke, Lieutenant-Colonel
    George Frederick Preston, 8, 223,
    226–232, 235–236, 246–247, 255
Bradley, Lieutenant J.R., 86
Brebner, Colin, 231
Brennan, Paul, 186
Britain (*see also* England, Great
    Britain, United Kingdom), 77,
    165, 170, 173, 185–186, 188,
    190, 194
British Commonwealth Air Training
    Plan (BCATP), 159

British Eastern Fleet, 177
British Empire, 37, 170, 180, 195
British Military Formations
  1st Parachute Battalion, 229
  3rd British Infantry Division, 232
  3rd Parachute Brigade (3 Para
    Bde), 229
  6th Airborne Division (6 AB
    Div), 229, 232
  7th Armoured Division, 172–173
Broadhurst, Air Vice-Marshal Harry,
  188
Brokenhead Reserve, 96, 107, 121–122,
  124
Brooke, Field Marshal Sir Alan, 246
Brookes, Air Vice-Marshal George,
  160, 162
Brown, Squadron Leader "Hilly," 185
Bulford, 234
Buller, General Sir Redvers, 29
Buxton, Sergeant Dick, 113
Byng, Sir Julian, 21

Cambridge, 22, 77
Canadian Army, 61, 196–197, 104, 106,
  109, 113–114, 199, 225–226, 228,
  239, 242, 245
Canadian Army Special Force
  (CASF), 96, 109–110
Canadian Army Training
  Memorandums, 224
Canadian Expeditionary Force
  (CEF), 59–62, 64, 72, 157
Canadian Football League (CFL),
  230
Canadian High Commissioner in
  London, 25
Canadian Military Formations (see
  also specific formations)
  1st Canadian Parachute
    Battalion (1 Cdn Para Bn),
    17, 97, 103, 106, 223–225,
    227–229, 233–235, 287,
    239, 246
  1st Field Park Company, 96

2nd Battalion, Princess Patricia's
  Canadian Light Infantry (2
  PPCLI), 109–111
2nd Canadian Infantry Brigade
  (2 CIB), 139, 142, 145, 148,
  202, 207, 209–213
2nd Canadian Parachute
  Battalion (2 Cdn Para Bn),
  228–229
3rd Battalion, Princess Patricia's
  Canadian Light Infantry (3
  PPCLI), 113–116
3 Naval (N) Squadron, 165
3rd (Special Service) Battalion,
  Royal Canadian Regiment of
  Infantry, 23
6th Canadian Mounted Rifles, 46
9 Parachute Battalion, 233
5 Squadron, 174
28 Squadron, 157–159
35 (RAF) Squadron, 155–156
47 Squadron, 170
66 Squadron, 157
126 Wing, 191
203 (RAF) Squadron, 170
249 (RAF) Squadron, 186
411 Squadron, 186, 188, 193
413 Squadron, 175–176, 182
421 Squadron, 188
426 Thunderbird Squadron, 161
Canadian Military Headquarters, 235,
  258–259
Cape Town, 27–29, 31, 45
Carey, Lance Corporal, 33
Carter Barracks, 235
Casino, 100–101, 210
Cawthra, Ann Mabel, 23
Ceylon, 175–180, 197
Charleston, 32, 40
Chief of the General Staff (CGS), 229,
  235
Chinese, 110–111, 115–116
Clark, General Mark, 104
Colarossi, Sergeant L.A., 177–178
Collishaw, Air Vice-Marshal

Raymond "Collie," 17, 155, 164–174, 195
Colombo, 176–178
Command (defined), 13–19, 200, 223–224, 247–248
Copp, Terry, 118
Corpus Christi, 22
Creelman, Corporal Richard, 239
Crocodile River, 56
Crocodile Valley, 42, 57
Cunningham, Admiral Sir Andrew, 83, 92

Dallaire, Lieutenant-General, Senator Roméo, 118–119
De Vries, Private Jan, 241
Director of Military Training, 224
Director of Personnel Selection, 225
Distinguished Flying Cross (DFC), 156, 158–159, 161, 170, 180, 183, 185–186, 188, 191–192
Distinguished Service Order (DSO), 48, 60, 83, 161, 169–170, 191, 199, 206–207
Dives, River, 233
Durban, 29, 31, 47

Eadie, Major Fraser, 8, 234–235, 240, 243, 245, 247
Easton, Allan, 78, 90
EG-9 (RCN support group), 75, 77, 83, 85, 87–88
EG-11 (RCN support group), 90
Emerlo, 42
England (*see also* Britain, Great Britain, United Kingdom), 21–22, 26, 45, 62, 78, 96, 106, 157, 159, 180, 184–185, 188, 192–193, 226–227, 229, 232, 234–235
Europe, 86, 95–97, 106–107, 125, 155–156, 160, 173, 232, 244, 246

Fancourt, Captain H.L., 81–82
Fauquier, Group Captain Johnnie, 162

Feduck, Sergeant John, 234, 236–237, 245
First Special Service Force (FSSF), 97–105, 228
First World War, 15, 48–50, 59, 61, 64, 78, 96, 158
Flint, Major George, 111
Fort Benning, 227–228
France, 46, 48, 59, 62, 104–105, 124, 158, 163, 165–166, 173, 184–185, 192, 233–234, 237–238
Free French partisans, 105

Gale, Major-General Richard, 231, 243
Genaille, Don, 123
German Military Formations
  132nd Grenadier Regiment, 100
  316th Division, 102
Germans, 48, 64–67, 69–70, 90, 100–103, 105, 140, 172–173, 202–208, 210–211, 234, 244
Gibraltar, 79–80, 175
Gilday, Lieutenant-Colonel Thomas P., 100–101, 103
Godega Airfield, 157
Gordon, Major W.D., 46
Governor General's Foot Guards (GGFG), 22, 24, 46
Great Britain (*see also* Britain, England, United Kingdom), 45
Great War (*see also* First World War), 49, 59, 77, 117, 160, 168, 173–174, 183, 192
Grierson-Jackson, Squadron Leader W.R.F., 156

Halifax, 23–27, 29, 31, 52, 84
Harris, Sir Arthur, 161, 163
Haslam, John, 96–97
Hepenstall, Robert, 110–112, 124
Hill 146, 115, 133
Hill 677, 111
Hill, Brigadier James S., 229–238, 242–244, 257
Hillborn, Major Richard "Dick," 235

HMCS *Matane*, 75, 78–79, 87
HMCS *Saint John*, 85–86
HMCS *Swansea*, 75, 89
HMS *Broke*, 81–83
HMS *Chelsea*, 79–80
HMS *Excellent*, 79
HMS *Indomitable*, 78
HMS *Malcolm*, 81
HMS *Osborne*, 77
HMS *Pelican*, 75
HMS *Salisbury*, 84
HMS *Zetland*, 83
Hoffmeister, Major-General Bert, 8, 16–17, 139–151, 199, 204, 217
Holm, Tom, 125
Hook, the, 115–116, 133
Howell, Thomas Easton, 36–37, 44, 54, 56
Hutton, Major-General E.T.H., 50

Îles d'Hyères, 104
Indian Act, 108–109
Indian Affairs Department, 109
Irving, Lieutenant-Colonel J.D., 46

Jamestown Line, 115
Japan, 180–182
Japanese, 99, 175–182, 196–197
Japanese First Air Fleet, 176
Jeans, Corporal Ernie, 240
Jenkins, Lieutenant William, 230, 241
Johnston, William, 115
Jolly, Commander R.F., 92
Jutland, Battle of, 78

Kapyong, 111
Kapyong Barracks, 122
Kardiner, Abram, 118
Kemp, John, 235
Kesselring, Field Marshal Albert, 99, 102
King George VI, 106, 109, 163
Kiska, 99, 104
Korea, 16, 95–96, 110, 112–114, 117, 119, 124–126

Korean War, 77, 109, 111, 115, 119–120

La Difensa, 100
Larose, Sergeant Roland, 238–240
Layard, Commander A.F.C.8, 16, 75–92
Le Mesnil, 233, 235
Leadership (defined), 13–19, 200–201, 217, 223–224, 248
Leigh-Mallory, Air Chief Marshal Sir Trafford, 189
Leinster Regiment, 23
Lennox, Al, 97
Linton, Flight Lieutenant Karl, 160–162, 192
Liverpool, 27, 80, 84, 91
London, 25, 27, 29, 46, 192, 235
Lord Minto, 25
Lord Strathcona, 25, 27, 37, 44
Lord Strathcona's Horse, 47, 52, 56
Luqa Airfield, 186

Mackenzie, Major-General J.P., 231
Macleod, Major Murray, 257
MacNichol, Raymond, 109
Madden, Captain John, 241
Maitland Camp, 28, 38
Malkin, Captain Hank, 156
Malta, 186–190
Management (defined), 14, 200, 217, 223, 246
Manitoba Museum of Man and Nature, 124
Mannock, Edward "Mick," 170
Marks, Wing Commander Jimmy, 155–156
McAndrew, Bill, 118
McArthur, Alex, 35–37
McEwen, Air Commodore Clifford Mackay "Black Mike," 17, 155–164, 195
McGillivray, Private, 43
McNair, Robert Wendell, 17, 155, 183–195, 197

McNaughton, Lieutenant-General A.G.L., 229
Mediterranean Sea, 78, 98
Merville Battery, 233
Miksche, Captain F.O., 224
Military Cross (MC), 158
Military Medal (MM), 95, 103, 106
Miller, Andrew, 37
Minister of Militia and Defence, 25, 61–62
Moll, Dr. A.E., 225
Montana, 97
Montgomery, Field Marshal Viscount Montgomery of Alamein, 139–140, 144
Montreal, 22, 26–27, 157, 159
Morrison, Private Doug, 230–231, 237, 240, 245
Munro, Lieutenant Brian, 111
Munroe, Ross, 70
Mussolini Canal, 102

Nagumo, Vice-Admiral Chuichi, 176
Natal, 29
Natal Field Force, 29
National Defence Headquarters (NDHQ), 19, 228
Nicklin, Lieutenant-Colonel Jevon Albert "Jeff," 8, 223, 227, 230–232, 234, 236–241, 243, 245–247
Niigata Camp, 181
No. 6 Group Bomber Command, 160
No. 62 Operational Base, 160
Normandy, 86, 163, 188, 191, 233, 235–239, 243, 247
North Africa, 81, 99, 171–173, 229, 237
North Atlantic, 16, 75, 79–80, 176
North-West Europe, 244
North-West Mounted Police (NWMP), 25, 38
Nova Scotia, 24, 51, 174, 183–184

O'Connor, Major-General R.N., 172
Ontario, 22, 124, 167, 174, 182, 184, 200

Onyette, Warrant Officer "Bart," 175–176, 178
Operation Chesterfield, 210
Operation Compass, 172
Operation Torch, 81, 229
Operational Training Unit (OUT), 185
Ortona, 16–17, 139–151, 203, 207, 209
Ottawa, 22–27, 29, 31, 33, 35, 62, 109, 183–184, 215
Ouistreham, 232

Paardeberg, 46
Parachute Training School, Royal Air Force Station Ringway, 226
Peacock, Lieutenant Robert S., 115–116, 124
Pearl Harbor, 175, 176
Peppard, Sergeant Herb, 228
Petawawa, Canadian Forces Base, 123
Petit, Claude, 115, 122
Pigeau, Ross, 200
Port Elizabeth, 29, 31
Port Hope, 22
Porter, McKenzie, 98–100, 112–113
Post-Traumatic Stress Disorder (PTSD), 8, 117–120, 125, 134–137
Prentice, Commander J.D. "Chubby," 90
Prince, Sergeant Thomas George, 8, 16, 95–138
Princess Patricia's Canadian Light Infantry (PPCLI), 17, 21, 48, 58, 109–111, 113–116, 119, 122–123, 145, 149, 151, 201–202, 210, 212, 217, 218
Proctor, Major Hilton D., 248

Rayner, Commander D.A., 89–90
Regia Aeronautica, 171–173
Reid, Ellis, 167, 169
Richardson, Sergeant A.H.L., 35–38, 47
Richthofen, Baron Manfred von, 168, 183

Ringway (*see also* Parachute Training School), 97, 226

Ripstein, Howard, 161

Ross, Corporal John, 230, 240

Royal Air Force (RAF), 155–156, 159, 163, 170–171, 173, 175, 179, 185–186, 191, 226

Royal Canadian Air Force (RCAF), 155–156, 159, 162–163, 174–175, 181, 183–185, 193

Royal Canadian Engineers (RCE), 96

Royal Canadian Navy (RCN), 83–85, 164, 174

Royal Canadian Naval Reserve (RCNR), 78

Royal Flying Corps (RFC), 157, 165–166, 170

Royal Military College of Canada (RMC), 7, 182, 235

Royal Navy (RN), 78, 84–85, 91–92, 164

Royal Winnipeg Rifles, 230, 234

Rustigno, 159

Salerno, 99, 102

Salt, Lieutenant G.E.S., 53, 55

Sarcee, Camp, 109

Saskatoon Light Infantry, 226

SC 94 (convoy), 81

Scapa Flow, 85–86, 173

Scotland, 173, 185

Seaforth Highlanders of Canada, 139, 141, 204

Sealey, Bruce, 121

Second World War, 16, 75, 77, 91–92, 94, 96, 118–119, 124, 155–156, 159, 182, 192, 212, 217

Seine River, 234, 246

Sergeant Tommy Prince Army Training Initiative, 123

Shilo Camp, 243

Simpson, Commodore G.W.G. "Shrimp," 85

Sinclair, Verna, 121

Smith, Donald, 25

Somerville, Admiral Sir James, 175

South Africa, 22, 24–33, 37–41, 43–50

South African Light Horse, 32

St Croix, Commander B.J. de, 84

St. Vincent, 28

Standerton, 32–33, 35, 37

Steele, Lieutenant-Colonel Sam, 25, 42, 45, 56, 62

Stewart, David Morrison, 27–28

Stone, Colonel James, 111

Strickland, Inspector D'Arcy, 25

Stuart, Major-General Ken, 229, 235

Submarines (*see also* U-boats), 86

Swetman, Group Captain Bill, 161

Taylor, Robert, 226

Tedder, Marshal of the Royal Air Force Lord (Arthur W.), 171–172

Terraine, John, 172

Thomson, Colonel S.W. "Syd," 139, 141, 147, 151

Thomson, Rear-Admiral G.P., 259

Tiger Force, 164

Tommy Prince Barracks, 123

Tommy Prince Drill Hall, 123

Trenchard, Major-General Hugh, 165

Trenton, RCAF Station, 159

Trinity College, 22

Tucker, Lieutenant Alf, 238, 260

Turner Stan, 186

Tuxford, Lieutenant-Colonel George Stuart, 15, 59–73

U-311, 92

U-448, 75

U-boats (*see also* U-bootwaffe and submarines), 16, 77, 80, 86

U-bootwaffe (*see also* U-boats and submarines), 86

United Kingdom (*see also* Britain, England, Great Britain), 170

United States Military Formations
    2nd Corps, 104
    5th Army, 99–100, 102, 104
    6th Army Group, 104

United States Army Air Force (USAAF), 163
United States Presidential Unit Citation, 111

Varaville, 233
Victoria Cross (VC), 33, 37, 47, 113
Vyvere, Peter Van de, 121

Wainwright, Camp, 109, 123
Walker, Captain F.J. "Johnny," 78, 81, 90, 92
War Office, U.K., 46
Ware, Lieutenant-Colonel Cameron "Cammie," 17, 199–218
Washington, D.C., 182

Watervaal, 41
Weeks, Brigadier F.G., 224
Wellington Barracks, 23
Western Front, 15, 21, 59–61, 64, 168
Winnipeg, 95–96, 106–107, 118, 120–124, 184, 234
Winnipeg Blue Bombers, 230, 238
Wismar, 244
Wolf-pack tactics, 86
Wolve Spruit, 33, 37, 40–42
Woodhall, Group Captain "Woody," 186–187

Yokohama (prisoner of war camp), 179–180

Marquis Book Printing Inc.

Québec, Canada
2007